I CAN DO ALL THINGS

AF271263

by

Barry Stebbing

Dedicated to Elizabeth

Elizabeth was in one of our beginning painting and drawing classes in Wichita, Kansas. Even though the children were supposed to be at least five years of age, she was still only four, with her birthday just a few days away. Whenever I tried to help her, she would sigh and say, "I really can't draw that well." or "I really didn't do a good job with my painting." However, she kept working as hard as she could, always striving to do the very best job possible. Because of this, we dedicate "I Can Do All Things" to Elizabeth White (homeschooled, Kansas).

Copyright 1999

Revised 2006

How Great Thou ART Publications

(Lessons within HGTA texts are reproducible for "in home use" only)

Dear Boys & Girls, Moms & Dads, Grandpops & Grandmoms:

Welcome to our beginning book on drawing, color and painting. This text is intended for 5 year olds all the way to 100 year olds! *I Can Do All Things* is a beginner's art book and has been created for everyone who wants to learn how to draw and paint.

We hope you enjoy this book and that you learn much about drawing, color, and painting. Learning to draw and paint is a discipline. Therefore, it is important to have a good attitude. Much of what you learn comes from determination. Take one step at a time. Build "precept upon precept." And remember, "I can do all things through Christ who strengthens me." (Philippians 4:13)

We would love to hear from you. Please write us a letter and send us copies of your art work. We will be glad to evaluate it for you and tell you all the things you are learning to do correctly.

In Christ,

Stebbing

Barry F. Stebbing
P.O. Box 48
McFarlan, NC 28102

I CAN DO ALL THINGS

by

Barry Stebbing

Dedicated to Elizabeth
Elizabeth was in one of our beginning painting and drawing classes in
Wichita, Kansas. Even though the children were supposed to be at least
five years of age, she was still only four, with her birthday just a few days
away. Whenever I tried to help her, she would sigh and say, "I really can't
draw that well." or "I really didn't do a good job with my painting."
However, she kept working as hard as she could, always striving to do the
very best job possible. Because of this, we dedicate "I Can Do All Things"
to Elizabeth White (homeschooled, Kansas).

Dear Boys & Girls, Moms & Dads, Grandpops & Grandmoms:

Welcome to our beginning book on drawing, color and painting. This text is intended for 5 year olds all the way to 100 year olds! *I Can Do All Things* is a beginner's art book and has been created for everyone who wants to learn how to draw and paint.

We hope you enjoy this book and that you learn much about drawing, color, and painting. Learning to draw and paint is a discipline. Therefore, it is important to have a good attitude. Much of what you learn comes from determination. Take one step at a time. Build "precept upon precept." And remember, "I can do all things through Christ who strengthens me." (Philippians 4:13)

We would love to hear from you. Please write us a letter and send us copies of your art work. We will be glad to evaluate it for you and tell you all the things you are learning to do correctly.

In Christ,

Stebbing

Barry F. Stebbing
P.O. Box 48
McFarlan, NC 28102

"I CAN DO ALL THINGS"

"I can do all things through Christ who strengthens me."

Philippians 4:13

ART Materials

1. Set of 12 Colored Pencils

2. 1 Extra Fine Black Marker

3. Set of *"Washable"* Markers

4. White Poster Board
   (22" x 28")

5. Acrylic Blending Paints:
   Primary Colors
   (Yellow, Red, & Blue) and White

6. 3 Brushes: Large, Medium, Small

7. Inspirational Classical Music

8. Folder*

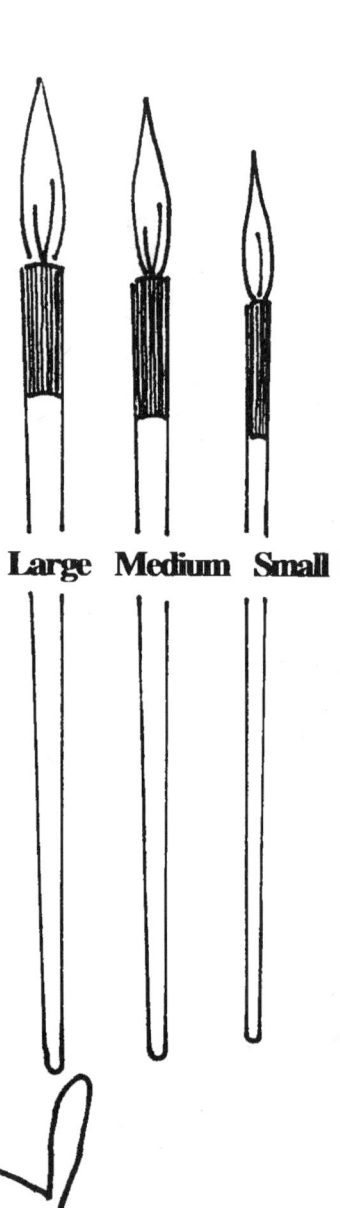

Large   Medium   Small

*Note: It is recommended that you have a folder to keep your paint cards organized.

Introduction.....Pointers for Teachers

Dear Parent and Teacher:

Before beginning with the first lesson in *I Can Do All Things*, let's review some important pointers for producing quality artwork:

Colored Pencils: First, we encourage your students to work with bright colored pencils. Children love to use bright colors! Many times their artwork is weaker than it should be because it has been done with an inexpensive brand of colored pencils. In general, an inexpensive colored pencil has a hard lead and produces a very light color. A more expensive colored pencil has a soft, yet durable lead, and produces a much brighter color. Scholar Prismacolor offers an excellent set for our purpose.

Colored Markers: Colored markers produce bold colors and create wonderful results for children. Many of the lessons in this text will be done with colored markers. For now, a basic set of *washable markers* will do. I like the Prang or Crayola *Instant Watercolor* markers with the bold tips. They are water soluble and can be used for all of our marker assignments. Regular paper is not a good surface for colored markers, as the colors often bleed to the other side. We recommend white poster board, *Bristol board,* or *110 index stock paper,* which can be purchased at office supply stores and is reasonably priced. This type of paper is thick enough to prevent markers from bleeding through to the other side and also affords a sturdy surface which will not wrinkle or bubble up as easily as paper.

Structuring an ART Curriculum: If students have an average interest in art, let them have one hour of art per week. If your students express a great deal of interest, you may want to give them two or three hours a week. If the students seem to be totally emerged in art, let them have as much art as they desire outside of their regular studies.

You will find that many students age 4 through 7 tend to be very creative and productive, able to do picture after picture on their own. Encourage and nurture this. Give younger students art materials like paper, poster board, colored pencils, markers, and free time to express themselves along with the structured program in this text. Even at an early age, it is wise to place *some* structure in their art time. For example, you may want to give your younger students 30 minutes on their own and, for the rest of the art period, have them do more structured assignments from the text.

Preserving ART Work: Many parents are continually looking for ways to store and preserve the large quantities of artwork their children produce. Some homes have reams of childrens' drawings and colorful pictures literally piled in stacks, where they become ripped or wrinkled. That is why it is good to contain most of the child's work in a sketchbook or a text like, *I Can Do All Things.* This helps to preserve the artwork and allows the student to compile a nice presentation.

Developing a Curriculum: Develop your art curriculum by going in and out of the chapters. For example, set up monthly or weekly lesson plans offering drawing one day, painting another, colored markers another and even a little art appreciation! Some students lose enthusiasm when they simply plod from cover to cover. We have found that variety will assist in generating their interest. Finally, many families end the school week with art. Try starting your week with art!

Learning to Expand Your Curriculum: Don't just work from the text. Use the creativity that God has given you to broaden many of the lessons. This will lengthen and enrich your curriculum. For example, if a child has done well on a drawing assignment, you may ask him to do it over again in colored pencils or colored markers, or even create a children's story from it. However, be discerning. Many students do not want to repeat an assignment they have just finished. If this is the case, encourage them to do it again a week or two later.

Your Main Purpose as an Art Teacher: An art teacher has two main purposes: to *inspire* and to *encourage*. To inspire means to instill in the student the desire to do the work. To encourage means to nurture the student, praising the good work he has done along with directing him through each assignment, sometimes even assisting in the completion of the work.

We recommend the parent or teacher *review* any new art curriculum with the student. After reviewing, you may want to ask him what he thinks of the curriculum. Does he think he can do the entire program? If he says *yes,* hold him to this commitment to complete the text from cover to cover. Most students are inspired by new art books and materials, but with time they may have a tendency to become complacent. It is up to the educator to keep the student inspired to do the work, especially during the younger years (ages 4 through 7).

Inspiration, encouragement and enthusiasm are key ingredients to being an effective teacher, especially in the arts. Many parents ask how can they be an inspiration to their children. I tell them that our greatest source of inspiration is God. Pray over the work of your children's hands and ask God to enrich both their understanding and abilities. Likewise, classical music is a good source of inspiration during art time. You can also go to the library and study works by the great masters. Finally, venture outside to do some of the art classes in God's creation as Nature can be a wonderful source for this.

*"The mediocre teacher tells.
The good teacher explains.
The superior teacher demonstrates.
The great teacher inspires."*

William Arthur Ward

"When we fail to praise a man who deserves praise, two sad things happen; we run a chance of driving him from the right road for want of encouragement, and we deprive ourselves of one of the very happiest of our privileges, the privilege of rewarding labor that deserves a reward."

John Ruskin

Encouragement: The younger the student, the more encouragement will be needed in order to have him working effectively in a structured program. The responsibilities of the art teacher are to review each lesson, explain the objectives, and be there to direct and encourage when the need arises. Many parents/teachers believe they can give the student the text and let him do the work on his own. Most younger children are not capable of this. Students work much better under the supervision of an older sibling or parent. More than anything, it is the juxtaposition of another person that gives him comfort and encouragement. Give your student the task to do (one of the assignments) and then check on him periodically to see how he is doing. Remember, it is important to *inspire* the student to do the task and to *encourage* him to complete it. Be nearby and continually offer praise and encouragement.

Student & Teacher: Elbow to Elbow

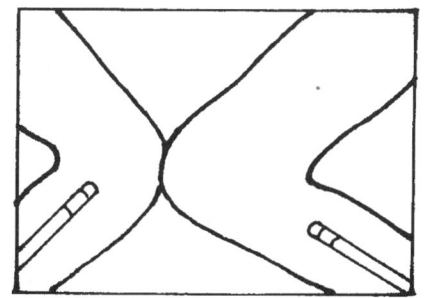

Whenever the parent or teacher actually sits alongside the student and does the artwork with them, they discover this to be some of the most precious quality time afforded during the day. Parents actually enjoy learning art just as much as their children, and the time together is quite memorable. Finally, we believe the teacher/parent be "hands-on," assisting the student by showing them how to do a certain part of their drawing or painting and making the corrections directly on the students artwork.

Student Frustration: Art is different than most of the academics. The teacher has to realize that no two art students are alike. Just as every snowflake that falls from heaven is different, so is every art student. One student may have a great amount of ability, and the next very little. One may have a good attitude, and another a poor attitude. One may be meticulous, and another impatient. Each student needs to be handled differently and with discernment. If a student becomes frustrated with an assignment, help him with it. When I was teaching in the classroom, I would go around and actually assist the student with their drawings and paintings to get them back on track and encourage them to complete the task. This builds their confidence and increases their productivity. If the frustration persists, you may want to go to another lesson or gently ease out of art for the day, returning to it when the student is in a better mood. Art, like God, cannot be forced on a child.

"The best way to cheer yourself is to cheer someone else up." Mark Twain

"It takes as much courage to have tried and failed as it does to have tried and succeeded."

Ann Lindberg

How To Evaluate Your Student's Artwork: Many parents/teachers do not feel confident in evaluating their students artwork. They do not feel knowledgeable in this area and therefore tend to be evasive and offer nothing but praise, saying, *"Oh, that's nice!"* and then hang the work on the refrigerator. All praise and no criticism will eventually grow wearisome and our students will be able to see through it. Offer praise for the quality of the artwork and then give constructive criticism where improvements may be needed. Use the *specific objectives* for any given assignment as guidelines for evaluating the work. Just like a cookie — sandwich one layer of criticism between two layers of praise. *Nurture* your confidence in giving constructive criticism! God has given each and every one of us a heart, and our hearts can be used for evaluating. Finally, have the student look at his artwork in a mirror. This reverse image should reveal many of the mistakes made in the drawing.

Spoon Feeding Beginning Drawing/Ages 5, 6 & 7

It is very important to know that a majority of younger children will struggle with the Beginning Drawing lessons. This is because their motor skills are not yet developed. There will also be difficulty because we are teaching a structured program based on "fundamentals" (such as shading with lines), which can be somewhat tedious for younger children. We encourage you to spoon-feed these drawing lessons (i.e. thirty seconds a day, then forty-five seconds a day, etc.) and spend more time in beginning painting, colored markers, and colored pencils until their motor skills are better developed.

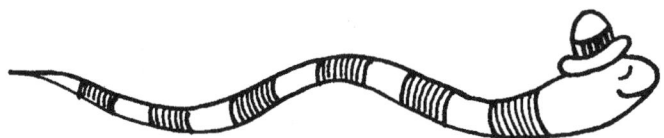

Preliminary studies are also good for the student to do. A preliminary study is a drawing done by the student to give him a better idea of how his composition is going to look. It also solves some of the drawing problems. When you have approved of the preliminary sketch, you may want to have the final artwork done in a sketchbook or on a piece of poster board. This will give the final artwork a nicer presentation.

Rules & Regulations: Every educator should begin each course with a set of guidelines. When rules and regulations are established in the classroom, students will understand what is expected of them concerning their behavior and the care of their materials. Once your rules and regulations are established, they should be adhered to. As soon as you waver, you may not regain the structure you desire. For example, you may want to establish rules about behavior: the students will do their artwork during art time; students are not to ridicule other student's artwork; and students are to respect their art materials, taking care of them and storing them properly.

Introduction to Drawing:

Practice Exercises from **A** to **Z**

A B C D E F G H I J K L M

N O P Q R S T U V W X Y Z

"I drew and I drew and I drew some more." Michelangelo

Introduction: *Practice Exercises*

Drawing is a learned *discipline.* The more you practice the better you will become. *Fundamentals* are the basic building blocks in art. When you practice basic fundamentals, such as learning how to draw a straight line, or a circle, it will make you a better artist. It may be good for you to prepare for the drawing assignments in *I Can Do All Things* by practicing these basic fundamentals. If you apply yourself and take your time with the 26 exercises (A to Z) it should give you more confidence in doing the other lessons in the book. So sharpen your pencils and get ready!

Practice Exercise **A:** *Drawing Straight Lines_____Connecting the Dots.....*

For your first exercise, let's practice drawing straight lines. Learning to draw a straight line (without the use of a ruler) is one of the most important fundamentals in drawing. Using your colored pencils, connect each pair of dots below (A) with *horizontal* lines (straight across from left to right). Draw each line as straight as you can, using a different color for each.

When you are finished, connect the next series of dots (B) with *vertical* lines (straight up and down), using a different colored pencil for each. Finally, draw l-o-o-o-n-g, horizontal lines that connect the dots on the bottom of the page.

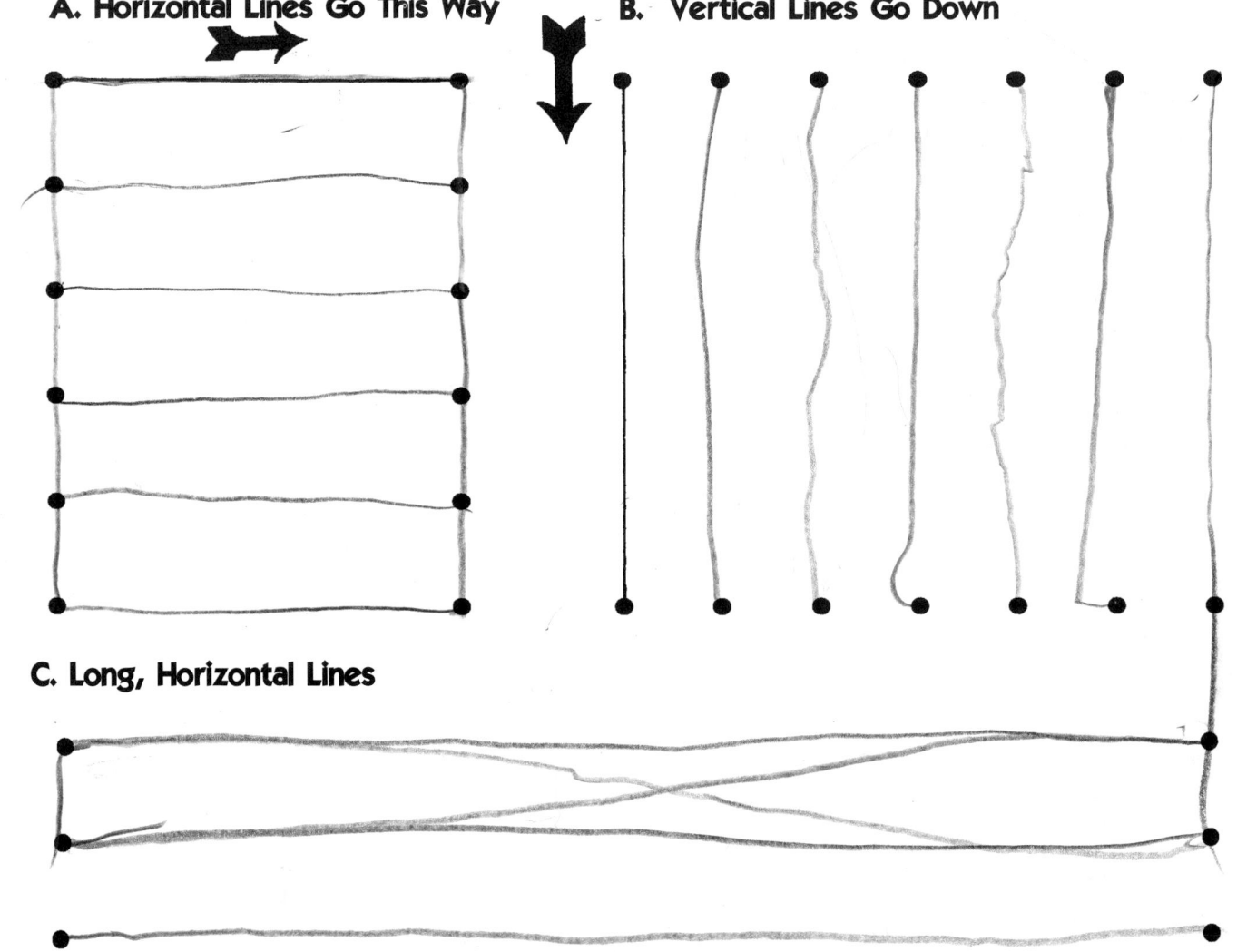

A. Horizontal Lines Go This Way

B. Vertical Lines Go Down

C. Long, Horizontal Lines

Practice Exercise B: *More L-o-o-o-n-g, Straight Lines*

Let's practice drawing some more straight lines. First, connect the feathers with the arrowhead by drawing two, long lines with your brown colored pencil (A). Can you add nice, parallel lines in the feathers as illustrated in A? Then, draw the entire arrow on your own with nice, straight lines (B). When you are finished, connect the point of the pencil to the eraser with two, long, straight lines (C). Finally, draw your own pencil (D). (Notice that the two lines that go around the top of the pencil are curved because the pencil is round.)

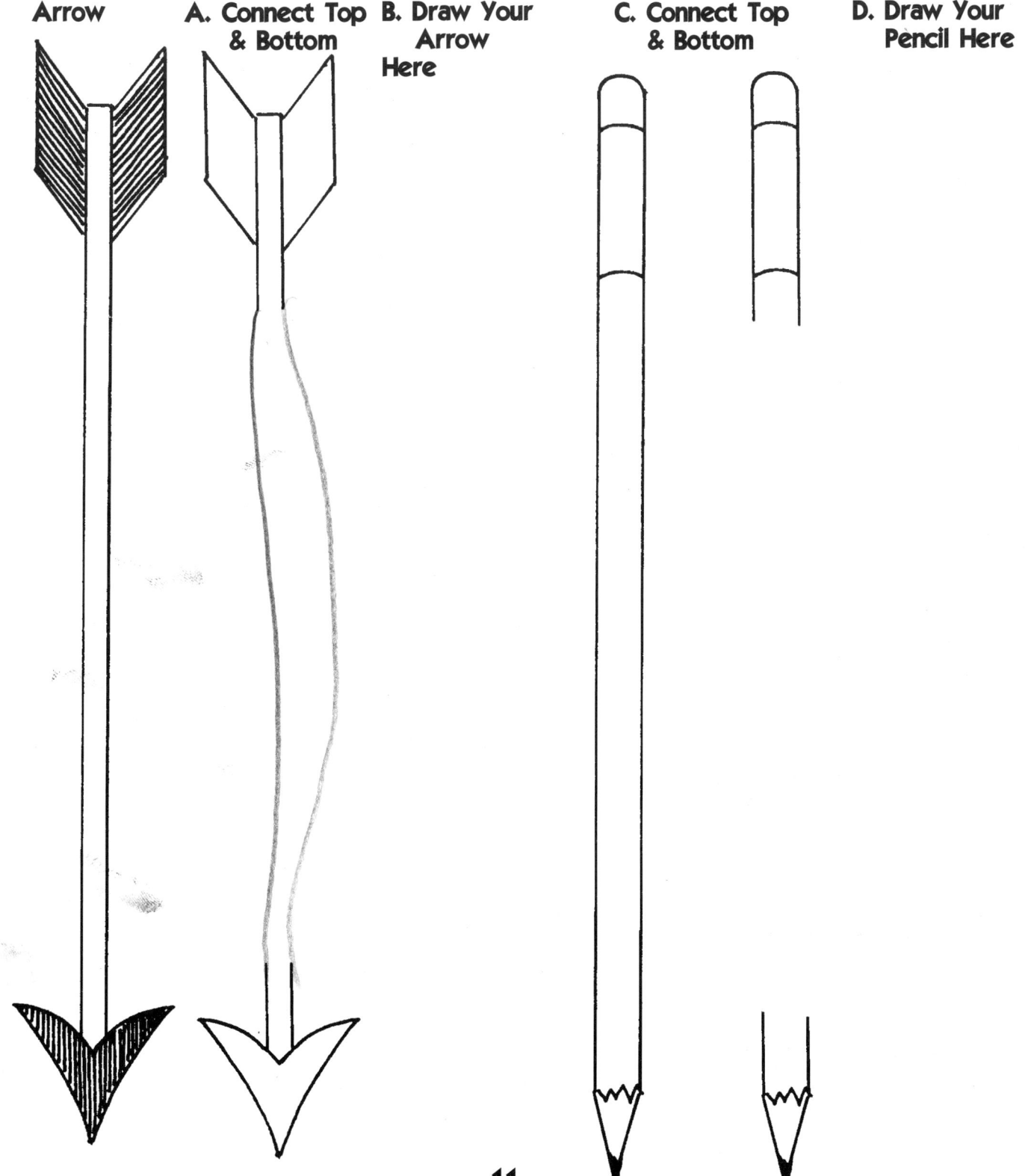

Arrow

A. Connect Top & Bottom

B. Draw Your Arrow Here

C. Connect Top & Bottom

D. Draw Your Pencil Here

Practice Exercise **C:** *Drawing Wally the Worm*

Now let's draw *Wally the Worm.* He is easy to draw if you know how to draw straight lines! Using your black pen, draw one long, horizontal line for the bottom of his belly and then draw another line coming up from his tail, making it wider as it goes towards his head (A). Draw a curved line connecting the top and bottom of his body for his head. After you have drawn his body, give him a smiley face and a hat. Then, add stripes to his body by drawing curved lines going around, because his body is round (B).

First, complete *Wally the Worm* (A) by drawing his entire body, face, hat, and stripes. Then draw *Wally the Worm* on your own (C). When you are finished, draw *Wally the Worm* going in the opposite direction, facing the *Wally the Worm* you just drew (D). Next, see if you can draw *Wally the Worm* and his reflection in the puddle as shown below (E). Finally, complete the drawing of the paint brush by drawing two long, horizontal lines that connect the tip of the handle with the hairs of the brush (F). Last of all, draw your own paint brush on the bottom of the page (G).

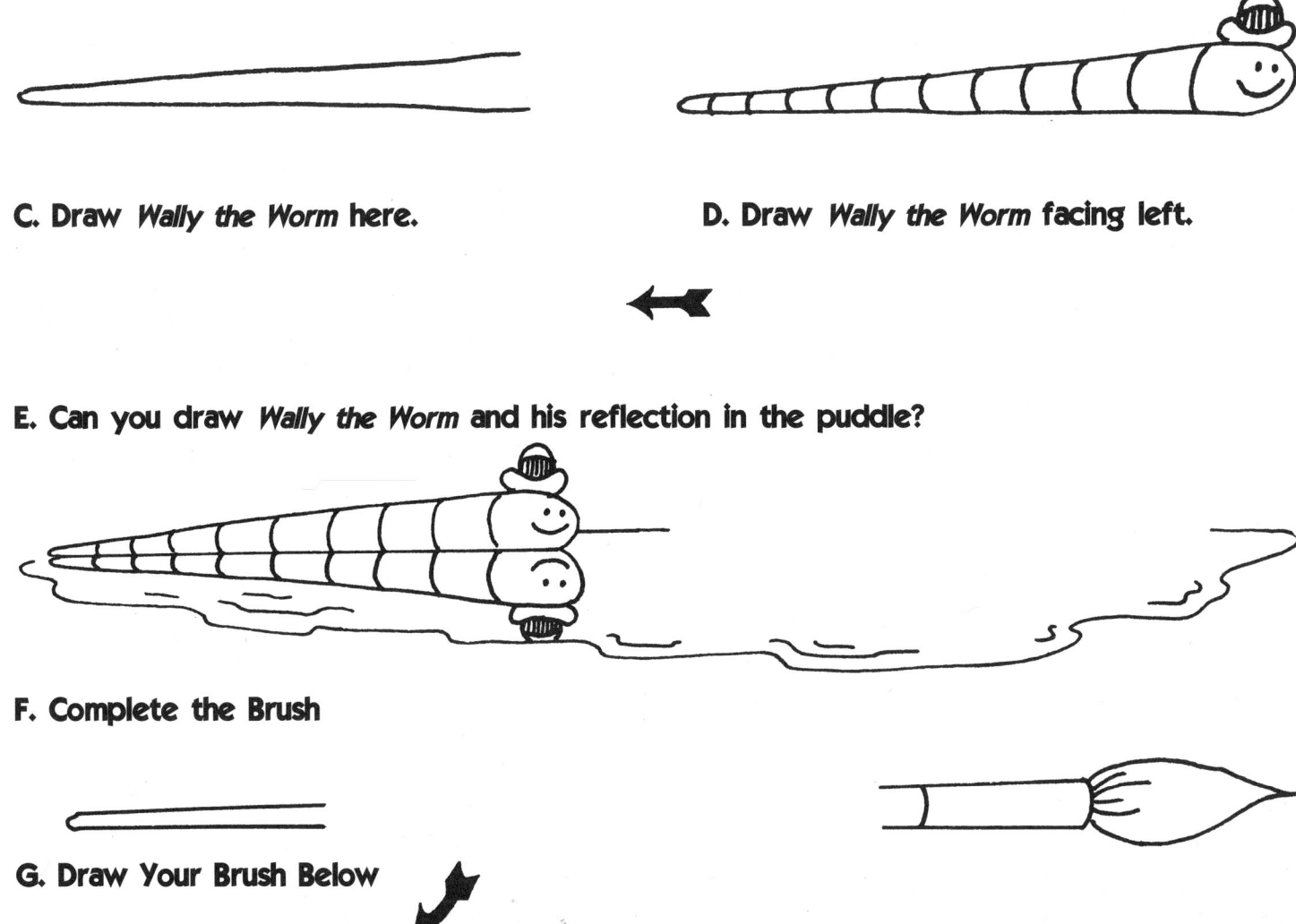

A Two Long, Straight Lines

B. Add a Smiley Face, Hat & Stripes

C. Draw *Wally the Worm* **here.**

D. Draw *Wally the Worm* **facing left.**

E. Can you draw *Wally the Worm* **and his reflection in the puddle?**

F. Complete the Brush

G. Draw Your Brush Below

Practice Exercise D: *Railroad Tracks & Picket Fences*

Now let's draw railroad tracks below with straight, horizontal lines. However, when drawing things that go back in the distance become closer and closer together the farther back they go until, finally, they seem to be touching each other (A). Using your black colored pencil, add railroad tracks in the picture below (B). When you are finished, draw vertical lines close together with your blue and green pencil for the distant trees (B). Then draw the entire picture with railroad tracks and distant trees below (C).

Next, using your black pen, complete the picket fence by drawing straight, vertical lines that connect the tops to the bottoms (D). Finally, on the bottom of the page, complete the entire fence by drawing rest of the picket slabs (E).

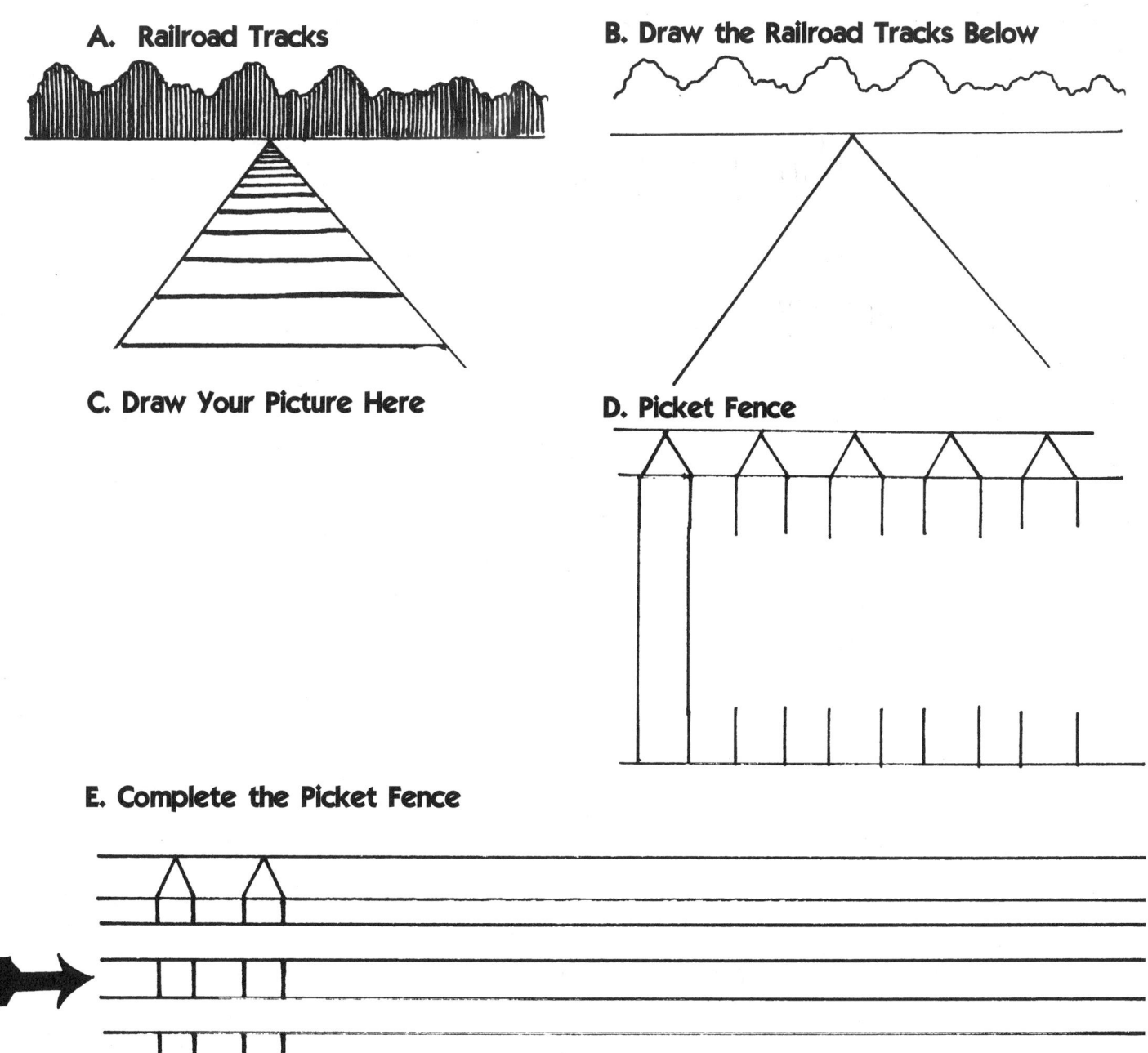

A. Railroad Tracks

B. Draw the Railroad Tracks Below

C. Draw Your Picture Here

D. Picket Fence

E. Complete the Picket Fence

Practice Exercise E: *Log Cabins and Long Lines*

Can you draw a house? Using your yellow pencil, draw a square (A) and add a triangle to the top for a roof (B). Draw a door and two windows and then go over your entire drawing with your brown colored pencil. It is always good to start your drawings *lightly* which will help in preventing mistakes. Finally, let's change the house into a log cabin by drawing horizontal lines from one side to the other, keeping your lines parallel and the same distance apart (C). Draw your log cabin in below (D).

When you are finished, draw a log cabin on the hill in the figure box (E). Can you draw another tree, cloud in the sky and some flowers in the foreground? Use your black pen and color your picture when finished.

A. Square   B. Square + Triangle   C. Log Cabin   D. Draw Your House Here

E. Draw Your Cabin on a Hill Below

cartoon hands

Practice Exercise F: *Stick People*

hot dog feet

Do you know how to draw people? Many young students draw *stick people*. For this exercise, draw three stick figures below: one standing (A), one sitting (B) and one walking (C). Don't forget to give each of your figures hands and feet.

For hands, let's start with a cartoon hand. Cartoon characters have three fingers and a thumb (above). First, draw a circle for the palm of the hand and then add three long, hot dog shapes for the fingers and a short, hot dog shape for the thumb. Complete your stick figures by giving them a smiley face. Draw your three stick figures on the bottom of the page with your black colored pencil.

A. Standing

B. Sitting

C. Walking

D. Draw Your Three Stick People Below

Practice Exercise G: *Hot Dog Figures*

Now let's draw *hot dog* figures by putting meat on the bones of our stick people. First, using your yellow pencil, draw the stick person below (A). Next, take your orange pencil and draw a hot dog shape for his *torso* (B). The torso is the stomach and chest area without the arms and legs. Finally, add two long thin hot dog shapes for each arm and leg (C). To complete your hot dog figure, add cartoon hands, short hot dog shapes for the feet and a happy face. Draw your hot dog person below (D). When you are finished, draw each of the stick figures on the bottom of the page and then add hot dog shapes for the different parts of their bodies.

A. Stick Person B. Torso C. Arms & Legs D. Draw Your Hot Dog Figure Here

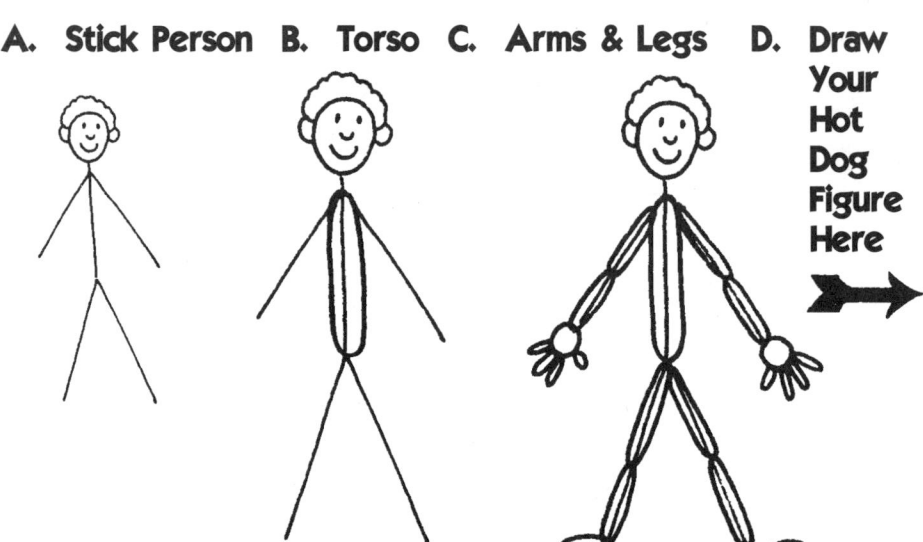

E. Fill the Figure Box with Hot Dog Figures

16

Practice Exercise H: Rectangular Man

Now let's draw *Rectangular Man*. Once again, we will start with a stick figure but this time we will add rectangular shapes for the parts of the body instead of hot dog shapes. Again, start by drawing the stick figure with your yellow pencil. Then, taking your blue pencil, draw a rectangular shape for the torso (A). Add arms and legs by drawing two, long, thin, rectangular shapes for each (B). Finally, draw the feet and hands by adding short, rectangular shapes (C). Draw a small circle for the head, add the fingers to each hand, and give your rectangular man a smiley face. Draw your person below (D). When you have finished, draw the stick figures again in the large figure box (E) with your yellow pencil and then draw rectangular shapes for the parts of their bodies, along with hands, feet, and smiley face.

A. Torso B. Arms & Legs C. Hands & Feet D. Draw Your Figure Here

E. Fill the Figure Box with Rectangular People

Practice Exercise I: *Geometric Shapes*

Geometric shapes are: triangles (A), circles (B), squares (C), and rectangles (D). Drawing geometric shapes is a good exercise for learning to draw. See if you can draw each geometric shape correctly. Start by using your light yellow pencil. Make sure to draw your lines as straight as possible for the square and the rectangle without using a ruler. To draw a circle, simply go around and around, four or five times with your pencil until you have made it perfectly round. After you have drawn each geometric shape, go over them with a darker colored pencil. Finally, stack your geometric shapes together to make a nice *composition* on the bottom of the page. Composition simply means the way you place things in your picture. Be creative in the way you stack them! Start your drawing lightly with your yellow pencil and then add other colors.

A. Triangle

B. Circle

C. Square

D. Rectangle

E. Stack Your Geometric Shapes Here

Practice Exercise J: *"Charlie Contrast"*

A. Light Against Dark

"Charlie Contrast" is a cartoon character. The peculiar thing about *Charlie Contrast* is that when standing in front of a dark background, his face is light (A). When standing in front of a light background, his face is dark (B). Whenever you place light areas against dark, or dark areas against light, it is called *contrast* and can create bold effects in your drawings.

B. Dark Against Light

To start, draw *Charlie Contrast's* face in the figure box (C). Start by drawing a circle. Then add a watermelon-shaped smile and two egg shapes for his face. Next, darken the background behind *Charlie Contrast* in the second figure box (D) with your black colored pencil. Finally, in the third figure box (E), shade his face with vertical lines very close together, leaving the background light (as shown above). Make sure to use nice, controlled vertical lines. The closer you place them together the darker the value will be.

C. Draw *Charlie* Here **D. Darken the Background** **E. Darken *Charlie's* Face**

Now let's draw *Charlie Contrast's* entire body. However, the funny thing about *Charlie Contrast* is that he doesn't have a body! His arms and legs go right to his head (F). Draw *Charlie Contrast* in the space below (G), giving him hands and feet. Make *Charlie Contrast* as creative as you like! You might want to draw him as a cowboy, farmer, baseball player, or anything else you can imagine.

F. *Charlie Contrast*

G. Draw Your *Charlie Contrast* Here

Practice Exercise K: *Balloons & Clowns*

Let's practice drawing some more circles by drawing balloons! Remember, the more you practice basic fundamentals like *lines* and *circles,* the better you will become in drawing. For this assignment you are going to draw three balloons. Remember, to draw a circle, go around and around lightly with your pencil until you have made a nice, round circle. Draw a tip on each balloon and also a *highlight*. A highlight is where light is reflected the most. Draw a highlight by placing a small, curved window on the upper right side of each balloon (A). When finished, color your balloons with vertical lines (B), using at least two colors for each to make a new color. Draw your three balloons in the long figure box (C).

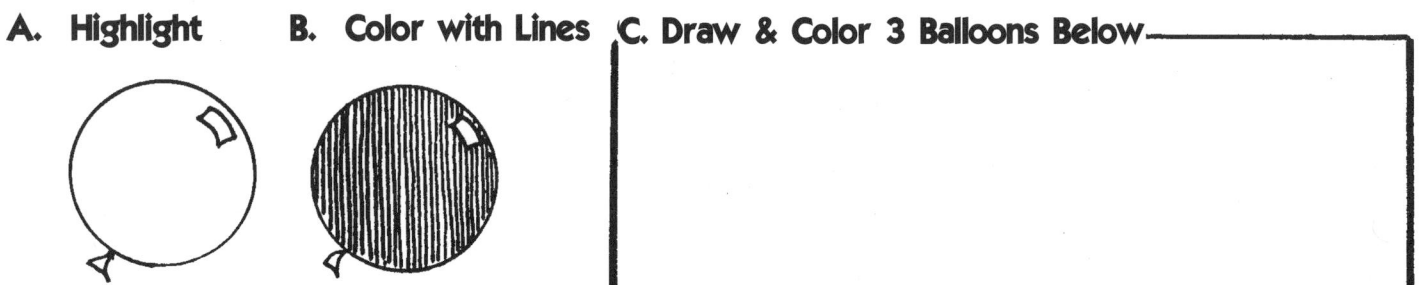

A. Highlight **B. Color with Lines** **C. Draw & Color 3 Balloons Below**

Finally, can you draw a clown's face in the space below? First, give him a round head by drawing a circle. Then draw a circle for his nose and two small circles for his eyes. Finally, draw a string going up in the air and connect it to a balloon. Color your clown with your colored pencils when finished.

Draw Your Clown Here

Practice Exercise L: Overlapping

Overlapping is placing one object slightly in front of another to create *depth,* or distance, in your picture (A). Before beginning, draw another triangle, rectangle, and square beneath the ones illustrated (B, C & D).

When finished, draw three more geometric shapes. However, this time overlap by placing *Wally the Worm* behind each (E). Start by drawing lightly with your yellow colored pencil and then add darker colors. Draw *Wally the Worm* with your red pencil behind a triangle, rectangle, and square. Don't forget to add curved stripes to his body, a smiley face, and a hat.

A. Overlapping

B. Triangle   C. Rectangle   D. Square
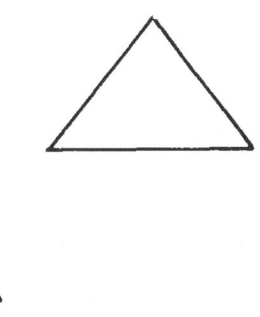 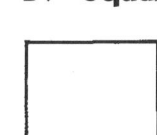

E. Overlapping

F. Draw *Wally the Worm*
   Behind a Triangle Here

G. Draw *Wally the Worm*
   Behind a Rectangle Here

H. Draw *Wally the Worm*
   Behind a Square Here

Practice Exercise M: *Designs on Balls*

Let's draw some more circles and make beach balls out of them by placing colorful designs on each (A). Remember, if you want to put a stripe on a ball, the stripe has to go *around* because the ball is round (B). Using your orange colored pencil, draw three beach balls in the figure box below (C) and place creative designs on each.

When you are finished, draw two more beach balls on the bottom of the page. Have *Wally the Worm* crawling over one (D) and crawling behind the other (E). When you are finished, go over your drawings with other colored pencils.

A. Beach Ball

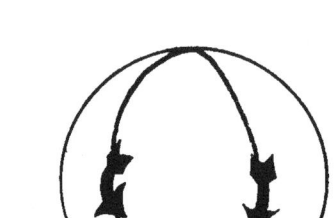

B. Stripes Go Around

C. Draw Your 3 Beach Balls Here

D. *Wally the Worm* Crawling Over a Ball

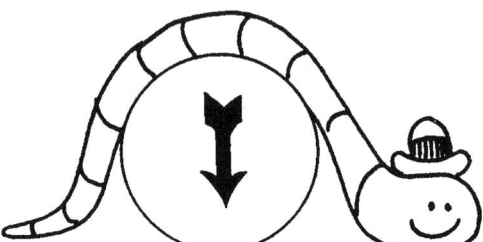

D. *Wally the Worm* Crawling Behind a Ball

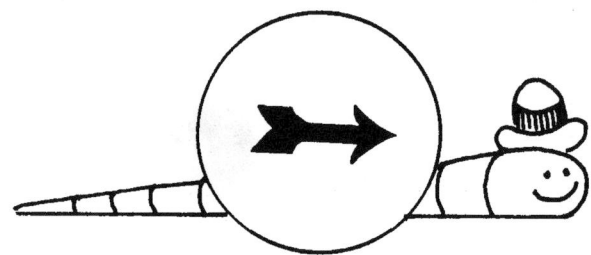

Practice Exercise N: *Texture: Wood & Water*

Do you know how to draw *texture* on a tree? One way is by drawing long, vertical lines. However, as you draw your lines, break them occasionally to give your tree a more woodsy effect. Notice the way the lines are drawn on the tree below (A).

For the first part of this exercise, add texture to the tree (B) by drawing long, broken lines. Use your violet and orange pencils to give your tree trunk more color. Make sure your lines are close together. Then, *overlap* by placing two cartoon characters behind the tree. Draw part of a circle and part of an oval for their heads and give them cartoon facial features. Use your red pencil for one and your blue pencil for the other. For the fingers, simply draw three small circles to suggest each hand as your characters look around the tree.

Do you know how to draw water? One way is by drawing long, broken horizontal lines (C). Broken lines will add a nice sparkle to your water and is similar to the way you drew texture on the tree; however, these lines will be horizontal instead of vertical. The farther away the water, the closer the lines will be to each other. (This is similar to the way we drew the railroad tracks in a previous exercise.) Draw your water in the figure box below (E) using your blue and violet colored pencils. The line in the distance is what separates the water from the sky and is called your *horizon line*. Can you draw a sailboat on the horizon line with your black pen?

A. Woody Texture

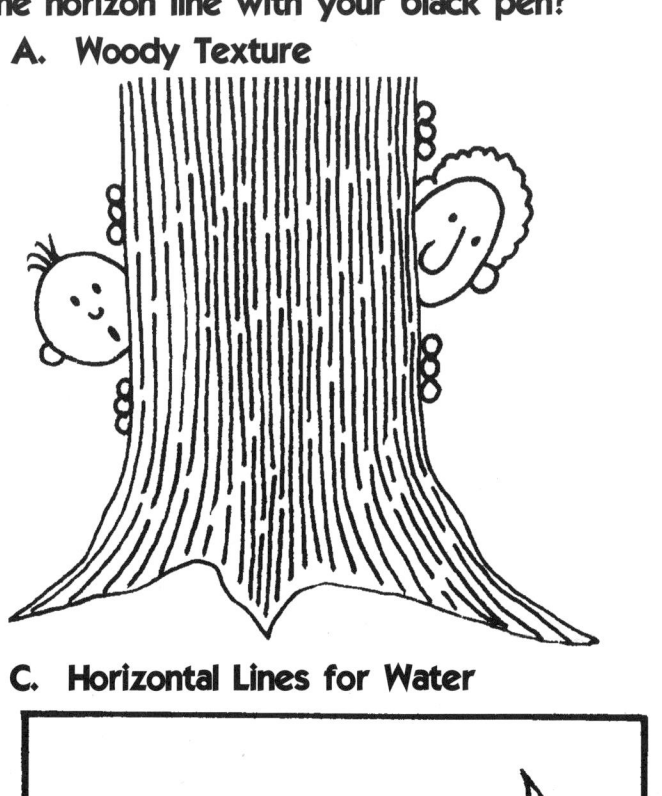

B. Complete Your Tree Here

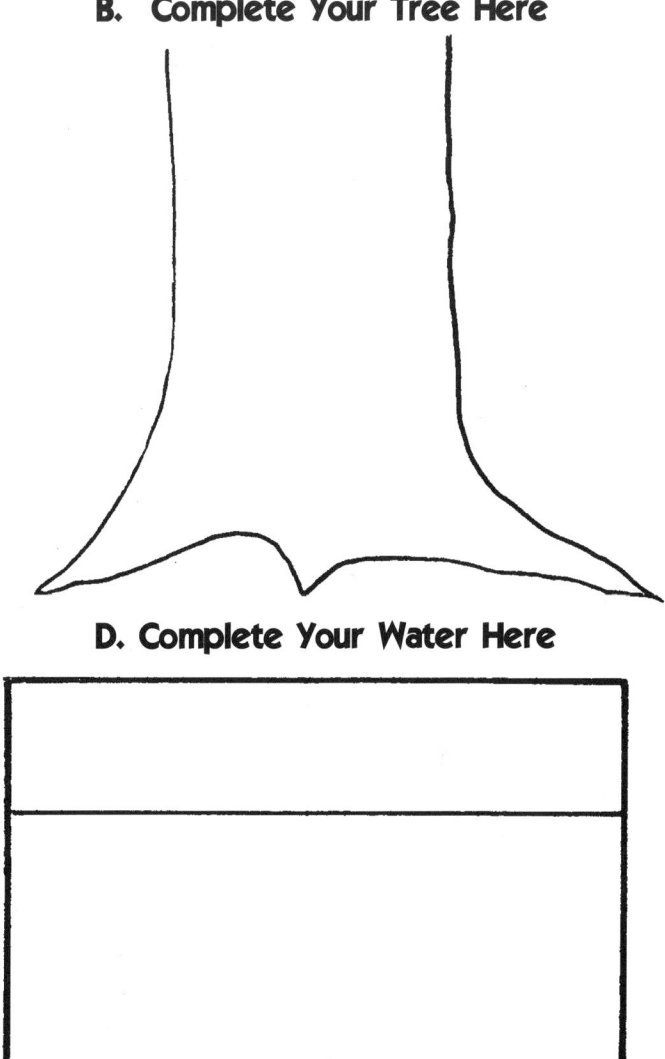

C. Horizontal Lines for Water

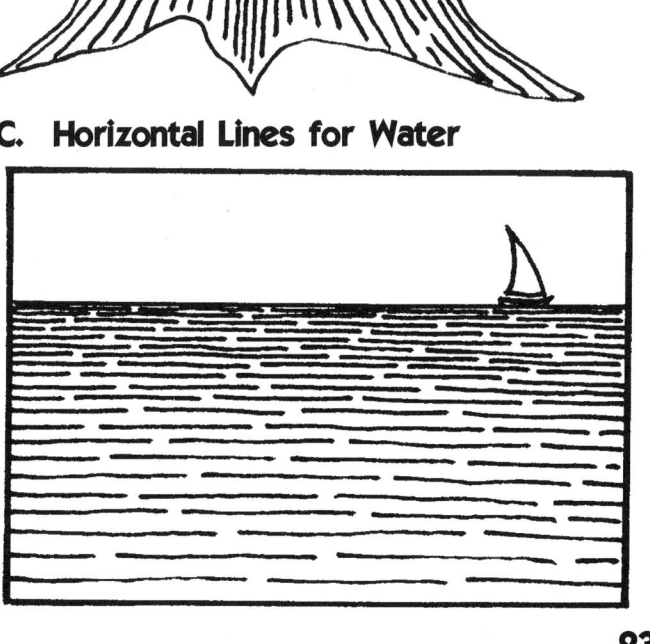

D. Complete Your Water Here

Practice Exercise O: *Whiskers & Fur*

Now let's practice drawing short strokes. First, draw a teddy bear and put fur, or texture, on his body by drawing short strokes (A). To draw the teddy bear, use your orange colored pencil and draw a circle for his body and a smaller circle for his head (B). Then add smaller circles for his arms and legs and two very small circles for his ears (C). Go over your teddy bear with your brown pencil. Add fur by placing short strokes close together with the point of your pencil, giving your teddy bear a furry texture. After you have completed the teddy bear below (C) draw your own teddy bear in D.

Next, let's practice your strokes by giving the cowboy on the bottom of the page (E) hair, mustache, and a beard. Using your black pen, draw long curved lines for his hair and short curved lines for his mustache (F). Then make shorter strokes for the beard.

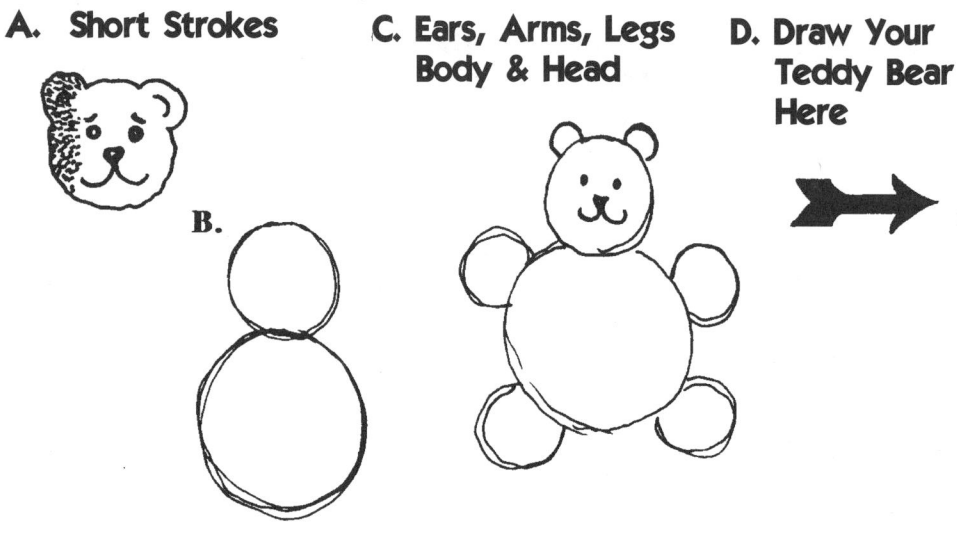

A. Short Strokes

B.

C. Ears, Arms, Legs Body & Head

D. Draw Your Teddy Bear Here

E. Practice Here

F. Cowboy

Practice Exercise P: *Practicing Shading with Lines*

Whenever you practice fundamentals in drawing you should practice them as much as possible. Remember, the more you practice the better you will be and the better you will do the lessons in this book.

For this exercise, let's practice *shading with lines*. Notice the can (A), the box (B) and the man peeking out of a manhole (C). They all have an opened area with a dark *value* inside. A good way to shade dark areas is with lines. First, take your black pencil and add a darker value inside the open can with controlled vertical lines. Then shade inside the box and manhole in the same manner.

A. Opened Can   **B. Opened Box**

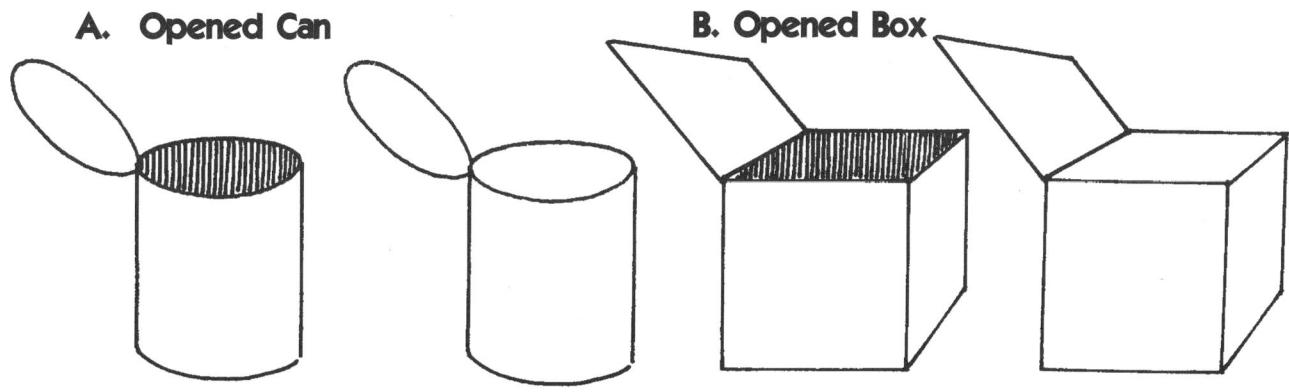

C. Man Peeking Out of a Manhole

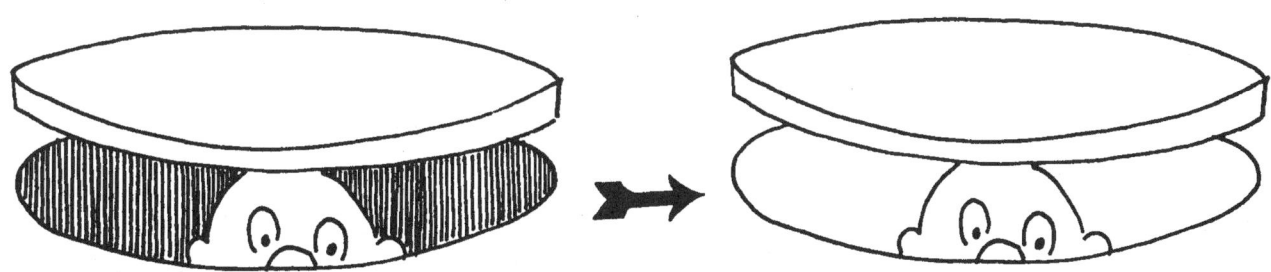

E. Silvery Moon

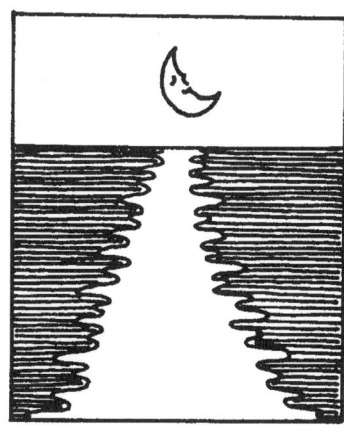

When you have finished, color the water on either side of the moon's reflection with *horizontal lines* with your blue colored pencil (E), making sure to place your lines very close together. Don't go over the reflection, leaving that area white. Last of all, shade the sunglasses by using *diagonal lines* with your black pencil (F). Diagonal lines are lines that are on a slant /////.

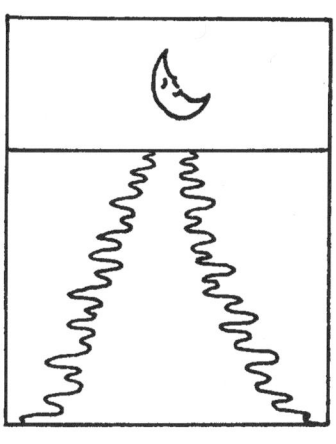

   **F. Sunglasses**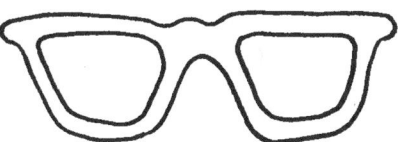

A.

Practice Exercise Q: *Ellipses*

Ellipses are another very important fundamental in drawing (like learning how to draw circles and lines), and should be practiced as much as possible.

An ellipse is simply a circle seen on an angle (A). There are hundreds of things around the house that are drawn with ellipses, such as lamps, cups, glasses, pots, bottles, and jars. To draw an ellipse, lightly go around four or five times with your pencil to form a perfect pancake shape (B).

For the first part of this exercise, practice drawing ellipses in the long figure box below (C). Use a different colored pencil for each and make them as perfect as you can. Fill the entire figure box with ellipses!

* ELLIPSES * ELLIPSES * ELLIPSES * ELLIPSES * ELLIPSES * ELLIPSES * ELLIPSES *

C.

D. Fish Bowl

Draw Your Fish Bowl Here

Finally, see if you can draw the fish bowl (D) and the flower pot (E), making sure to use an ellipse for the top and bottom of each. Start by drawing lightly with your yellow pencil and then use darker colors.

E. Flower Pot

Draw
Your
Flower
Pot
Here

26

Practice Exercise R: *Drawing Objects with Ellipses*

Ellipses are not easy to draw and will take practice. Remember, the more you practice the fundamentals, the better you will become in drawing. Let's practice creating objects with ellipses by drawing the objects below. Start by lightly drawing each with your yellow pencil, making sure to draw a nice ellipse for the top and bottom of the objects, going around and around four or five times. Notice that the label and the lid on the jar are also drawn with ellipses. After you have drawn each object correctly, go over them with your brown or black colored pencil.

A. Basketball Rim

B. Cup

C. Glass with Toothbrush

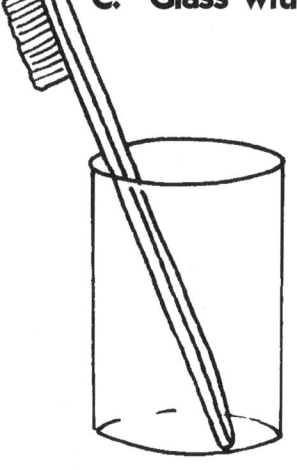

D. Bowl

E. Bottle

F. Jar with Lid & Label

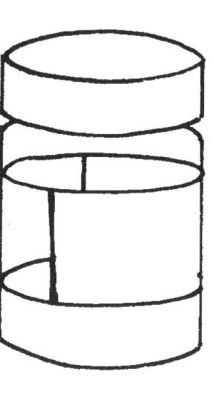

Practice Exercise S: *Drawing Ovals*

Now that you have learned how to draw *circles* (A) and *ellipses* (B), let's practice drawing *ovals*. Ovals are egg-shaped and are not as round as a circle. However, it is drawn in the same manner, going around and around four or five times to make a nice oval shape (C). An oval is a good shape to draw when you are drawing someone's face. To start, draw three ovals below in the figure box (D).

A. Circle   B. Ellipse   C. Oval   D. Practice Drawing Ovals Here

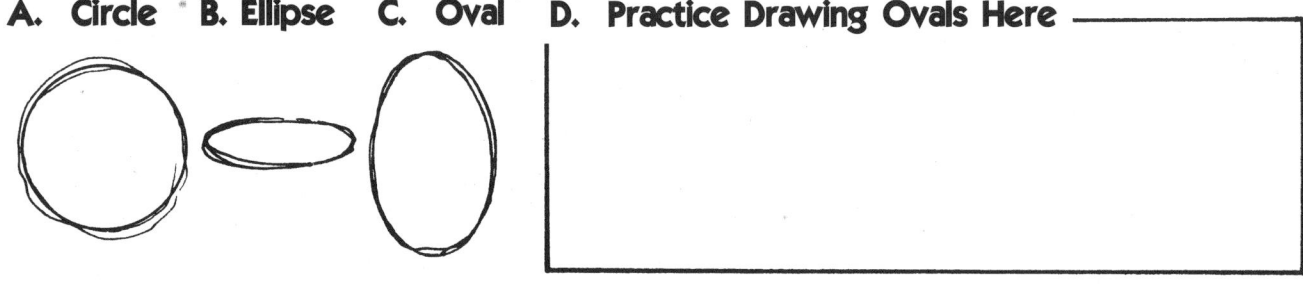

Now, let's see if you can draw an oval face for some of the cartoon characters below. Remember, an oval is not as round as a circle or as thin as an ellipse. Start off by lightly drawing four ovals in the figure box below (E). When you are finished, take out your black colored pencil and complete each face by adding cartoon faces and hair.

Ovals * Ovals * Ovals * Ovals * Ovals * Ovals * Ovals * Ovals * Ovals *

E.

Practice Exercise **T:** *Water & Ripples*

Let's practice drawing *wavy lines*. Wavy lines take just as much control to draw as straight lines. First, draw some more fish in the figure box below. Then, using your blue colored pencil, practice drawing wavy lines by filling the fish tank with water as illustrated (A).

A.
Fill the
Fish Tank
with
Wavy Lines

Next, draw a ripple in the water bucket. First, draw a raindrop dripping into the pool of water and then draw the ripples. Notice that the ripples become larger and larger and that they are drawn with ellipses.

B.
Rain Drop
Dripping
in a Pot

D. Draw Your Little Girl Here

C. Little Girl with Wavy Hair

Finally, draw the little girl to the left (C). Start by drawing an oval with your yellow pencil for her head in the space to the right (D). Then, using your other colored pencils, draw her hair using wavy lines for curls and then draw her facial features, making sure to give her a big, bright smile.

Practice Exercise U: *City Lights & Country Lights*

Silhouette means outline. During the night many times you can only see the outline, or silhouette, of things. First, draw the outline of the city and the little town of Bethlehem in the figure boxes with your black pen. Also, draw the windows, stars, and moon with your black pen and then color them yellow. You may want to color a yellow circle, or halo around the moon and stars. Then, add a darker value to your city scape and the little town of Bethlehem by coloring the skies blue by blending blue and violet. Finally, color the city and the little town of Bethlehem by blending blue and black together.

A. Silhouette of a City

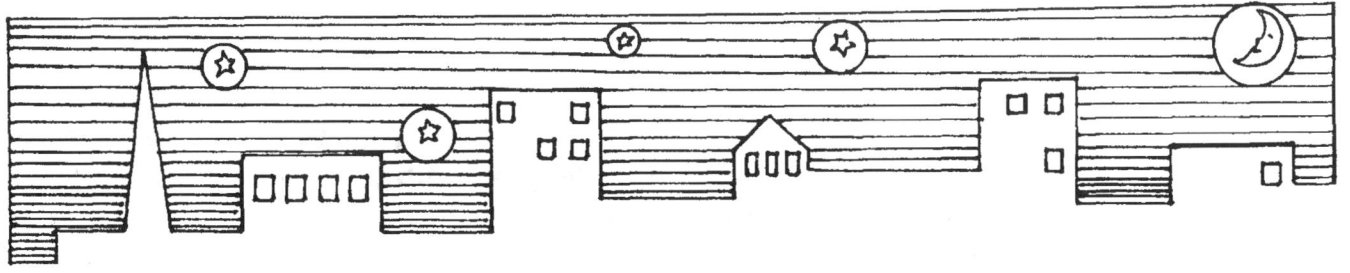

B. Little Town of Bethlehem

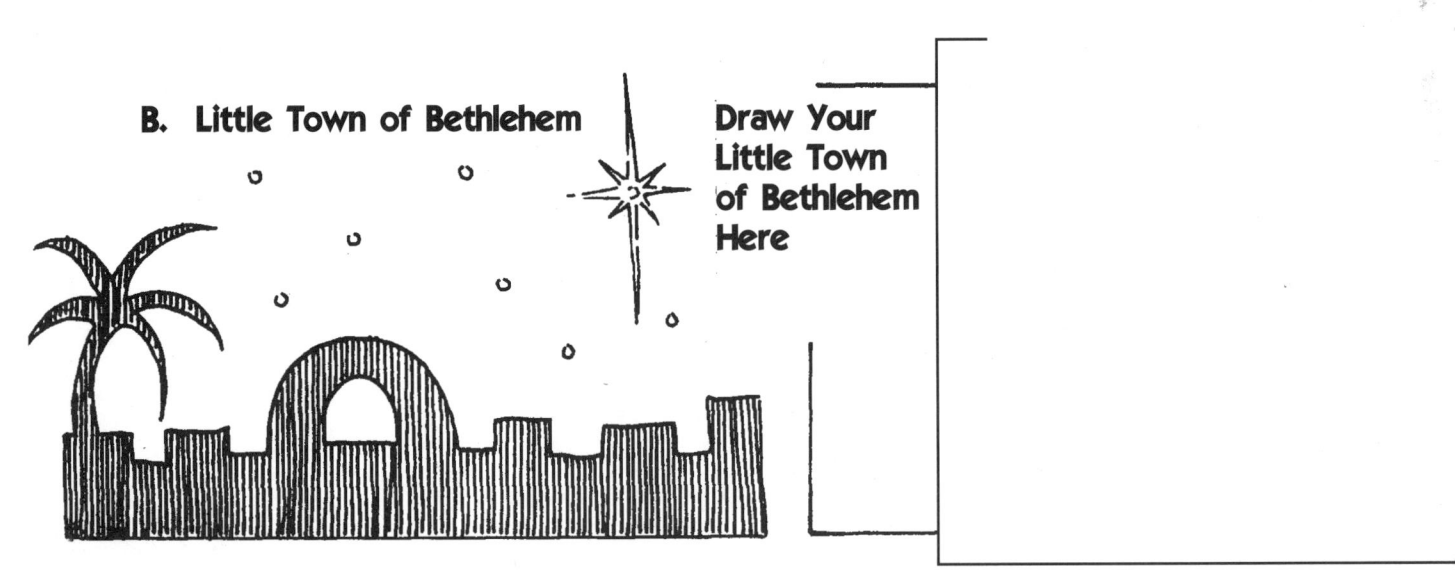

Draw Your
Little Town
of Bethlehem
Here

Practice Exercise V: *Figure Boxes & Picture Frames*

Placing drawings in *figure boxes* can make interesting little pictures. Many students do not know how to compose a picture on a large piece of paper finding it tedious to color in the entire background. Small figure boxes not only make for a nice little picture but also allow you to fill an entire page with them! Drawing a figure box is similar to drawing a square or rectangle (A) and you can draw them any size you like. However, make them look nice by drawing straight lines.

Another fun thing you can do with your figure boxes is draw a border around them to make a nice picture frame (B). For this assignment, lightly draw a figure box below (C) and place a picture frame, or border, around it. Fill your frame with creative designs and then draw a hot air balloon in it as illustrated. Color with your colored pencils when finished.

Finally, draw two more figure boxes on the bottom of the page and place a nice picture design around them with creative designs in each. Then find some treasures around the house like a teapot, flower pot, kitchen utensil, or candle and draw one of these objects in each of your picture frames.

A. Figure Box   **B. Figure Box with Border**   **C. Draw Your Figure Box Here**

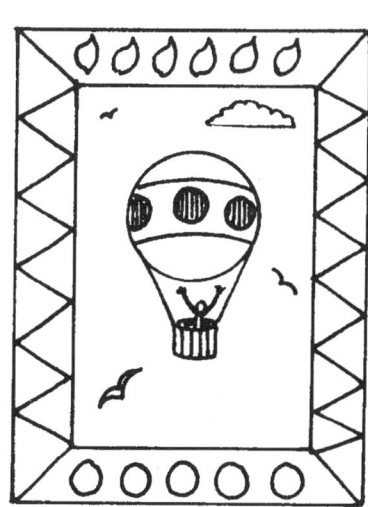

D. Draw 2 figure boxes below and then draw objects around the house in them.

Practice Exercise W: *Cubes, Boxes & Paper Bags*

Now let's see if we you make some three-dimensional boxes, look as though they have *depth*. First, draw a rectangle. Then add short diagonal (slanted) lines extending from the three corners as shown (A & B). Make sure all three diagonal are drawn at the same angle, like this //////. Next, connect the top two lines with a straight horizontal line and the two lines on the side with a straight vertical line (C). Draw your three-dimensional box below (D).

If you know how to draw a box, it is a simple matter to draw a paper bag. Again, lightly draw the rectangular shape you did in D, adding wavy lines to the side and a jagged top (F). You have just drawn a paper bag (G)! Draw your bag below (H) with your yellow pencil and then go over it with your brown pencil.

Finally, let's make a *cube*. A cube is like a square box. First, draw a square (I). Then extend the three diagonal lines out a little more and connect them just as you did with the first box (J). To draw a lid to your box draw one diagonal line coming out from the top left corner, and then a shorter diagonal line coming out from the far corner. Connect the two and you have made a top for your box (K). Draw your box below (L).

Finally, put some objects in the bag and box. You may want to draw *Wally the Worm*, or *Charlie Contrast* or anything else you like.

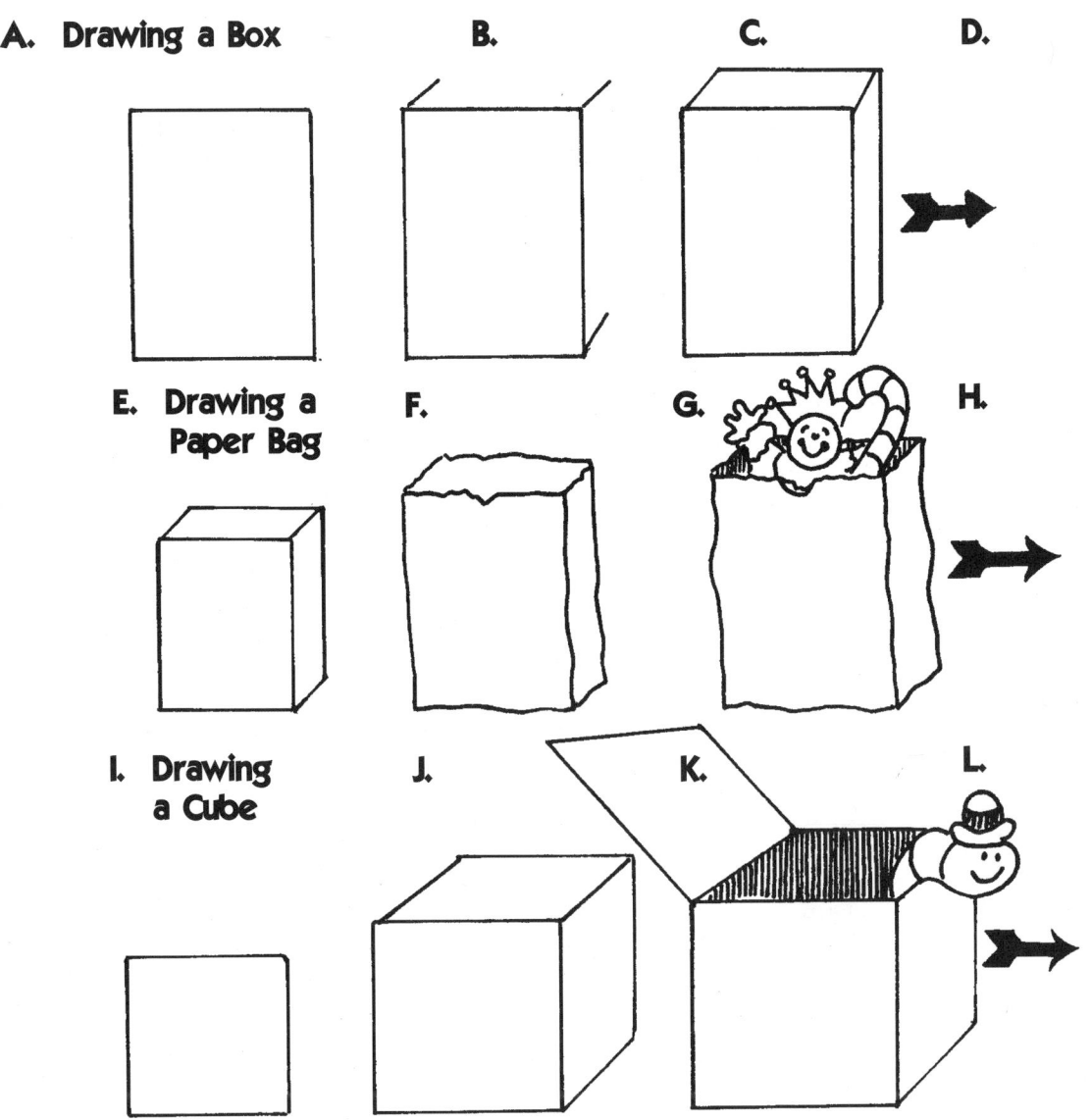

A. Drawing a Box   B.   C.   D.

E. Drawing a Paper Bag   F.   G.   H.

I. Drawing a Cube   J.   K.   L.

Practice Exercise X: *Small, Medium, Large*

Small Can of Beans

Have you ever noticed how many products come in different sizes? There is a *small* can of beans, a *medium* can of beans, and a *large* can of beans. There is also a *small* jar of jelly, a *medium* jar of jelly, and a *large* jar of jelly. Likewise, there is a *small* box of cereal, a *medium* box of cereal, and a *large* box of cereal. See if you can draw each of the objects below: *small, medium,* and *large.* When finished, draw and color labels on each with your colored pencils.

Medium Jar of Jelly

Large Box of Cereal

A Small Can of Beans

A Small Jar of Jelly

A Small Box of Cereal

A Medium Can of Beans

A Medium Jar of Jelly

A Medium Box of Cereal

A Large Can of Beans

A Large Jar of Jelly

A Large Box of Cereal

Practice Exercise Y: *Stripes & Waves*

For this exercise, complete the flag by drawing wavy stripes (A). Connect the dots from one side to the other with your yellow pencil. Make each wavy stripe exactly the same as the others. Then color in every other stripe red and the square behind the stars blue.

Finally, on the bottom of the page, use your blue and violet colored pencils to draw wavy lines behind Jonah and the big fish, filling the picture with lots of wavy lines (B). Remember, keep your lines close together and take your time. If you become tired, take a break and finish this assignment at a later time.

C. Connect the Dots....Make the Stripes

B. Wavy Lines & Water

Practice Exercise Z: *Review! Review! Review!*

Finally, let's review what you have learned. It is always good to repeat, or review, so you will remember these fundamentals and apply them to your drawings. For this last exercise, use any colored pencils you like. First, practice drawing lines by connecting the large dots below (A) with long horizontal lines and then long vertical lines going in the opposite direction so that they criss-cross. This will create a screen-like effect that is called *"cross-hatching."* Remember, keep your lines as straight as possible.

Next, shade inside the can (B), box (C), and opened manhole (D) on the top of the next page with vertical lines. Then see if you can draw a perfect circle (C), ellipse (D), and oval (E) and draw a funny face in each. Last of all, draw a jar (F), box (G), and flower pot (H), making sure to use nice ellipses for the jar and pot.

When you are finished, review what you have done by checking off the list on the bottom of the page. Do you still need to practice some of these fundamentals? If so, continue to practice whenever you feel like it. The more you practice the better you will become in drawing.

A. Connect the Dots with Long, Horizontal & Vertical Lines

B. Shade Inside the Can **C. Shade Inside the Box** **D. Shade Inside the Manhole**

 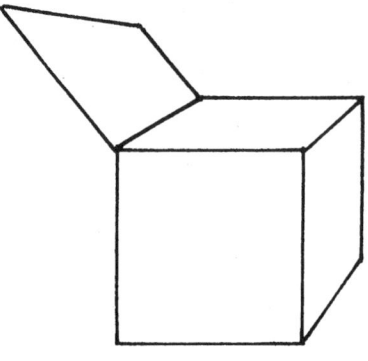 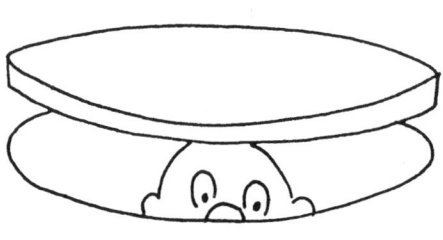

C. Draw a Perfect Circle **D. Draw a Perfect Ellipse** **E. Draw a Perfect Oval**

F. Draw a Jar **G. Draw a Box** **H. Draw a Flower Pot**

Check List:

_____Are your lines straight?
_____Are your circles round?
_____Can you draw a nice ellipse?
_____Can you draw a nice oval?
_____Did you take your time?
_____Are you ready to start I Can Do All Things?

****

ABCDEFGHIJKLMNOPQRSTUVWXYZ!!!

Now that you know your ABC's of beginning drawing, let's start the program. So, sharpen your pencils and keep a good attitude. Remember, *"I can do all things through Christ who strengthens me."*

Before We Begin.....

Before we begin *I Can Do All Things,* let's do a drawing assignment. Your drawing will help you see how much you have learned and how much better you have become by the end of the book. Use your black pen to draw a farm scene in the figure box below. Can you draw a farmer? A tractor? Some animals? Put as much detail in your drawing as possible adding anything else you like. When you are finished, write your name and age on the bottom of the page, and place the date on the top.

Today's Date is:_____

My Name is:_____   I Am_____Years Old

Let's Do One More Picture:

Let's do one more assignment before beginning *I Can Do All Things*. This time we will use colored pencils. (Do you like to color?) Color in the picture below anyway you like. Also, look in a mirror and draw a picture of your face in the picture frame to the left. This is called a self-portrait. Have fun with this. When you are finished, print your name and age on the bottom of the page and place the date on the top.

My First Self Portrait   **Today's Date is:**_____

My Name is:_____ **I Am** _____ **Years Old**

Beginning Drawing

"Man is a maker. This is part of what it means to be in the image of our Creator God. As we learn to collaborate with Him, He confirms and mightily blesses the work of our hands.... When we allow God to bestow His favor and beauty and delightfulness on the work of our hands, He makes artists of even the humblest among us."

Leanne Payne

Beginning Drawing

Drawing is commanding your pencil to do what you want it to do. This is not as easy as it sounds, especially if you are between the ages of 4 and 7. There are three things to consider when drawing:

1. As your *grow* older you will naturally have more control over what you want your pencil to do.
2. The more *patience* you have in drawing, the more your hand and pencil will do what you want them to do.
3. Drawing takes *practice*. The more you practice the better you will become.

Rules for Beginning Drawing

1. **Sharpen Your Pencil:** Always have a sharp pencil point. This is very important in drawing. The best way to have a sharp point is to use an electric or hand-held pencil sharpener.
2. **Store your Art Pencils Properly:** It is important to take care of your art materials. The best way to store your pencils is in a jar or cup with all the points facing up.
3. **Do Not Mix Drawing Pencils with Colored Pencils:** You will find that the two leads do not work well together. It is best to do your drawings either with all drawing pencils or with all colored pencils.
4. **Hold Your Pencil Away from the Point:** Most students like to hold their pencils tightly down near the point. Learn how to draw in a relaxed manner. Holding your pencil farther up from the point will help you relax more.
5. **Draw Lightly:** Most beginning students like to draw with a heavy hand and make dark lines. The student needs to learn how to start off his pictures by drawing lightly. A student must be taught to draw lightly. After everything is drawn in correctly he can go over this light drawing with a darker pencil.
6. **Refrain From Using a Ruler:** The student should learn how to draw lines *free hand.* This means drawing without the use of a ruler. This will teach you *control,* which is being able to make the pencil do what you want it to do.
7. **Refrain From Using an Eraser:** One of the first things I would hear in my beginning drawing classes was the sound of erasers! When I heard this it was a sign that the students did not have confidence in what they were drawing. When a student learns to draw lightly he will build up his confidence in his drawing skills.
8. **Listen to Classical Music!** Classical music can be very inspiring, especially during art time. Try to learn the composers as you listen.

Teacher's Note: Some of the drawing assignments are a little difficult for younger students (Lessons 12, 14, 15, 16, 19, 20, 21 & 23). If this is true with a student you are teaching, pass over those lessons that are difficult and return to them a little later when the child's motor skills have developed more.

Lesson #1: *Long Lines & Shoestrings*

A. No! ───────────────────────

B. No! ───────────────────────

C.   D. ═══════════════════════

Learning to draw is practicing *control,* or teaching your pencil to do what you want it to do. Let's practice control by drawing shoestrings. The best way to draw lon-n-n-n-ng lines is to patiently guide your pencil along with control. Take your time. *There is no rush!* However, do not inch your pencil across the paper like an ant walking through the desert (A). And don't be in such a hurry that your lines look sloppy (B). Draw a shoestring with stripes in the long figure box on the left (C) going down the side of the page. Make sure to use two lines to draw a shoestring to show its thickness. Draw stripes going *around* the shoestring just like the one above (D). Finally, draw a shoestring in the boot below just like the one on the left. Remember, take your time and practice control.

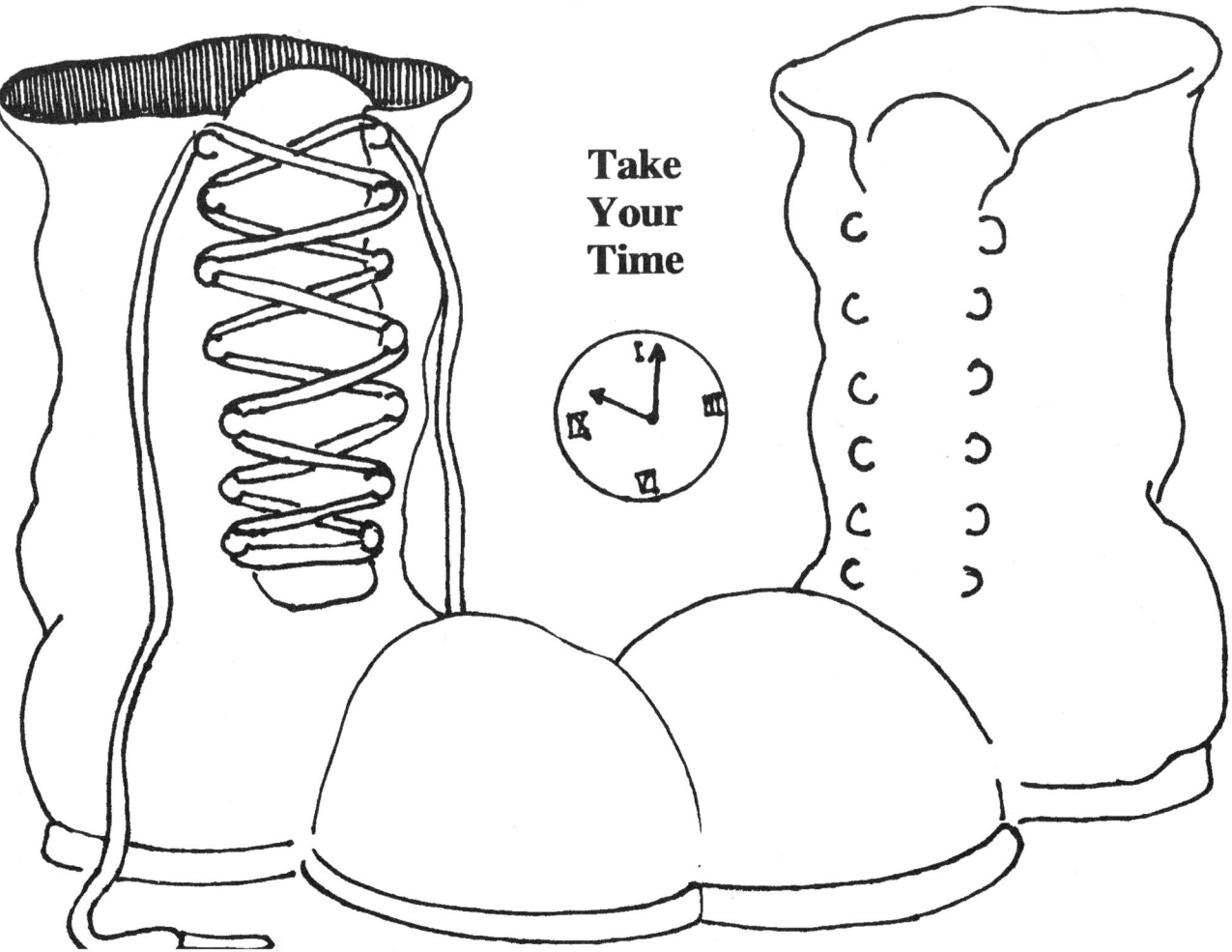

Take
Your
Time

Lesson #2: On a plain sheet of paper draw one of your shoes. Make sure to draw the shoestring with controlled lines. Start your drawing lightly with your yellow colored pencil and then go over it with your brown pencil. If you have problems drawing this have your mother or teacher draw it for you and then you can draw the shoestring.

Lesson #3: *Wally the Worm & Family*

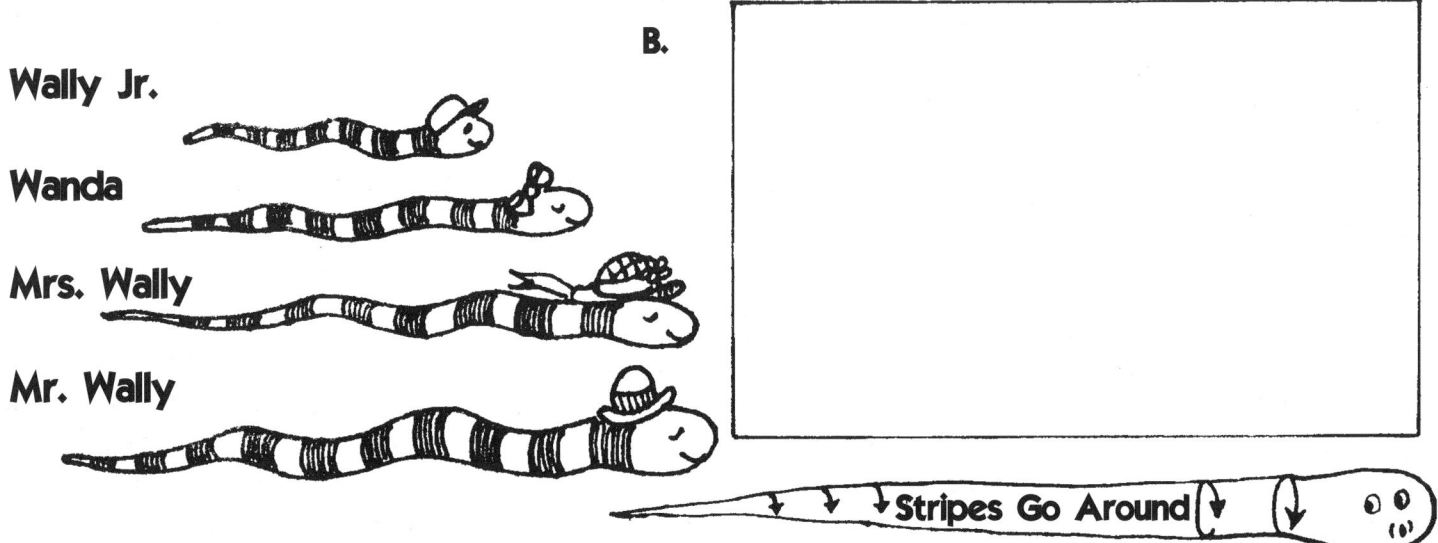

A.

Fatter to thinner, to thinner, to thinner......

Drawing Wally the Worm is like drawing a shoestring. However, the lines go from fatter to thinner to thinner as they meet at his tail (A). Draw Wally Jr., Wanda, and Mr. and Mrs. Wally in the figure box below (B) with your black pen. Take your time and practice drawing with *control*. Draw stripes on their bodies, making sure to show the stripes go *around*. Finally, place a baseball hat on Wally Jr., a bow on Wanda's head, a bonnet on Mrs. Wally, and a hat on Mr. Wally. Then complete Wally above by giving him a hat and drawing stripes going around his body.

Wally Jr.

Wanda

Mrs. Wally

Mr. Wally

B.

Stripes Go Around

Lesson #4: *Foreshortening*

Foreshortening means to draw things larger as they come forward and smaller as they go into the background. When we draw like this, it helps show *depth* in our drawings, creating *distance*. For this assignment, draw Wally as he winds his way forward on the paper (C). Start with a large "S" shape. (Don't forget, the closer he comes towards you, the fatter he will be.) Finally, on a piece of white paper, draw Wally the Worm winding through a flower bed. Show that he is much larger as he comes forward.

smallest

smaller

larger

largest

C.

42

Lesson #5: *Flower Stems & Wagon Wheels*

Grass and flower stems should not be drawn with one skinny line (A). Just like shoe-strings and Wally the Worm, flower stems are drawn with two lines (B). Can you add some petals and leaves to the flower below (C) with your black pen? Then complete the three flowers (D) by adding their stems and leaves. Grass also looks better if you draw it with two lines coming together at a point (B).

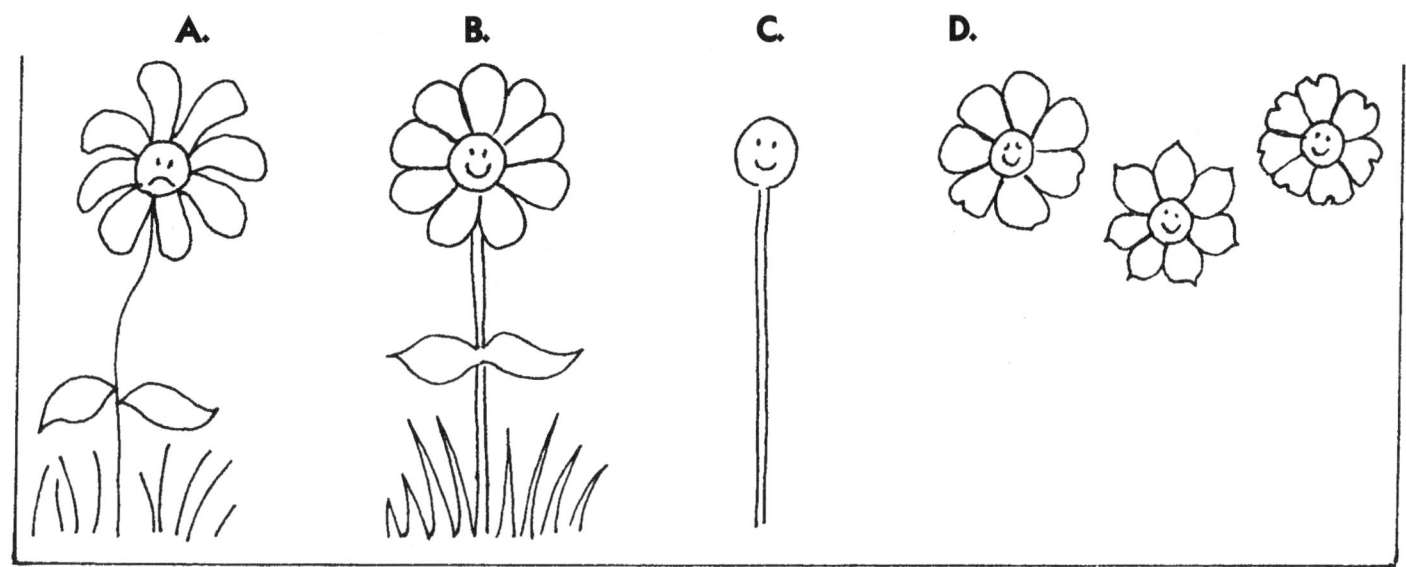

Lesson #6: *Wagon Wheels*

Drawing the spokes to wagon wheels is another way of practicing control. Notice the wagon wheel on the bottom of the page (E). The spikes are drawn with two controlled lines. See if you can draw spokes from the rim of the wheel to the center (F) with your black pen. Finally, draw some grass and flowers around the bottom of the wagon wheel.

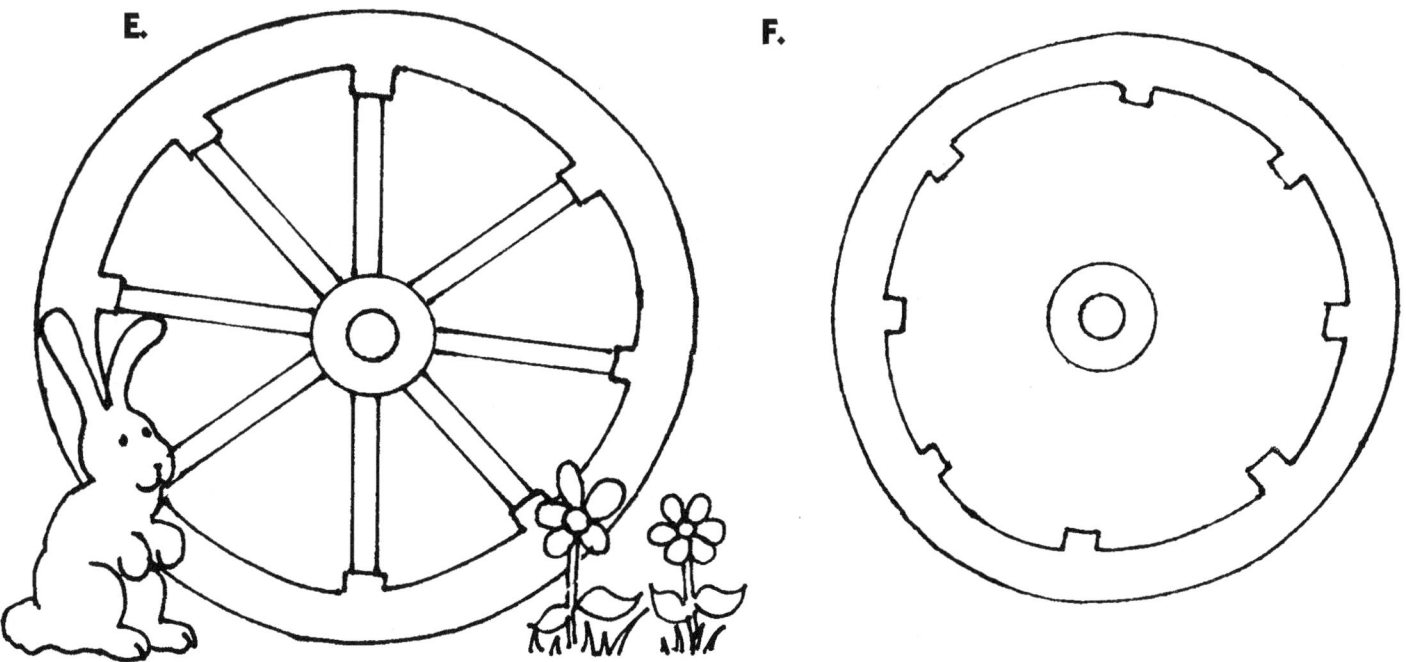

Lesson #7: *In & Out - Over & Around*

Let's put Wally the Worm through an obstacle course! Notice how much larger he looks when we see him through Grandpop's glasses (A), or how he looks coming out of a can (B), or the way he winds around a triangle (C). Using your black pen, draw Wally the Worm on the next page in each of the positions shown below.

A. Grandpop's Glasses

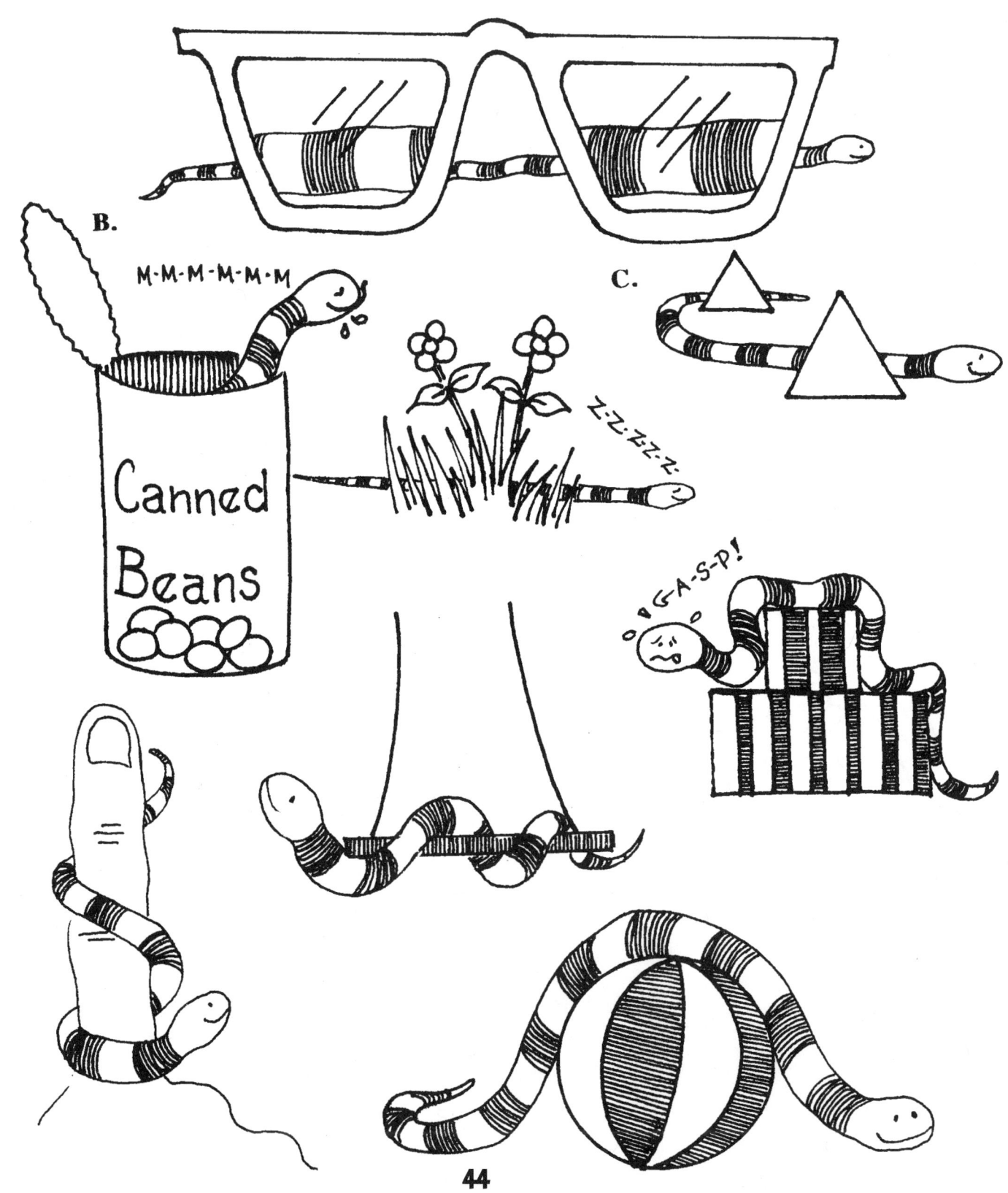

44

"Then God said, 'Let Us make man in Our own image, in Our likeness, and let them rule....over all the creatures that move along the ground."

Genesis 1:26

Draw Finger Below

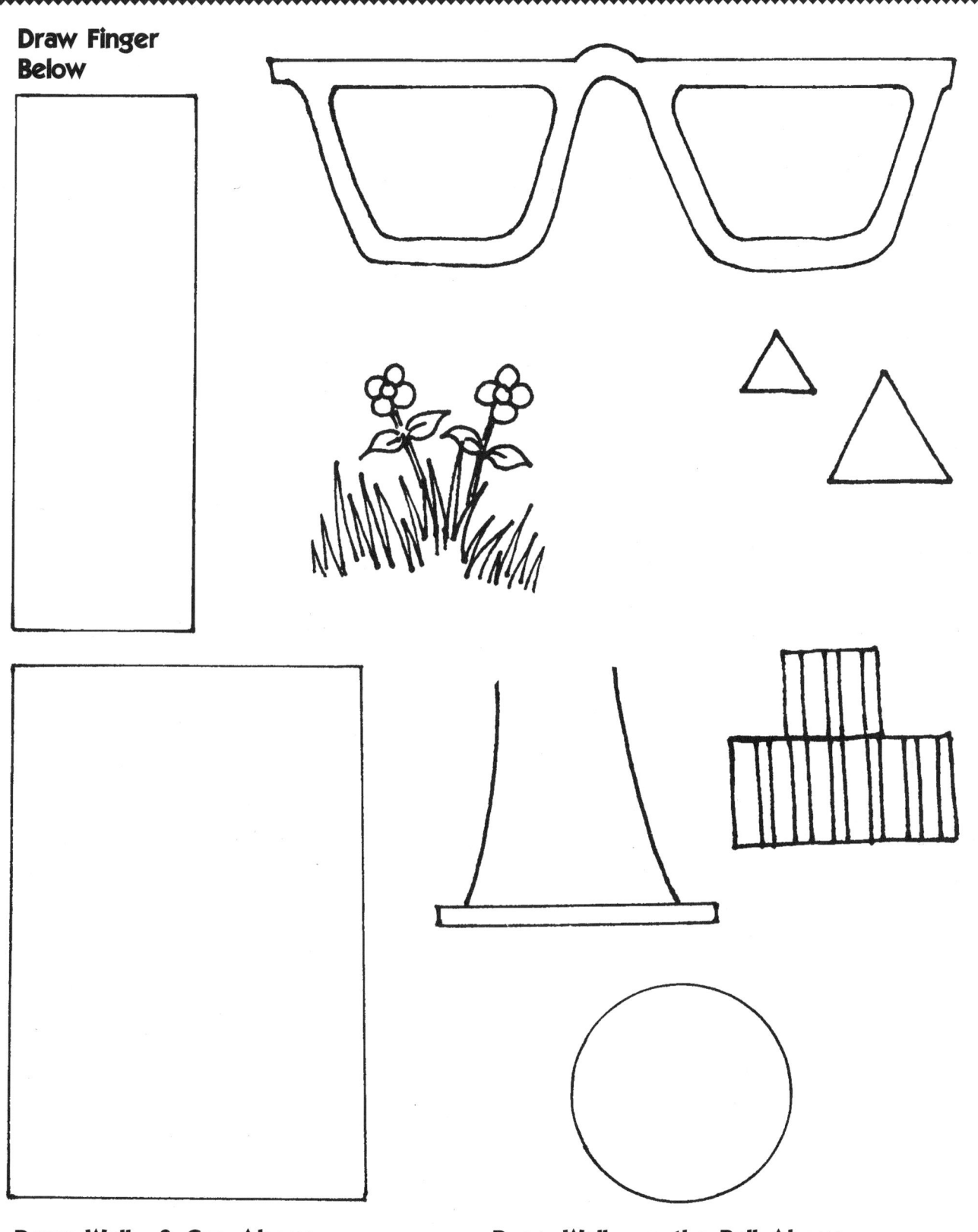

Draw Wally & Can Above   **Draw Wally on the Ball Above**

45

"The carpenter stretches out his rule; he marks it out with line..."

Isaiah 44:13

Lesson #8: *Once Upon a Line*

"Yes, sir!"

"I command you to go straight!"

Remember, in drawing we need to command our pencil to do what we want it to do. Learning control takes practice, time, and patience. The more you practice, the better you will be able to draw.

"I can't do this...."

For today's lesson, connect the lines of the roof on the barn below (B) with your black pen. Add windows and a barn door using controlled lines. Next, draw vertical lines (straight up and down) behind the barn as shown below (A) to make a nice background of distant trees for your barn. Can you draw a long clothesline connecting the two posts on the bottom of the page (C)? Finally, draw some clothes hanging from the line.

A.

B. Complete the Barn

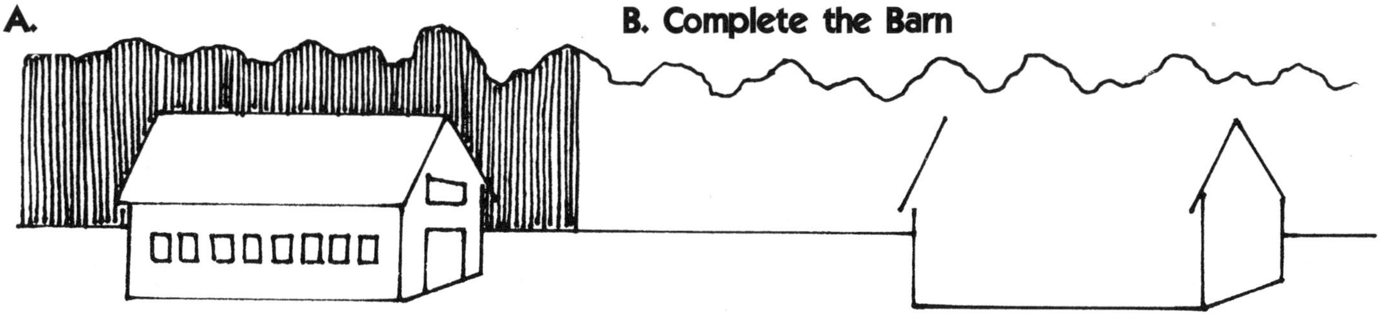

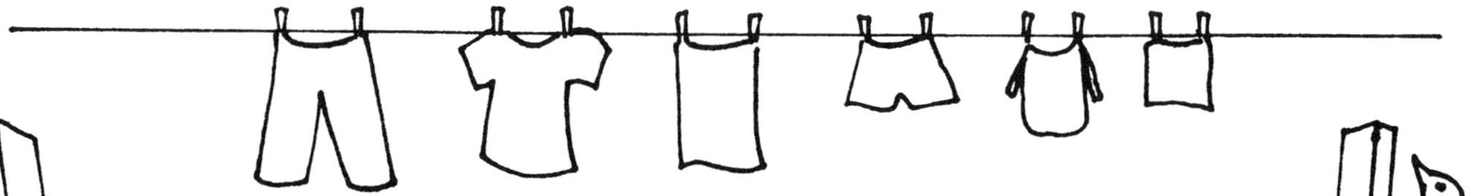

C.

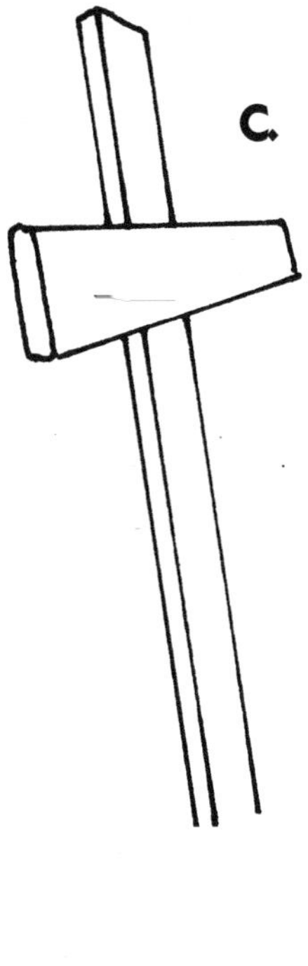

Can you draw a clothes line and add clothes to the line? Use your black pen and then color in the clothing, birds, and posts with your colored pencils when finished.

"Love comforteth like sunshine after the rain." William Shakespeare

Lesson #9: *Circles & Sunshine*

Just like lines, it is very important to learn how to draw a circle. (Remember, it is always good to start by drawing *lightly*.) Many students simply draw one heavy line and connect it (A). Other students draw something more like an egg shape than a circle (B). To draw a circle, hold your pencil above the paper and lightly go around four or five times until you have created a nice, round circle (C).

A. No!

B. No!

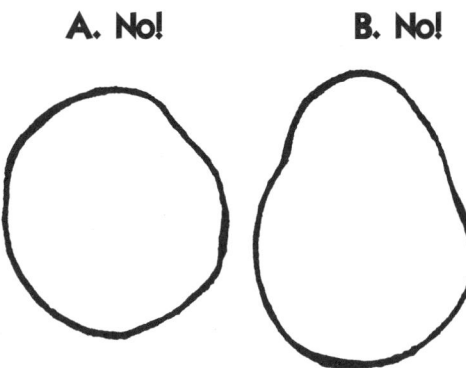

Don't be discouraged. Always draw lightly! Learning to draw circles is a fundamental and takes practice. Take a piece of paper and fill it with nice, round circles. Practice drawing them lightly, with your orange colored pencil, going around and around.

C. Yes!

Next draw a balloon, a sun, and a flower on the bottom of the page (D), making sure to draw each circle correctly. Color them in with your colored pencils when finished.

D. A Balloon   **Sunshine**   **A Flower**

Lesson #10: *Making a Snowman*

Now let's draw 3 circles with your blue colored pencil: a large circle, a medium size circle, and a small circle to make a snowman (A). Place one on top of the other in the figure box below to make a snowman (D). The smallest circle is for the head. After you have drawn your snowman, use your orange pencil and give him two branches for arms and place a broom in one of his hands. Remember, branches always become thinner and thinner the farther they extend out (B). Don't forget to give your snowman a carrot nose. Draw large coal buttons down his belly and give him two coal eyes and a big smile. Add a scarf and a hat to finish your snowman (C). Complete your picture by drawing three pine trees with your green colored pencil: a tiny one far in the distance, a larger one in the middle, and a much larger one in the foreground. Finally, add snowflakes with your blue colored pencil making sure to draw them perfectly round and drawing some in front of your snowman.

A. C. B. D.

Lesson #11: *Funny Faces*

A.

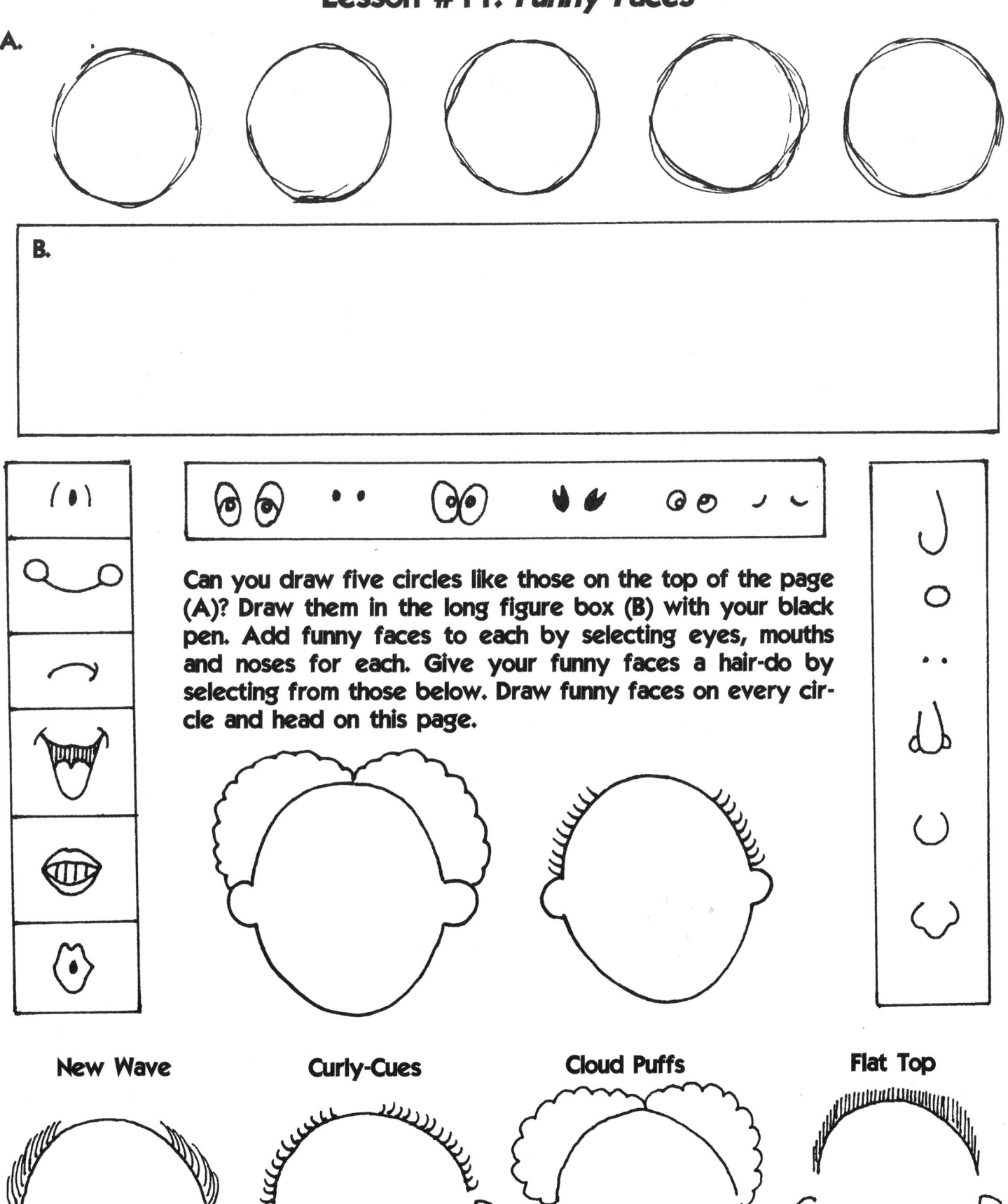

B.

Can you draw five circles like those on the top of the page (A)? Draw them in the long figure box (B) with your black pen. Add funny faces to each by selecting eyes, mouths and noses for each. Give your funny faces a hair-do by selecting from those below. Draw funny faces on every circle and head on this page.

New Wave   **Curly-Cues**   **Cloud Puffs**   **Flat Top**

Lesson #12: *Drawing Big Balloons*

Overlapping means drawing something slightly in front of something else. For instance, look at the three balloons below (A). One balloon has been drawn in front of the other two. Can you draw some balloons and overlap them? First, draw each circle lightly (B), just as we have been doing in previous lessons. Draw all the balloons (even the parts that go behind the other balloons). When you have all the balloons drawn in, take a different colored pencil and give your balloons a darker outline.

A.

As mentioned, *highlights* are little areas where the sunlight is reflected the most (A). You can draw a highlight on your balloons by placing a curved window on the upper right part of each. Finally, color each balloon with long vertical lines using two different colors for each balloon. The front balloon is done with vertical lines, the second balloon with horizontal lines, and the third balloon with diagonal lines.

B.

C. Overlapping Balloons

Draw three balloons in figure box C. Make sure to draw them by making nice round circles. Overlap the balloons by placing part of one in front of part of another as though they are see through or transparent. Can you draw a highlight on each? Finally, use vertical lines to color one, horizontal lines to color another, and diagonal lines to color the last one. Use two colors for each to make new color for the balloons.

Horizontal   Vertical   Diagonal

Lesson #13: Let's make a greeting card. Cut a piece of white poster board to the size of 11" x 7" and fold it to 5 1/2" x 7". Make a cheerful greeting card by drawing some balloons, flowers and a sunshine. Color with markers when finished and send it to a relative or friend.

"Do not have your concert first and tune your instruments afterward. Begin the day with God."

J.H. Taylor

A. Inside a Bell

B.

C. No!

D. Yes!

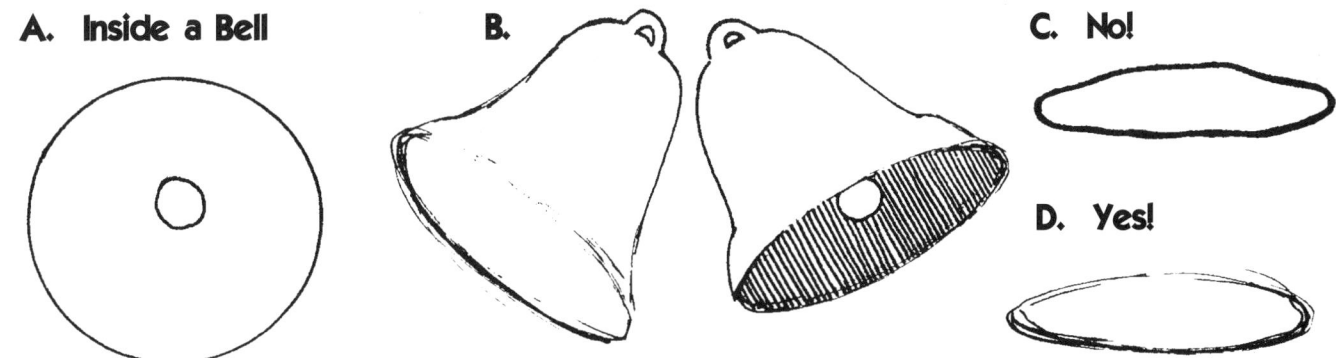

Lesson #14: *Drawing Ellipses*

E. Wishing Well

An *ellipse* is a circle seen on an angle. For instance, if you look straight up at a bell, it will look like a circle (A). However, as the bell swings back and forth, the circle becomes thinner (B). When a circle becomes thinner it is called an ellipse. Learning how to draw an ellipse is just as important as learning how to draw a straight line or circle. Remember, do not be heavy handed (C). An ellipse is drawn the same way as a circle, going around and around lightly four or five times (D). Whereas a circle is perfectly round, an ellipse is long and thin.

F. Your Wishing Well

Practice drawing several ellipses on another sheet of paper. Make some larger and some smaller. See if you can also draw the bell above (B), using an ellipse to show that it is round. Finally, draw a wishing well. Notice how the inside of the well is drawn with an ellipse, showing how the well goes around (E). Draw your wishing well in the figure box (F) with your orange colored pencil and color with other colors when finished.

51

Lesson #15:   *Fruit in the Bowl*

Can you draw a bowl? First, draw a large ellipse (A). Then draw a smaller ellipse directly under the large ellipse (B). Connect the two sides with a curved line and you have a bowl (C). See if you can complete the bowls in (A) and (B) with your black pen and then draw a bowl in figure box (D).

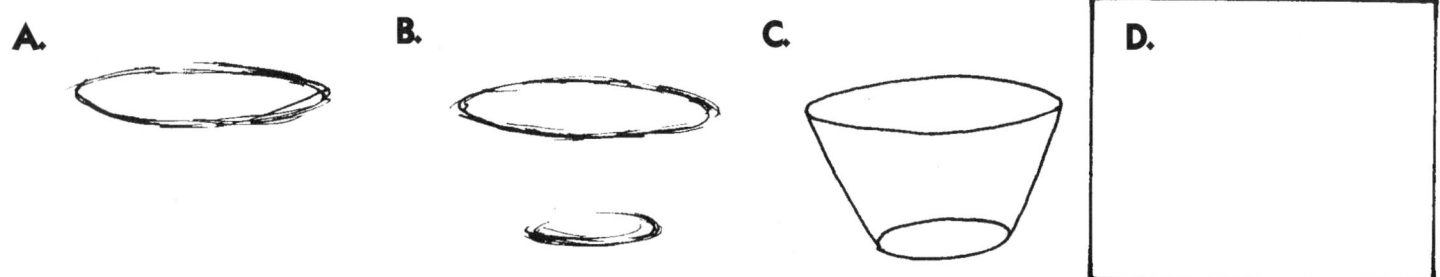

A.   **B.**   **C.**   **D.**

Below are two bowls. Let's pretend the first bowl is a glass bowl (E) and the second bowl is a ceramic bowl (F). Can you fill each bowl with fruit? In the glass bowl you will be able to see all the fruit in the bowl. In the ceramic bowl you will only see the fruit that comes out of the top. The ceramic bowl is not transparent, or see through. Fill the bowls with fruit, making sure to draw the fruit fairly large and to overlap, placing some fruit in front of others.

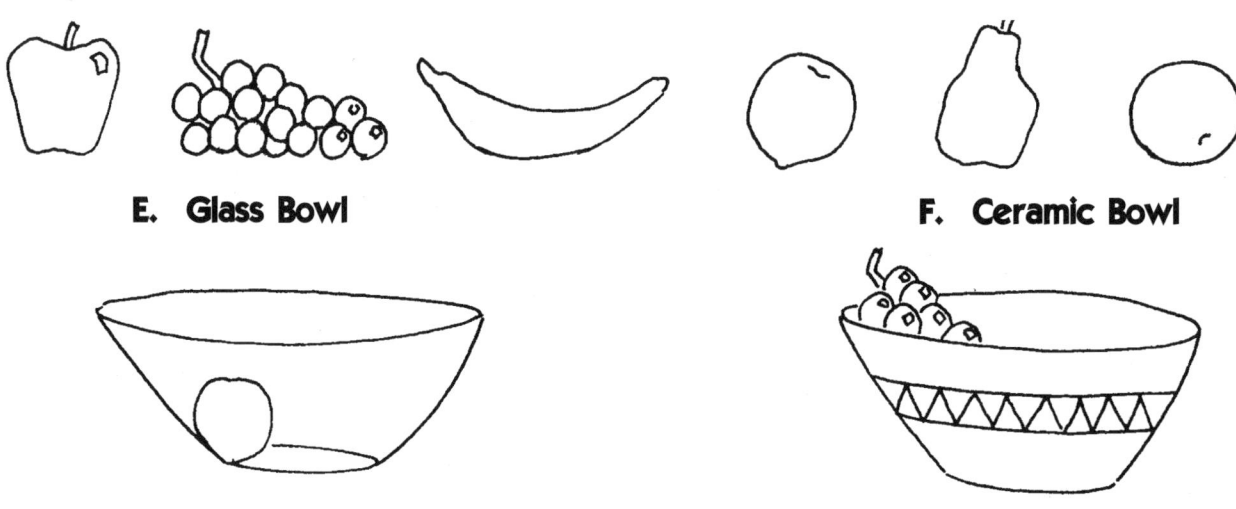

E.   Glass Bowl   **F.   Ceramic Bowl**

G.

Finally, can you draw a large glass bowl in the figure box (G) and fill it with fruit? Make sure to draw the bowl with ellipses and to overlap the fruit. Start with your orange colored pencil and then color in the fruit with your colored pencils when finished.

Lesson #16: A Bird's-eye View

Have you ever seen the entrance to a birdhouse? It is a little hole for the birds to go in and out of (A). We can make one of these by drawing an oval (it looks like an ellipse sideways). To show that it is a thick piece of wood, add another half ellipse to one of the sides (B). All that is left to draw is the bird (C). See if you can draw the entrance to a birdhouse in the figure box below (D). Make sure to draw it lightly. Then draw the bird. Finally, darken the hole behind the bird with vertical lines. Use your black pen.

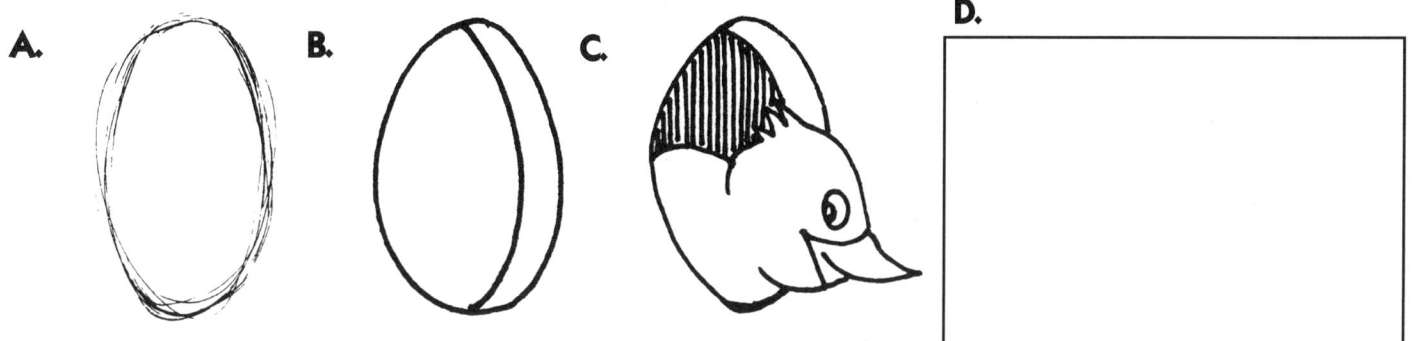

A.　　**B.**　　**C.**　　**D.**

Let's draw the front of a birdhouse. First, draw a square (E). Add a triangle to the top of it (F) and a pole to the bottom (G). Now add an entrance to the birdhouse. Draw your birdhouse in the figure box below (H). Can you add flowers and a vine growing up the pole? Use your black pen and color with your colored pencils when finished.

E.　　**F.** 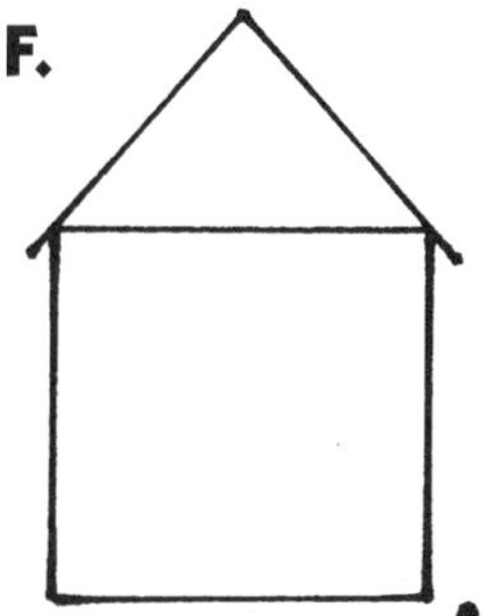　　**G.** 　　**H. My Bird House**

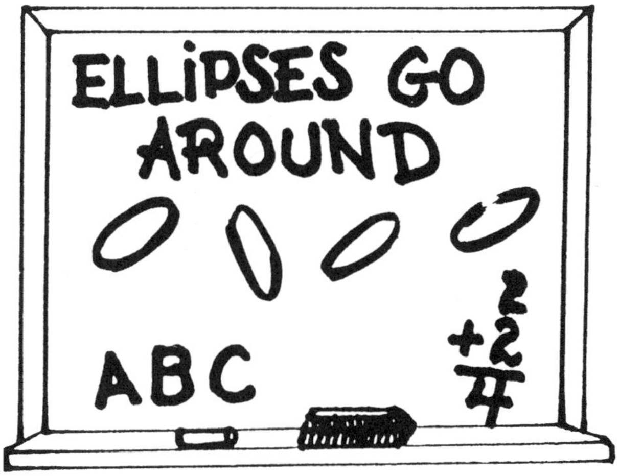

ELLIPSES GO
AROUND

ABC

$\begin{array}{r} 2 \\ +2 \\ \hline 4 \end{array}$

Lesson #17: *Drawing Egg Heads*

So far you have practiced how to draw lines, ellipses, and circles. Today let's practice drawing ovals. Ovals are good to use when drawing the human head. Try not to draw your ovals too fat like a circle (A) or too thin like an ellipse (B). Basically, an oval is *egg shaped* with the wider part near the top (C & D). Practice drawing five ovals in between the lines below (E) making sure to draw lightly, going around and around several times until you have the correct shape. Use your orange colored pencil. When you are finished, add funny faces to each with your black pen. You can use some of the facial features on page 28 or some of the expressions below. See if you can make some different faces like happy, sad, sleepy, and excited.

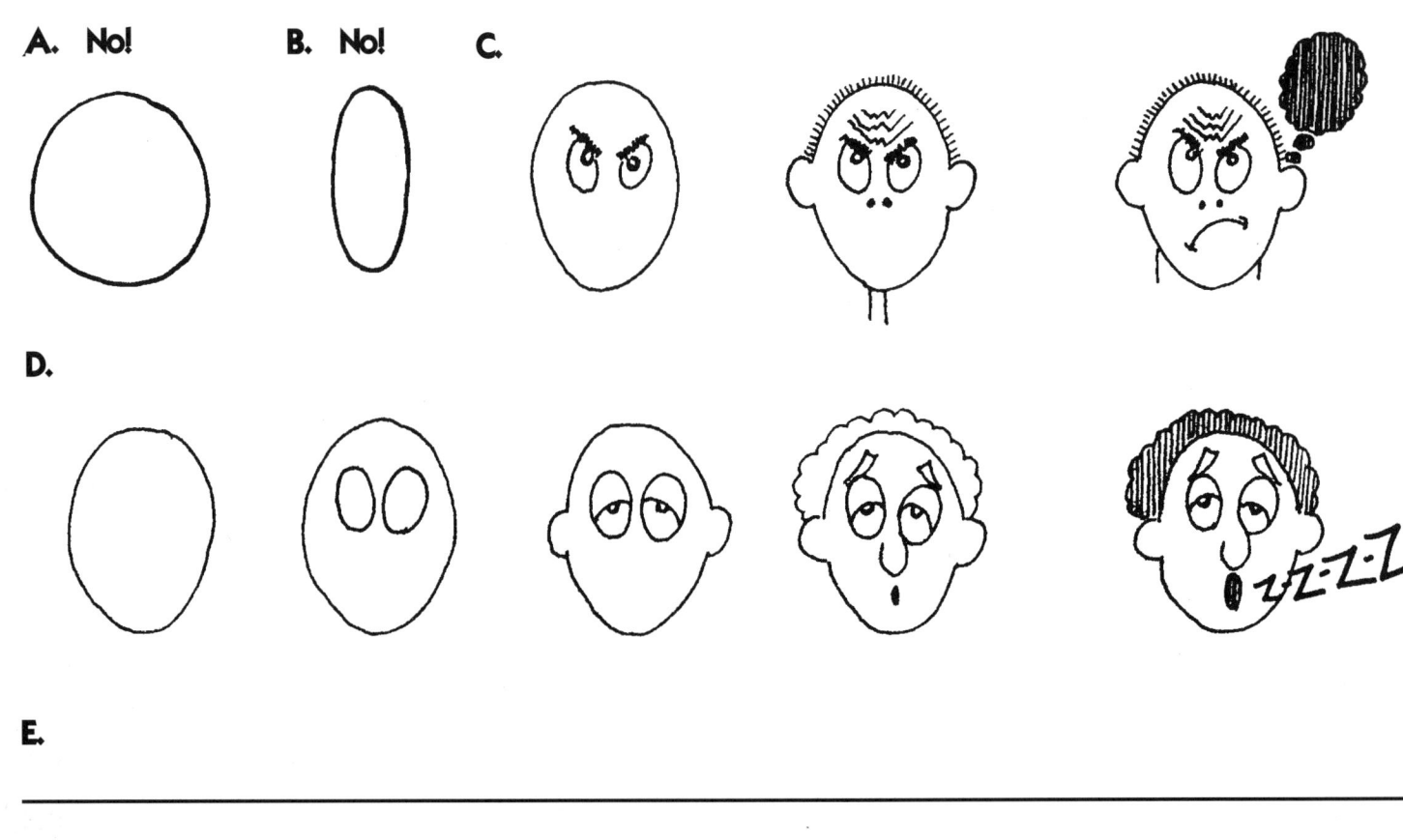

A. No!   **B. No!**   **C.**

D.

E.

_____

_____

Lesson #18: *Happy Faces Up & Sad Faces Down*

Copy the two clowns on the next page in the figure boxes provided. Don't forget to start off with a nice egg shape and draw lightly. Add the features to each clown. Notice that everything on the happy clown goes *up* and everything on the sad clown goes *down*. Put a striped background behind your happy clown and rain behind your sad clown when finished.

Lesson #18:   Happy Faces Up - Sad Faces Down

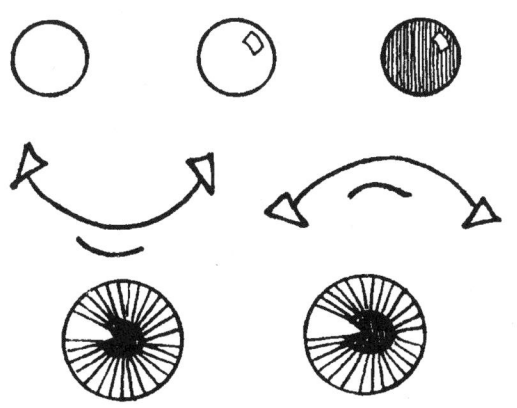

The shape of a clown's nose is round just like a balloon. One ear is a capital "C" and the other ear is a capital "D". The eyes are round with a dark pupil, or circle, in the middle. Draw little lines to the pupil like the spokes to a wagon wheel. Leave a little light area in each eye to give them a sparkle, or highlight. The happy clown's hat is basically a hot dog shape with a little hill on top of it. Add a flower and a band to the hat to give it decoration.

Lesson #19: *Cans, Jars, & Other Round Things*

There are many objects around the house that are *round* in shape. Most of these objects are drawn with ellipses to show they are round. Look at the objects below. Start by drawing an ellipse (A). Next, decide how long the jar is and draw another ellipse for the bottom. Make sure the ellipses are the same size and that one is directly under the other (B). Then, draw the sides of the jar with nice, controlled lines (C). To finish the jar, add a label by drawing two more ellipses (D). Can you draw two jars in the figure box (E)?

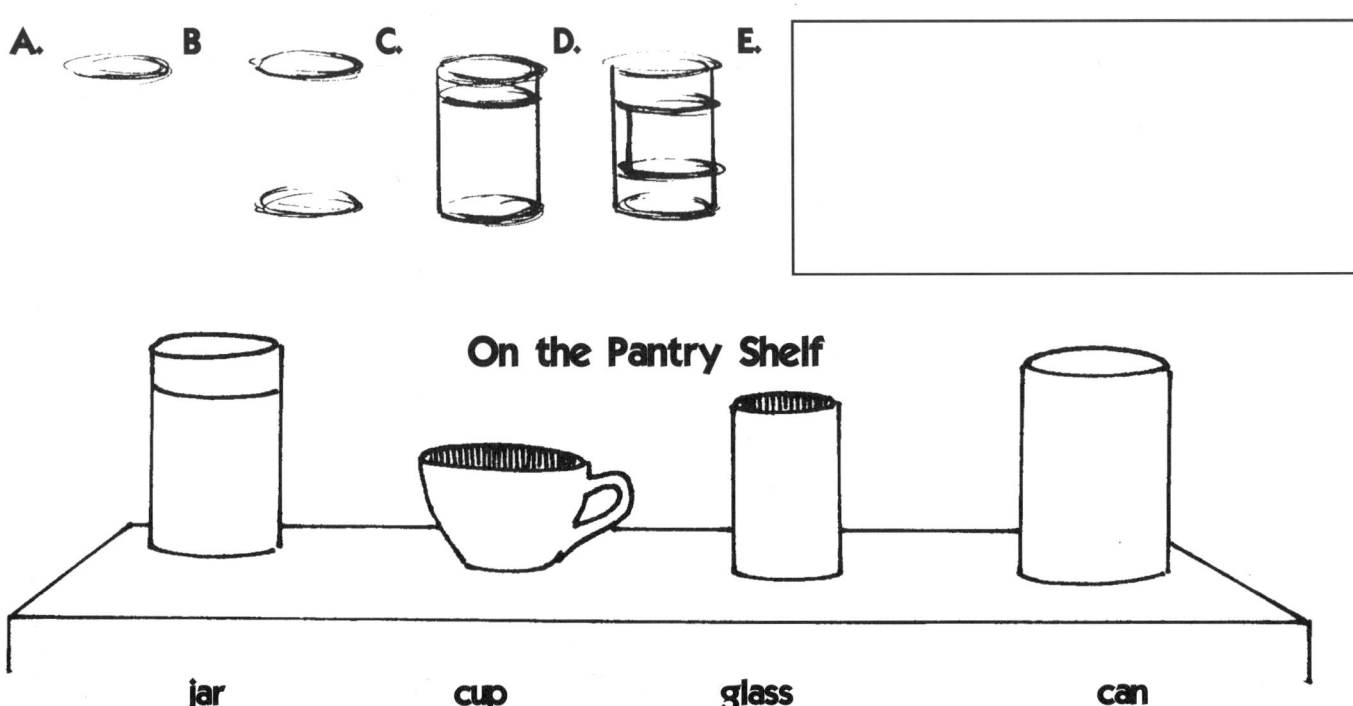

On the Pantry Shelf

jar   cup   glass   can

Notice the objects above: jar, cup, can, and glass. They are all drawn with ellipses to show they are round. Can you draw those four objects on the pantry shelf below (F)? If you draw straight, vertical lines inside the cup and glass, it will make them look opened and give your drawing a dark *value*. See if you can draw jars, cups, cans, and glasses below.

My Pantry Shelf

F.

Lesson #20: *Charlie Contrast*

A.

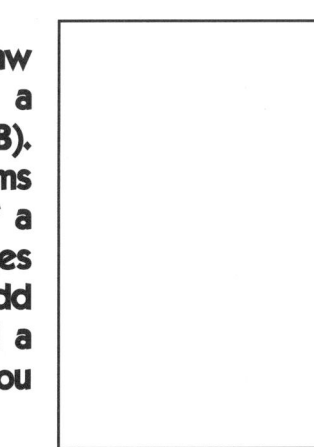
B.

Can you draw *Charlie Contrast?* Simply draw a circle and add arms, legs, hands, feet, and a smiling face (A). Draw him in the figure box (B). Make sure to use a double line to draw his arms and legs, just as you did to draw the stem of a flower in Lesson #5. Draw two hot dog shapes for feet. Draw a circle for each hand and add three little hot dog shapes for his fingers and a still smaller hot dog shape for his thumb. Can you give him a watermelon smile?

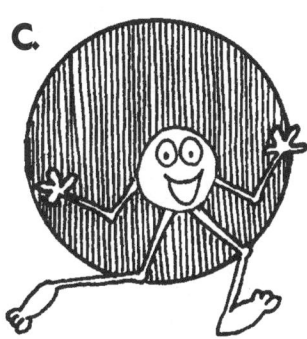
Cartoon Hands

C.

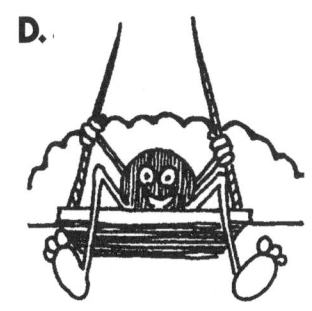

D.

Charlie Contrast has a bold personality. He always stands out. For instance, when he is standing in front of a dark background, he becomes light (C). And when he stands in front of a light background he becomes dark (D). Draw Charlie Contrast in four different settings below. Use vertical lines to show a dark background or to give Charlie Contrast a darker value when he is standing in front of a light background. Make sure to use double lines for his arms and legs. Use your black drawing pen.

Lesson #21: *Things that Go Around*

Many things that go *around* other things to show that they are round. Look at all the things that go around below and see if you can draw them on the next page. Make sure to use ellipses if you can.

A Tail Going Around

A Stripe Goes Around a Ball

A Candy Cane

Suspenders

A Collar

A Band on a Hat

A Sweatband

A Ribbon on a Finger

"To fill the hour — that is happiness." Emerson

Things That Go Around

Lesson #22: Boxes & Other Square Things

Can you draw a square (A)? Remember, when drawing lines, draw slowly and with *control.* To draw a three dimensional cube, or box, draw another square like the first one (B). Overlap it just like we overlapped the balloons in Lesson #12. Then connect the four corners to complete the box (C). Practice connecting the corners (D). Then, see if you can draw your own three dimensional box next to it (E) with your orange colored pencil.

A.   B.   C.   D.   E.

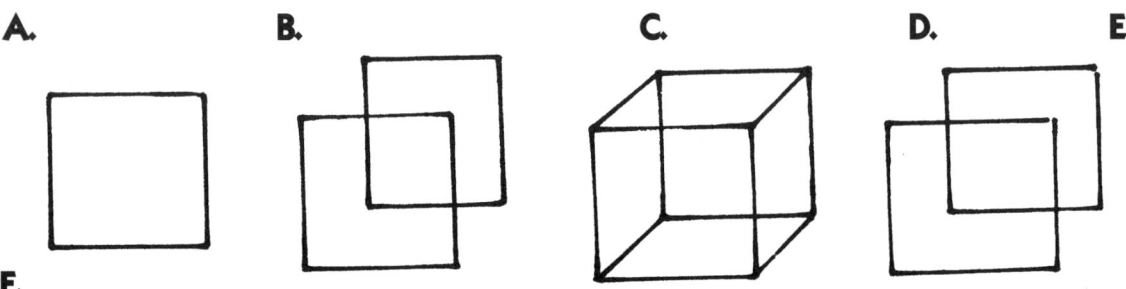

F.

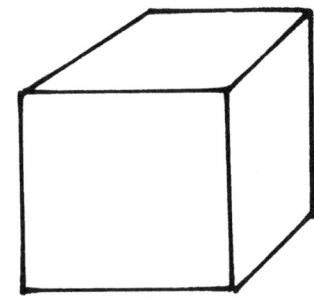

The box above (C) is like a glass box in which you can see inside. This is called transparent. Let's draw a box and give it sides that you cannot see through. This is called opaque. All we have to do is erase three of the lines inside the box (F). That is why it is important to draw *lightly* so your lines will be easy to erase when your drawing is nearly finished.

H.

G.

Shading with Vertical Lines

Shading with Horizontal Lines

Shading with Diagonal Lines

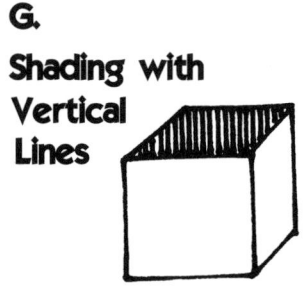

Now let's draw boxes with one side open, allowing us to see inside the open tops. To do this, *shade* inside all of the boxes with *lines.* Three ways of shading with line are: vertical lines (straight up and down); horizontal lines (lines that go sideways); and diagonal lines (or lines that are drawn at an angle). Draw three boxes to the right (H). Shade inside one with vertical lines, one with horizontal lines and one with diagonal lines just as the ones are shaded to the left (G). Finally, draw Wally the Worm coming out of each box.

Vertical   Horizontal   Diagonal

"It is not doing the things we like to do, but liking the things we have to do that makes life blessed."

Goethe

Lesson #23: *Let the Sunshine In*

It is good to draw objects and show light shining on them. To do this, we have to draw a *light* side and a *shaded* side. The best way to draw darker values, or the shaded side, is by using line. If you have an open box you can shade the outside with one value (A) and the inside of the box with another value (B). This can be done by *cross-hatching*. Cross-hatching is drawing a series of criss-crossing lines to make darker areas. Draw and shade a box below. Use cross-hatching to show the darker areas inside the box (C).

A.   **B.**   **C.**

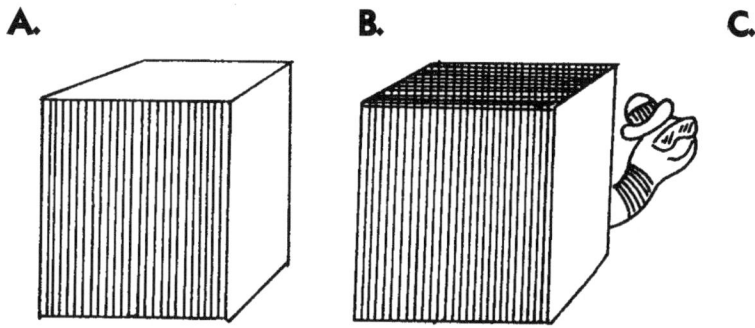

light source

Big Boxes, Small Boxes, Thin Boxes & Tall Boxes

Let's draw some boxes of different sizes: a big box, a small box, a thin box, and a tall box. You may want to make one box a cereal box and another one a match box. You can draw a big book (which is also shaped like a box). Draw your boxes below.

Big Box   **Cereal Box**   **Book**

Match Box

Lesson #24: Making A Block City

B. Windows & Doors

C. Stairs & Ladders

A. Block Upon Block

Now that you know how to draw a cube, let's make a block city by drawing one cube on top of another (A). Then add doors and windows (B). Also, add some stairs and ladders (C). Finally, add Charlie Contrast and his friends to your block city. Make sure to draw them light against a dark background and dark against a light background. Do your drawing of a block city below (D) with your black pen.

D.

Lesson #25: *Peek-A-Boo!*

We learned how to draw round objects such as cans, cups, and jars. We also learned how to draw square objects such as boxes. Let's see if you can draw Wally the Worm hiding in some of these objects. Draw round objects such as cans and cups; and square objects such as boxes, on the bottom of the page, showing part of Wally's body coming out of each. You can even draw Wally the Worm coming out of an apple. *"Peek-a-boo!"* Draw lightly with your orange pencil until you have drawn everything just the way you want it. Then darken your lines with your black pen. Use ellipses for round objects and nice controlled lines for square objects. Don't forget to show a darker value inside each object by shading with line. If you need more space for drawing, use your sketchbook in the back of the text.

"He is like a man building a house who dug down deep and laid the foundation on rock. When the flood came, the torrent struck that house but could not shake it, because it was well built."

Luke 6:48

Lesson #26: Rules & Measurements

Do you know how to use a ruler? A ruler can be a handy tool since there are many things that call for measurements. For today's lesson, place a ruler down on the line below (A). See if you can find these measurements on the line: 1 1/2", 1 5/8", 2 1/16", 2 3/4", 3 7/8", 4 3/16", 5 7/8" and 6 15/16". Draw a mark on the line for each measurement.

A.   Place Your
↙ Ruler Here

Measuring a Box

Now let's see if you can draw a box with exact measurements. Look at the box below (B). It is 11/4" wide and 2" tall. See if you can draw a box that is 2 1/2" wide and 3 1/2" tall in the figure box (C). Can you make a house out of the box by adding a roof (D)? Add windows and a door. Use your ruler for drawing all the lines. Sometimes when you use your ruler for drawing it is called a *technical drawing*.

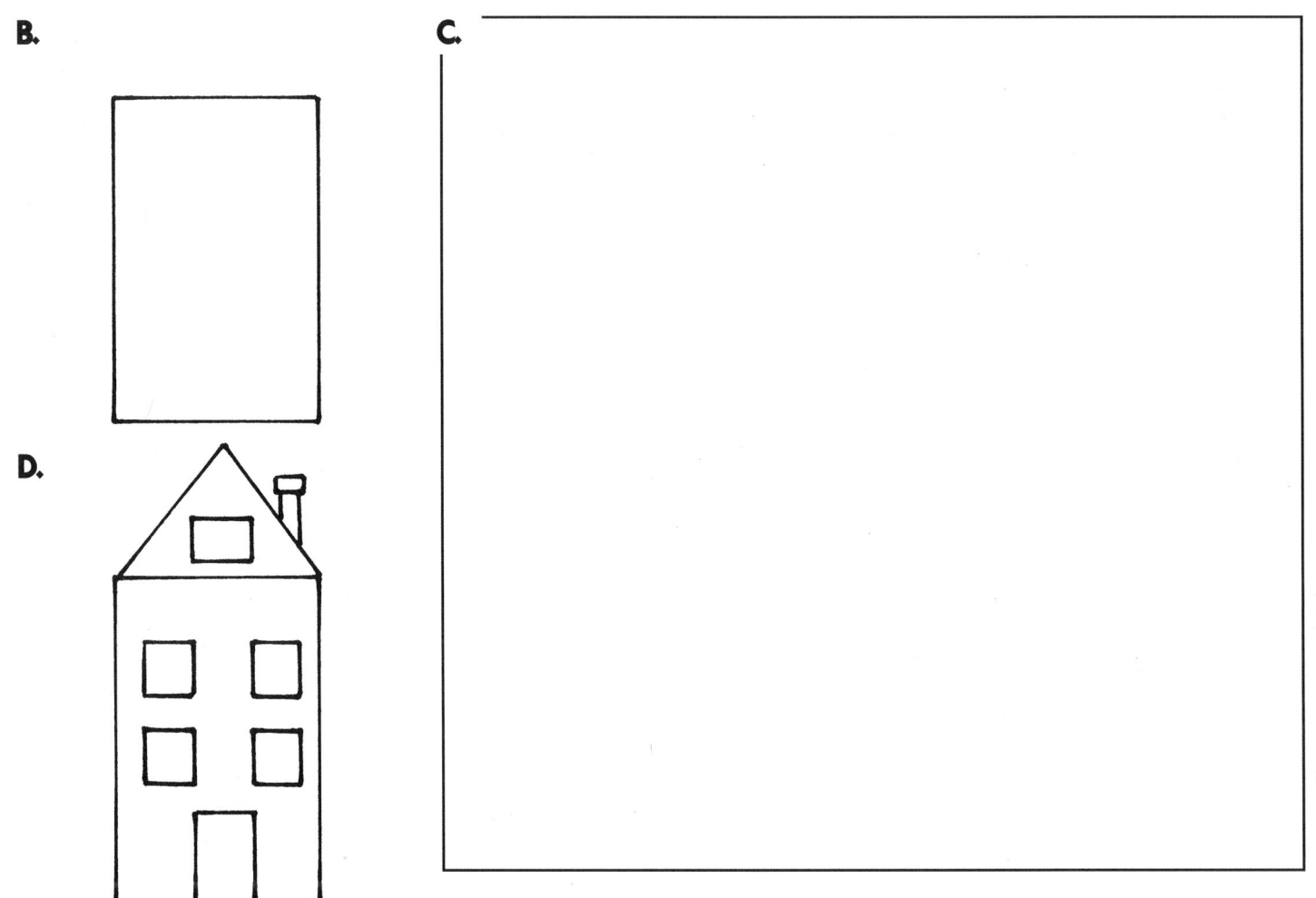

B.

C.

D.

Lesson #27: Animal Fluff and Woody Grain

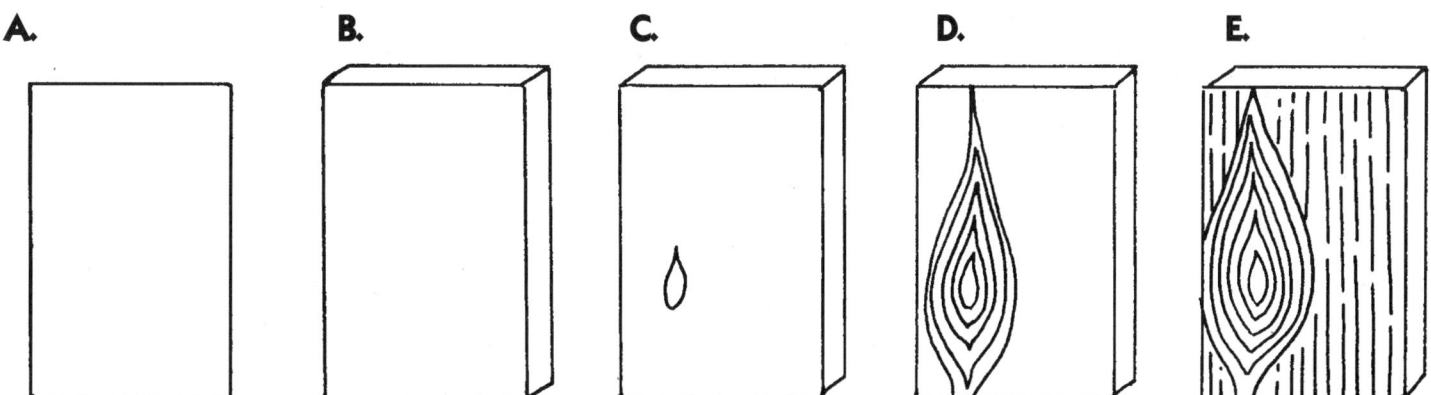

A. **B.** **C.** **D.** **E.**

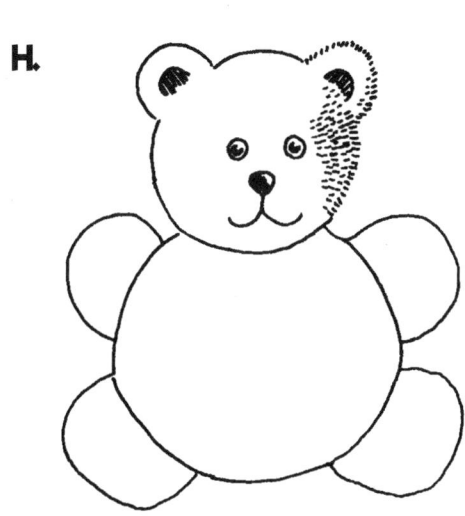

H.

Drawing *texture* can be fun. Texture makes your drawing look like the surface of what you are drawing. For instance, the surface of wood is grainy, the surface of a sponge is spongy, the surface of a teddy bear is fluffy. Today let's draw a piece of wood. First, draw a long box (A). Then add the backside to it, making it thicker (B). Draw a knot in the wood by first drawing something that looks like a candle flame (C). Keep going around the candle flame shape with other candle flames, making it larger and larger. This should look like a knot on a piece of wood when your are finished (D). Add to the rest of your wood by drawing long, vertical, broken lines (E). Draw your piece of wood below (G).

Let's have some fun with the piece of wood you just drew. See if you can draw two cartoon figures behind it like the ones below (F). Notice that the hands have been suggested again with three small circles. Finally, add some fluff to the teddy bear (H). Using your black marker put the rest of the fur on his body by adding short lines.

F.

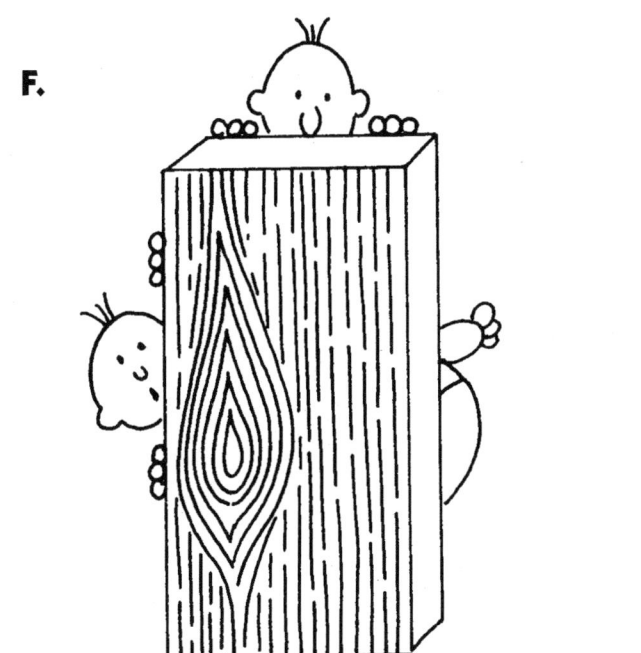

G.

65

Lesson #28: *Raining Cats & Dogs*

Below is a drawing done by Mereda Mason. She was seven and a half years old and was homeschooled in Charlotte, North Carolina. Her picture represents *raining cats and dogs.* Some of the cats and dogs Mereda made up from her imagination and others she copied from pictures. For this assignment, fill the next page with cats, dogs and rain drops. Turn your paper at different angles to draw your animals so they look like they are falling from the clouds.

"Raining Cats & Dogs"

Lesson #29:   *Trees & Tributaries*

Did you ever notice how the branches of a tree become thinner and thinner as they stretch to the sky. And have you ever noticed how streams become thinner and thinner as they flow away from a river? For this assignment, use your black pen and see if you can add some more tributaries (streams) to the river below (A) making them thinner and thinner. Then complete the tree by adding more limbs and branches. Make sure the branches become thinner as they stretch out. Color your water and tree more when finished.

A. Draw Some Streams Coming Out From the River

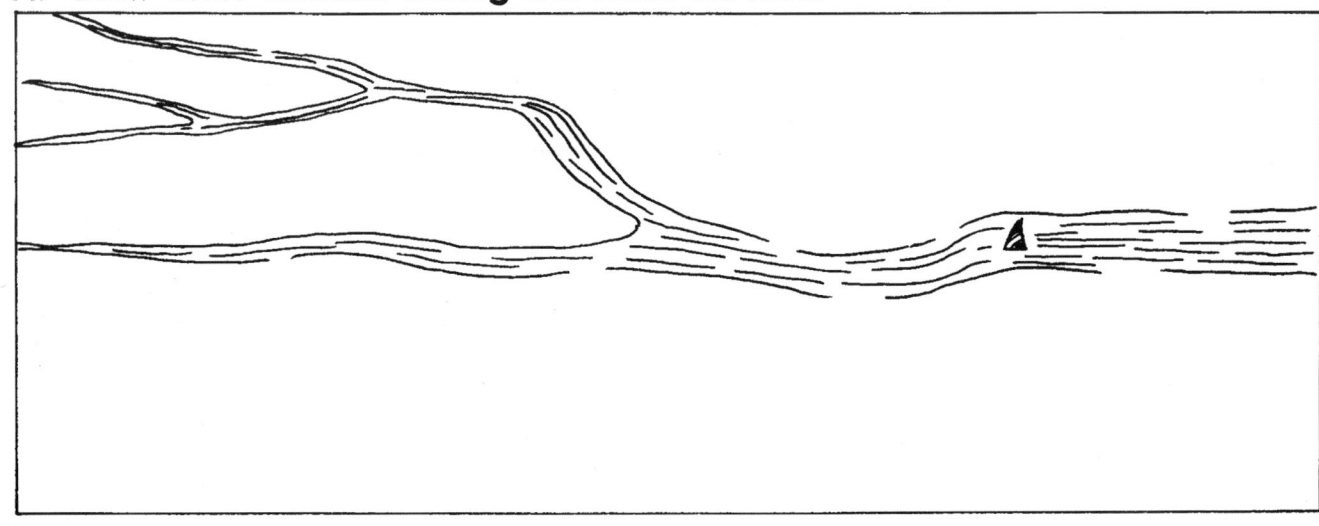

B.
**Complete the Limbs
& Branches of the Tree**

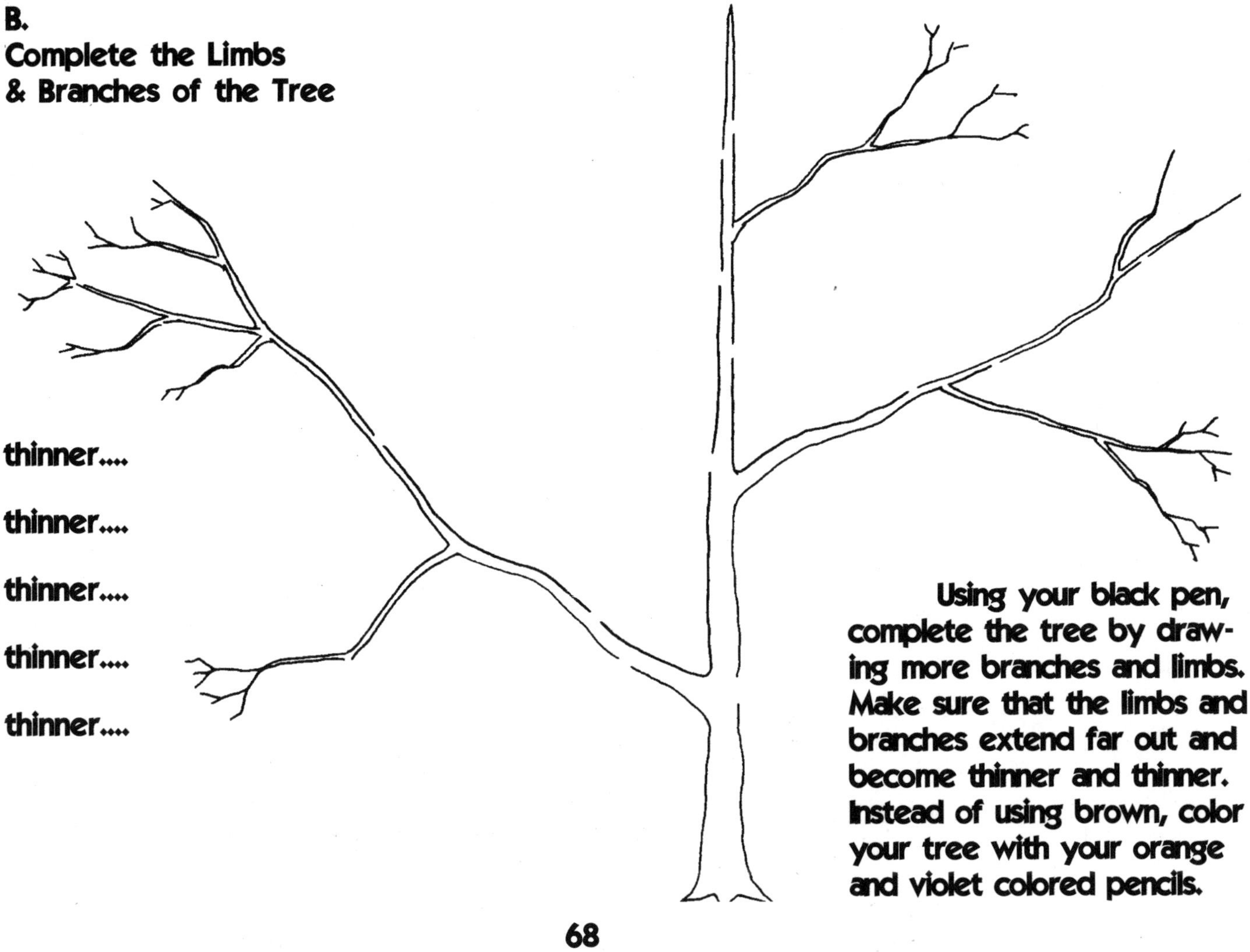

thinner....

thinner....

thinner....

thinner....

thinner....

Using your black pen, complete the tree by drawing more branches and limbs. Make sure that the limbs and branches extend far out and become thinner and thinner. Instead of using brown, color your tree with your orange and violet colored pencils.

Lesson #30: *Drawing People*

A.    **B.**

Let's draw some more people. However, this time let's draw them without making stick figures. First, draw a circle for the head and an oval shape for the body (A). Add arms and legs by drawing long, thin rectangles (B). For hands, draw a circle and add long hot dog shapes (C). Don't make your fingers too small and stubby (D). Finally, the feet can be fat hot dog shapes (E). Put it all together and you will have a simple human figure.

C.

D. No!

E.

F.

In figure box F, copy the stick figures on the top of the page by putting meat on their bones as shown. Start with your orange colored pencil and then go over your drawings with your black drawing pen.

Lesson #31: *Human Proportions*

Proportions simply means drawing everything the correct size. For instance, the hand of a mature adult is really the same size as the face from the top of the forehead to the bottom of the chin (A). That is the correct proportions for drawing a hand. Look at the figure below (B). The adult figure is eight head lengths long from the top of the head to the bottom of the feet. The hands extend down on the sides five head lengths from the top of the head. The mid-section of the figure is where the legs join at the bottom of the bowl shape, or pelvis.

A.

For this assignment draw eight heads, one on top of another, next to the figure (C). Then draw the adult figure in the space provided (D), making sure that it is eight head lengths long; that the hands extend down five head lengths; and that the legs join right in the middle of the body (four head lengths). Use your orange colored pencil.

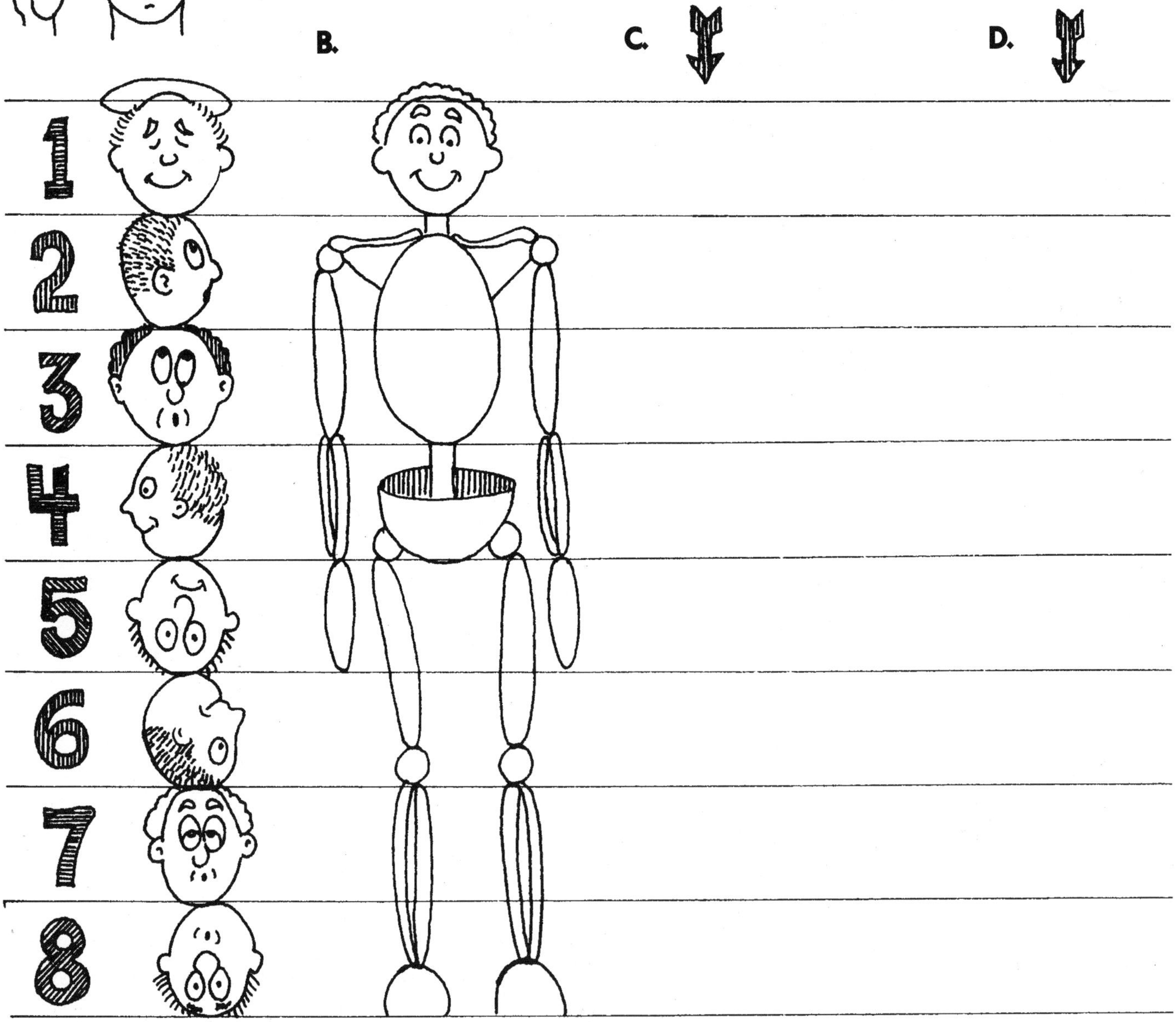

B.   **C.**   **D.**

1
2
3
4
5
6
7
8

70

Lesson #32: *Paper People*

Let's practice drawing more human figures, putting meat on their bones. However, this time we will draw them on paper such as a paper roll (A), or an envelope (B), or a plain piece of paper (C). Draw people on the pieces of paper below, making sure they have meat on their bones. Use your black pen.

A.

B.

C.

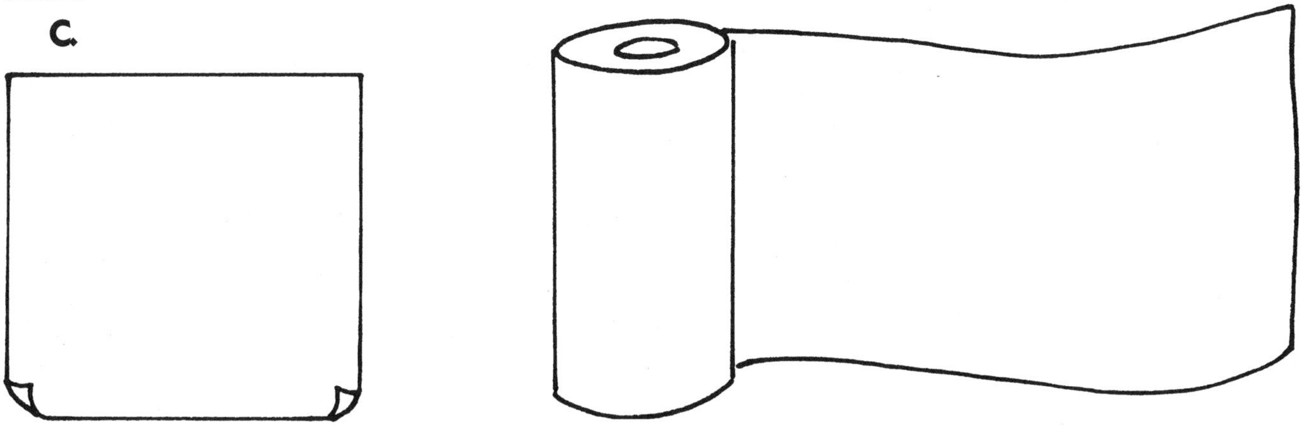

D.

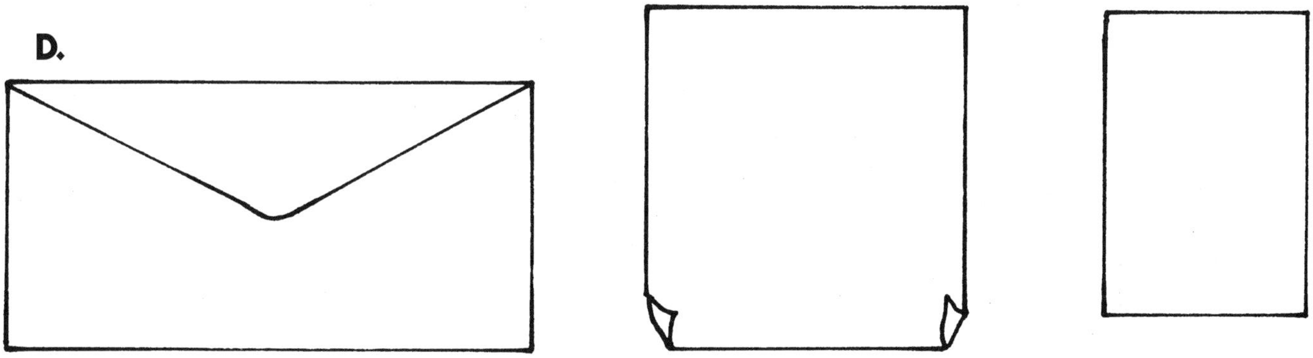

Lesson #33:

Let's make a flip book. Draw a character in action like the one below (E). To do this, cut small pieces of paper all the same size. Then draw the character below on each small sheet, tracing both positions by holding the paper to the window and tracing the images with your black pen. Staple the collection of figures together at the top, and then flip through the pages to see him go!

E.

Lesson #34: Drawing Hands & Fingers

A. Cartoon Hand

Let's draw some more hands. Remember, to draw a cartoon hand all we need is a circle for the palm, three hot dog shapes for the fingers and a smaller hot dog shape for the thumb (A). See if you can draw two cartoon hands in the figure box (B) with your black pen.

B. Cartoon Hands

Now let's draw some hands doing different things like holding a flower (C); holding a book (D); or pointing (E). Draw each hand in the figure boxes.

C. Holding Flowers

D. Holding a Book

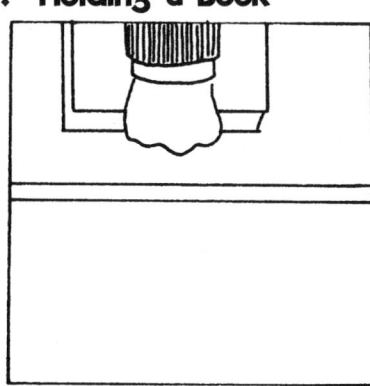

E. Pointing a Finger

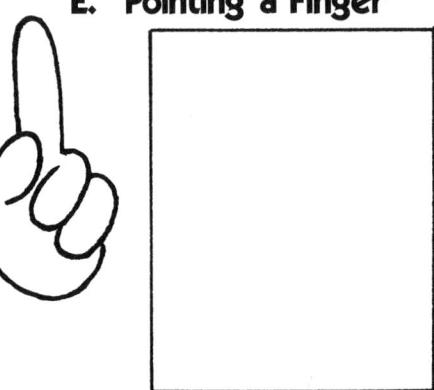

Another simple way to draw hands is to suggest the fingers by drawing little circles. This is good to do when showing hands holding something. Draw the figures below (two behind the rectangle and one reading a book), show their fingers by drawing little circles.

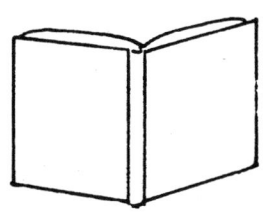

F.

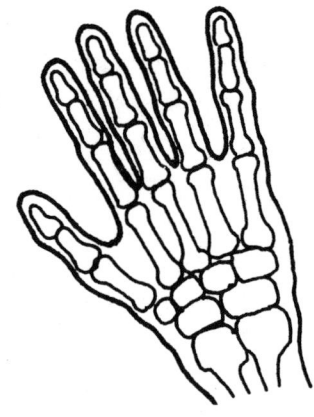

Finger Bones

Look at your hand and feel the bones in your fingers. Draw the skeleton on the left (F) and put the flesh on the bones in the figure box on the right (G). Notice the finger bones go into the palm with three bones showing in each finger and only two bones in the thumb. You may need help in drawing the bones.

G.

Lesson #35: *Bible Stories*

Bible stories can be wonderful to draw! Great artists of the past such as Michelangelo, Carl Bloch, and Rembrandt have done great paintings and drawings of stories from the Bible. For this assignment, let's see if you can illustrate the story of Samson when he was blinded by the Philistines. You may want to show when he was brought before a great audience of Philistines outside the temple of his captors. Or you can show when Sampson was pulling down the pillars of the temple. Try to be creative with your drawing and put as much detail in it as possible. Use your black pen and, when you are finished, show it to someone and see if they can recognize which story it is. Read the story below and then do your illustration in the figure box.

"While they were in high spirits, they shouted, 'Bring out Samson to entertain us.' So they called Samson out of the prison, and he performed for them.

While they stood him among the pillars, Samson said to the servant who held his hand, 'Put me where I can feel the pillars that support the temple, so that I may lean against them. Now the temple was crowded with men and women, all the rulers of the Philistines were there, and on the roof were about three thousand men and women watching Samson perform. Then Samson prayed to the Lord, 'O Sovereign Lord, remember me. O God, please strengthen me just once more, and let me with one blow get revenge on the Philistines for my two eyes.' Then Samson reached toward the two central pillars on which the temple stood. Bracing himself against them, his right hand on the one and his left hand on the other, Samson said, 'Let me die with the Philistines!' Then he pushed with all his might, and down came the temple on the rulers and all the people in it. Thus he killed many more when he died than while he lived." Judges 16:25-30

Lesson #36: *Let's Keep an ART Journal!*

Do you know what an art journal is? It is a book which you write in (like a diary), and draw in (like a sketchbook). Today we are going to write the first page in our journal. Things you may want to write about are: What are you learning in school? What is the weather like? What things did you do during the day? Most of all, try to write about your artwork: what are you learning, what are you doing, and what do you want to learn? Along with writing about your day, draw things around you. How about a tea pot, a bowl of fruit, some flowers, a lamp, etc. Write about your day on the lines below and do your drawings in the open space with your colored pencils.

_____

_____

_____

_____

_____

_____

_____

_____

_____

_____

_____

_____

_____

_____

Colored Pencils

COLOR iS LEARNING

ABC

"It is not how much color you use, it's how you use it." Phillip Jamison

Colored Pencils

Colored pencils are great for the young student to use for many reasons:

1. They are like drawing with a pencil.
2. They are not messy and are easy to store.
3. They can be used on regular drawing paper.
4. They can be carried with you wherever you go.
5. They can teach you about color.
6. And many of the same rules for drawing apply to coloring with colored pencils.

Rules & Regulations

1. **Sharpen Your Pencils:** Just like drawing pencils, make sure you have sharpened colored pencils.

2. **Store Your Pencils Properly:** It is best to store your colored pencils in a solid jar or cup (points up), just like your drawing pencils. This will prevent them from being lost or rolling off the table and breaking.

3. **Do Not Mix Drawing Pencils & Colored Pencils:** The lead from a drawing pencil is shiny and does not blend well with colored pencils, so use only one or the other. Choose one of the colors from your color pencil pack to draw with and then color with the rest of your pencils.

4. **Draw Lightly:** Just like with drawing pencils, start by drawing *lightly*. This is best done by using a light colored pencil like yellow or orange. After the drawing is finished, begin using darker colors.

5. **Color with Line:** Learn to color with *line* as we learned to shade with line in some of the drawing lessons. Learn to color with vertical, horizontal, or diagonal lines. Color with lines of one color, and then add lines of a different color between the first colors.

6. **Do Not Use Too Much Black or Brown:** Most students use their black and brown colored pencils too often. These colors are dark and overwhelm the other colors. Do most of your coloring with your other colored pencils. See if you can make some nice browns and other dark colors by mixing various colors together. Your black and brown pencils can also make excellent drawing pencils.

> *"A picture is an unusual combination of lines and colors that set one another off."*
>
> Edgar Degas

Lesson #37: *Let's Make Lots of Colors!*

Making a *color chart* will show you the great variety of colors you can mix and blend together other than the colors in your colored pencil pack. Let's make two color charts below. The first one will be mixing colors with line. The second color chart will be mixing colors by blending.

A. Yellow Plus Red Lines **B. Horizontal Lines** **C. Diagonal Lines** **D. Cross-Hatching**

   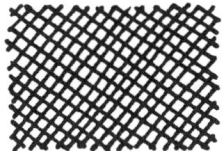

Mixing with Line: To mix colors with line, first color a series of lines with one color. Place another series of lines with another color between the first series of colors (A). For example, you may want to draw a series of vertical lines with a yellow pencil. Add a series of red vertical lines between the yellow lines. Practice different types of lines like *vertical* (A), *horizontal* (B), and *diagonal* (C). Try practicing *cross-hatching,* which is a series of lines that criss-cross the first series of lines (D). See how many colors you can create in the flowers below by mixing different colors with line.

Color Chart with Lines

Let's make another color chart by blending one color over another color. Lightly place a color in the balloons below. Then, lightly place another color on top of each to see how it changes. See how many colors you can make by blending two or three colors together.

Color Chart with Blending

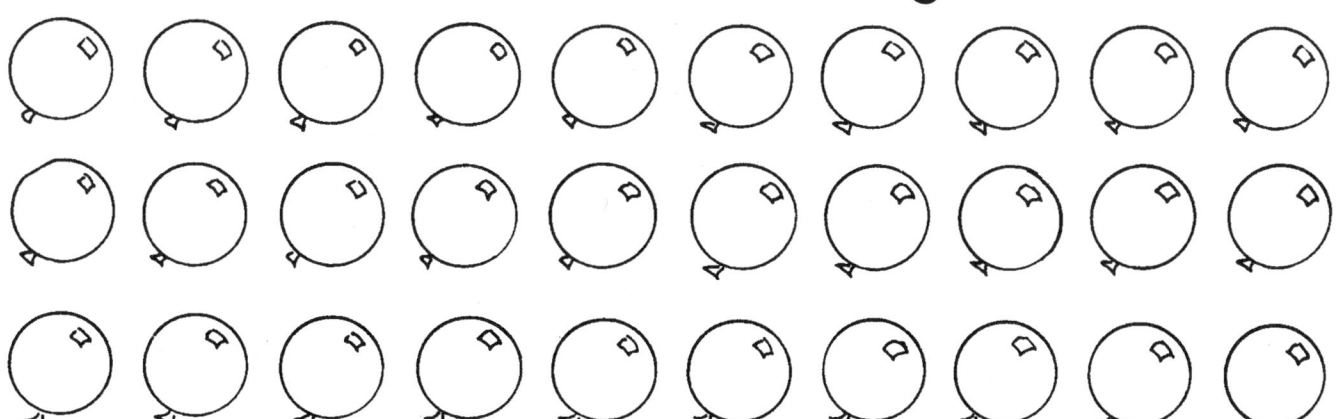

Lesson #38: *Doodle Bugs*

Can you draw some *doodle bugs?* Doodle bugs are simply bugs that you have created. You can make them very cute and colorful. Fill the next page with doodle bugs. Draw their houses. Have some crawling on the ground and others flying in the air. Draw them with your yellow and orange pencils. Then color them with colorful colors. Look at the colors on your color chart to see what colors you would like to use. Can you place some creative doodle bugs inside the frame around your picture?

Lesson #39: Large doodle bugs! Fill a large 22" x 28" sheet of white poster board with doodle bugs using a colored marker to draw them. Make some large and others larger. Create a doodle bug community. Color with your markers when finished.

Doodle Bug Country

"But now I see through a glass though dimly...."   I Corinthians 13:12

Lesson #40: *Outside My Window*

Can you draw and color what is outside your window? Many times there are interesting pictures to do just by drawing what is outside. Take *I Can Do All Things* and your colored pencils and sit next to a window in your house. Draw and color a picture of what is outside in A. Add a lot of yellow to brighten your picture, making it sunny. Color the window panes with blue, brown, and purple to show a contrast between the light outside and the dimness inside. Then do another picture on the bottom (B) of something outside that you have made up in your mind. You may want to show a park scene, a winter scene, or a farm scene. Be creative and colorful! Finally, select the picture you like best and do it large in the window on the next page with bright colored pencils.

A. Outside My Window

B. Inside My Mind

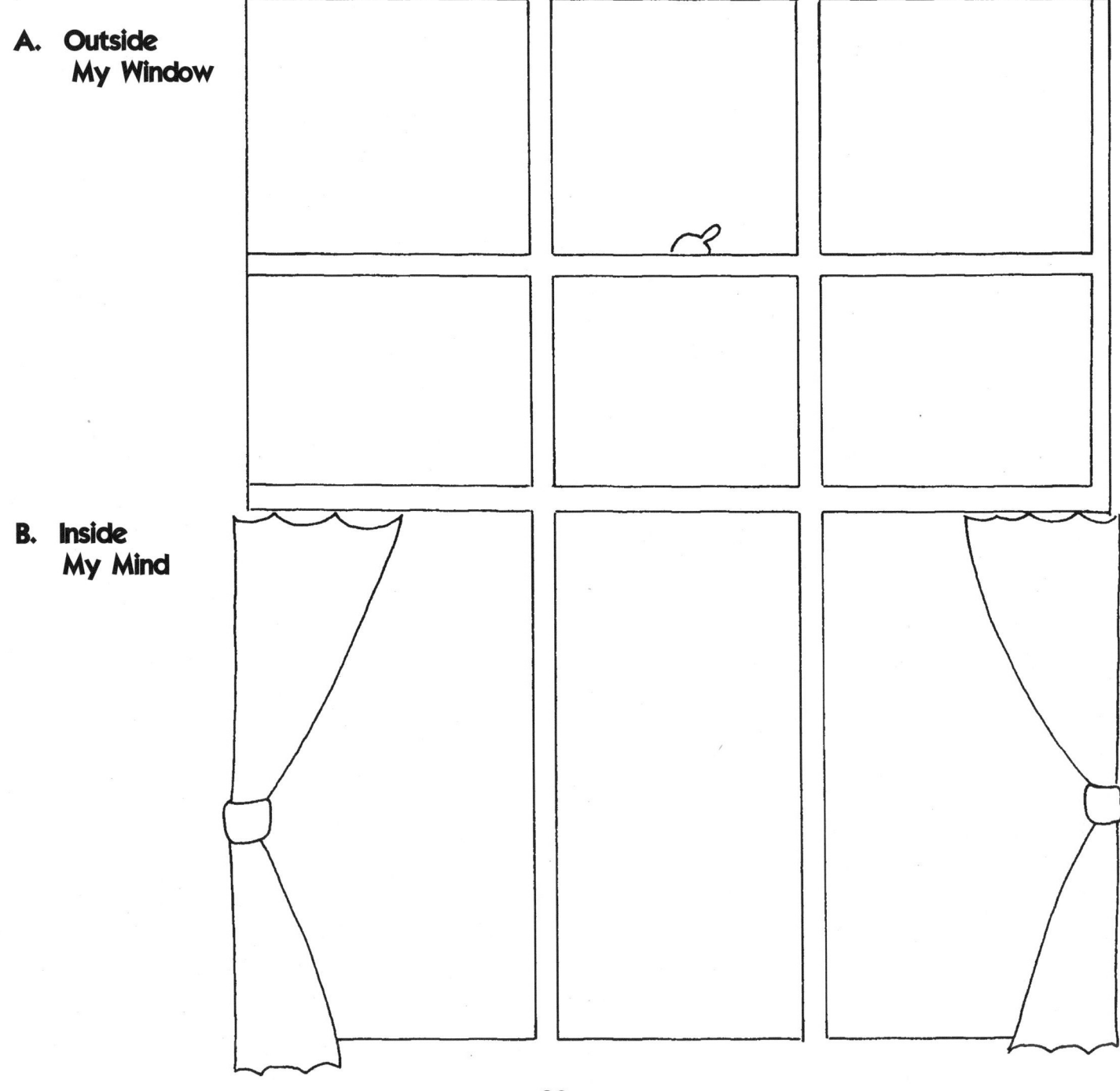

Looking Outside

Lesson #41: *Drawing & Coloring Butterflies*

Do you know what *warm colors* are? Warm colors are red, yellow, and orange. Warm colors create a bright and lively picture. Using your colored pencils, color in the picture of the butterfly below with warm colors (A), coloring with dots, lines, and blending. See how many warm colors you can make. Then, on the bottom of the page (B), draw your own butterfly with your black pen. Make sure to draw him *large* and color him with bright and cheerful colors! Draw and color some more flowers around the frame. (Did you see the butterfly that Elizabeth White drew on the first page of the book?)

A.

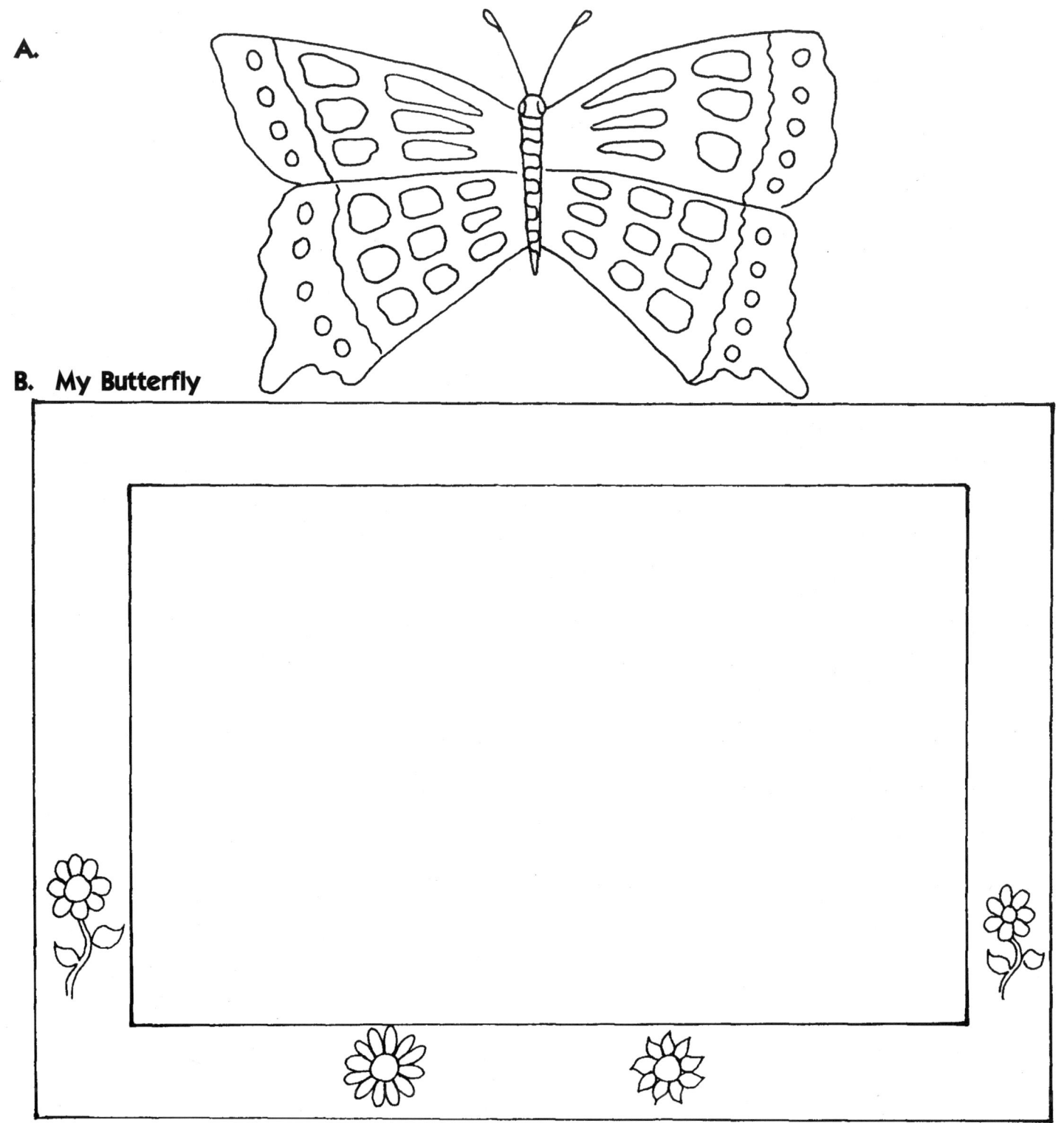

B. My Butterfly

Lesson #42: *My Neighborhood*

For this assignment, take *I Can Do All Things* outside and draw four pictures of your neighborhood. Do you want to draw a picture of the park? Your backyard? Where you go swimming? The library? The neighbor's house? The swing hanging from the tree? Draw and color each picture in the figure boxes below. If you have a good memory, you can draw the pictures of your neighborhood at home. Be colorful and color with lines!

Lesson #43: *Coloring Pretty Flowers*

A. Vertical Lines

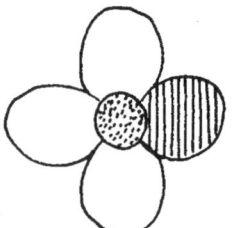

B. Diagonal Lines

C. Horizontal Lines

Flowers, like butterflies, are bright and colorful. Draw and color some more flowers in the frame below. Color each flower with vertical (A), diagonal (B), or horizontal lines (C). Add one color inside another. For instance, add yellow lines inside of violet lines; red lines inside of blue lines; or orange lines inside of red lines. Make sure your lines are close together. Color the center of each flower with dots of yellow and orange. Complete the three flowers on the top of the page (A, B, & C) using two colors in each, and then draw and color three of your own flowers in the large figure box below (D). Can you add some colorful butterflies flying above the flowers?

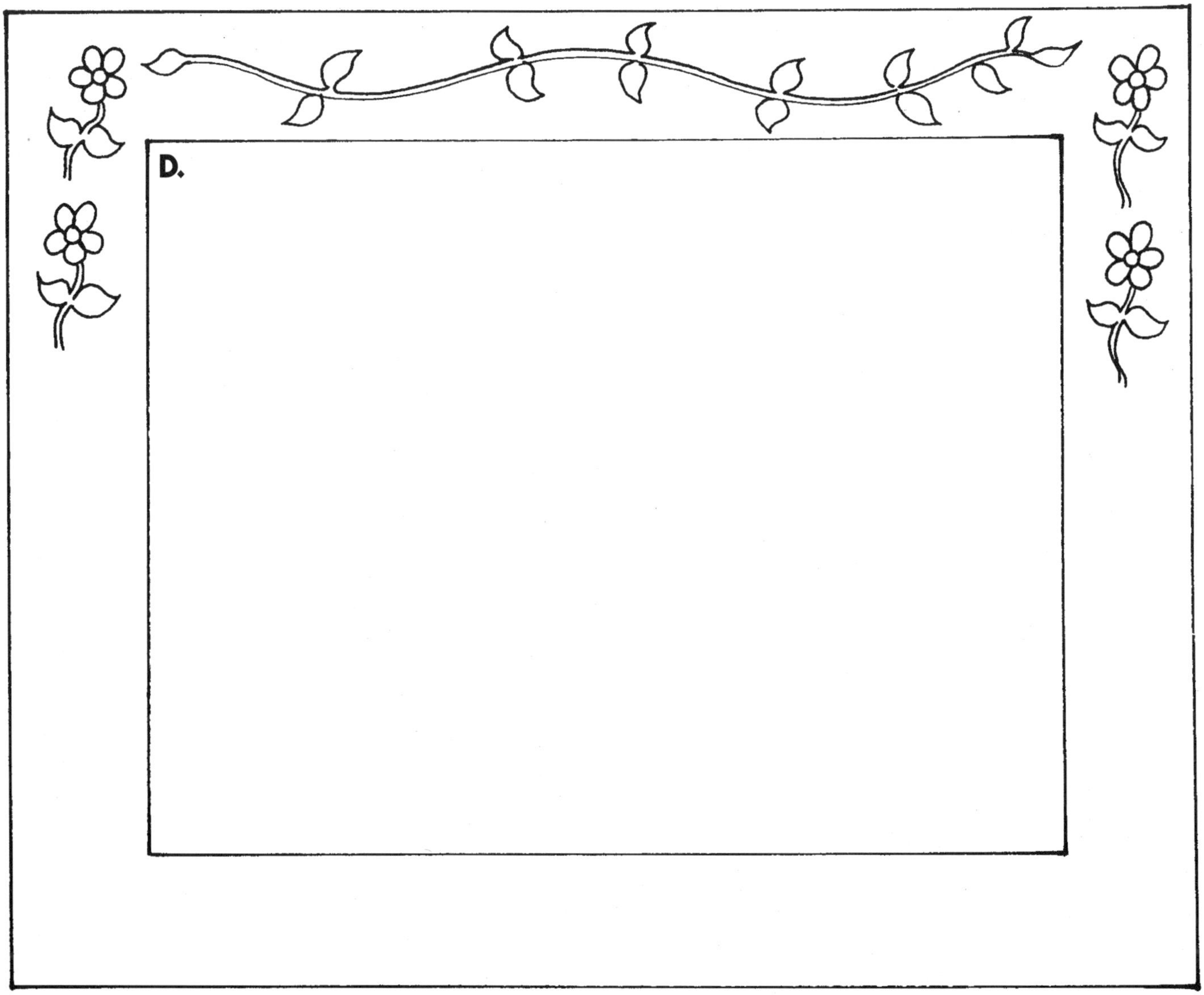

D.

Lesson #44: *Coloring Trees*

Do you know how to draw and color a tree? First of all, let's see how many different greens you can create by mixing different colors together. Color the trees below (A) with an assortment of greens. You can make a green by coloring the tree yellow and then adding a blue over it. Then try coloring a tree yellow and adding green over it. You may even want to mix yellow plus blue, and then place some green over that. You can make a dull green by adding a touch of red to green. You can even blend a little black with green. Experiment with your greens on the five trees below.

A. Yellow/Blue   Yellow/Green   Yellow/Blue/Green   Green/Blue   Green/Blue/Red

Let's learn to color our trees with sunshine! First, draw a little sun to show which direction the light is coming from. Then color your entire tree yellow. (Yellow will add a bright color to your greens!) Divide your tree into three parts: the part in sunshine; the part in shade; and the middle tone, between the sunshine and the shade (B). Remember, color with lines. Draw and color your tree in the figure box below (C). Color the grass in the sunshine with a lot of yellow and a very light green. Color the grass in the shade with a lot of dark blue and dark green. Remember, a good way to draw grass is with short vertical strokes.

B.

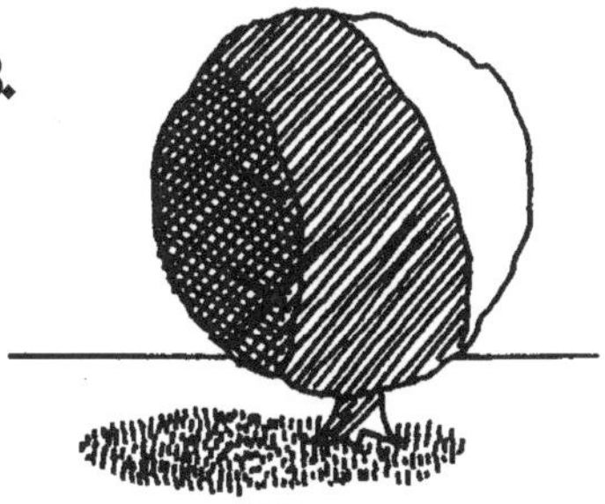

C. **Draw Your Tree Below**

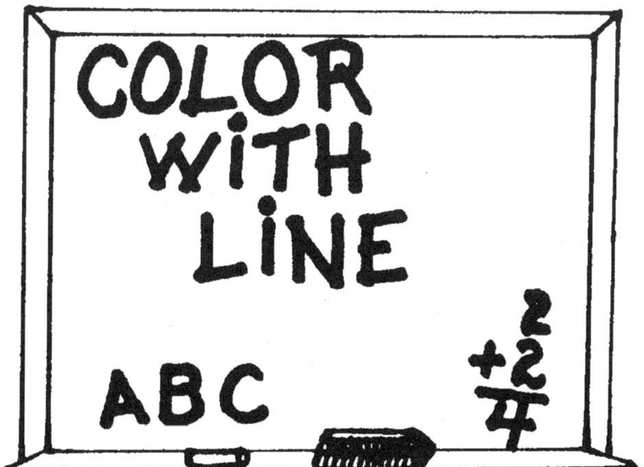

COLOR
WITH
LINE

ABC $\begin{array}{r} 2 \\ +2 \\ \hline 4 \end{array}$

This is a
good
way to
draw
grass.

"......Let your light shine before men, that they may see your good deeds and praise your Father in heaven."

Matthew 5:16

A. Yellow Duck

B. Place Your Duck Here

Lesson #45: *Let There Be Light!*

Look around you and you will see that everything has light on it! When objects have light on them it changes their color and also gives them a *light* side and a *shaded* side. For instance, the duck (A) is lighter on the side in the sunlight. The light side could be colored a bright yellow. The shaded side of the duck could be colored with yellow and a little violet. However, keep your violet light when you color over the yellow. If it is too dark, go over it again with more yellow. First color the duck above and then draw a duck (B) with your black pen, coloring it with light and shaded areas showing the sun shining on it.

Next, draw and color an apple in the space below (D).

C. Apple

First, color the entire apple orange. Then add red over all the orange. When you are finished add a brighter red over the middle portion and the shaded side of the apple by applying more pressure to your red pencil. Finally, add some blue, and violet to the shaded area (C). Leave a white highlight to show where the light is reflecting the most.

Finally, draw and color a mouse (E). Color him a light brown and blend some black on the light side, adding some dark blue with brown to the shaded side. Draw and color your mouse below (F).

D. Your Apple

E. Brown Mouse

F. Your Mouse

Lesson #46: Blending with White

A. Pink Flower

Have you ever looked at your white pencil and wondered what it was for? You can't color with it on white paper because you would not be able to see it! One of the main purposes for having a white pencil is for *blending*. You can make some wonderful colors when you blend with white: a pink, violet, light blue, or even a flesh tone. To begin, see if you can make a pink by blending white with a very little red in the flower above (A). Color the center of each flower with yellow and orange. In the next flower make a very light violet by coloring the petals lightly with violet and blending white into it (B). Next, see if you can create a light blue by coloring the flower lightly with your blue pencil and blending white over it. Finally, see if you can make a flesh tone by coloring the face first with a very light red. Then add a little bit of yellow and blend everything with white. This may take some practice. If you don't have a white colored pencil lightly blend the colors with an eraser.

B. Violet Flower

C. Light Blue Flower

D. Skin Color

Let's color a light gray mouse by mixing a lot of white with a little black (E); a light blue sky with a lot of white and a little blue (F); and a peach by mixing a lot of white with a little yellow and red. Remember, *blend, blend, blend* with white or by gently erasing the color.

E. Light Grey Mouse

F. Light Blue Sky

G. A Light Peach

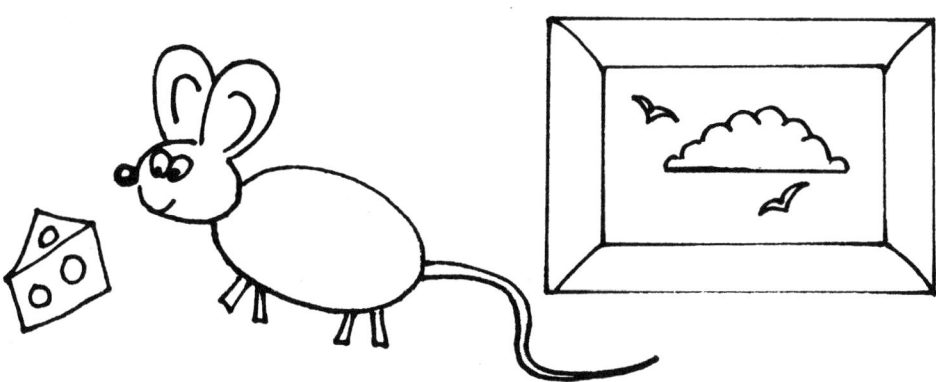

"I praise You because I am fearfully and wonderfully made." Psalm 139:14

Lesson #47: Coloring People!

Let's draw some more people. However, this time we are going to draw them a little differently than we did in previous lessons. You learned how to draw people with long rectangular shapes (A). Today let's learn how to draw them with long hot dog shapes (B). This will make their bodies more round. Start by drawing the circle for the head and the hot dog shapes for the body, arms, and legs. Do not make them too fat. You can draw two hot dog shapes for each arm and leg to show where they bend. Put in the details by drawing little hot dog fingers. Draw the features in the face, and give your figure clothing (C). Draw one of your hot dog figures below (D) with your black pen.

Can you draw two hot dog figures below? First, draw each figure lightly with your yellow pencil. Put clothes on your figures and color them with a nice skin tone.

Hot Dog Figure #1   Hot Dog Figure #2

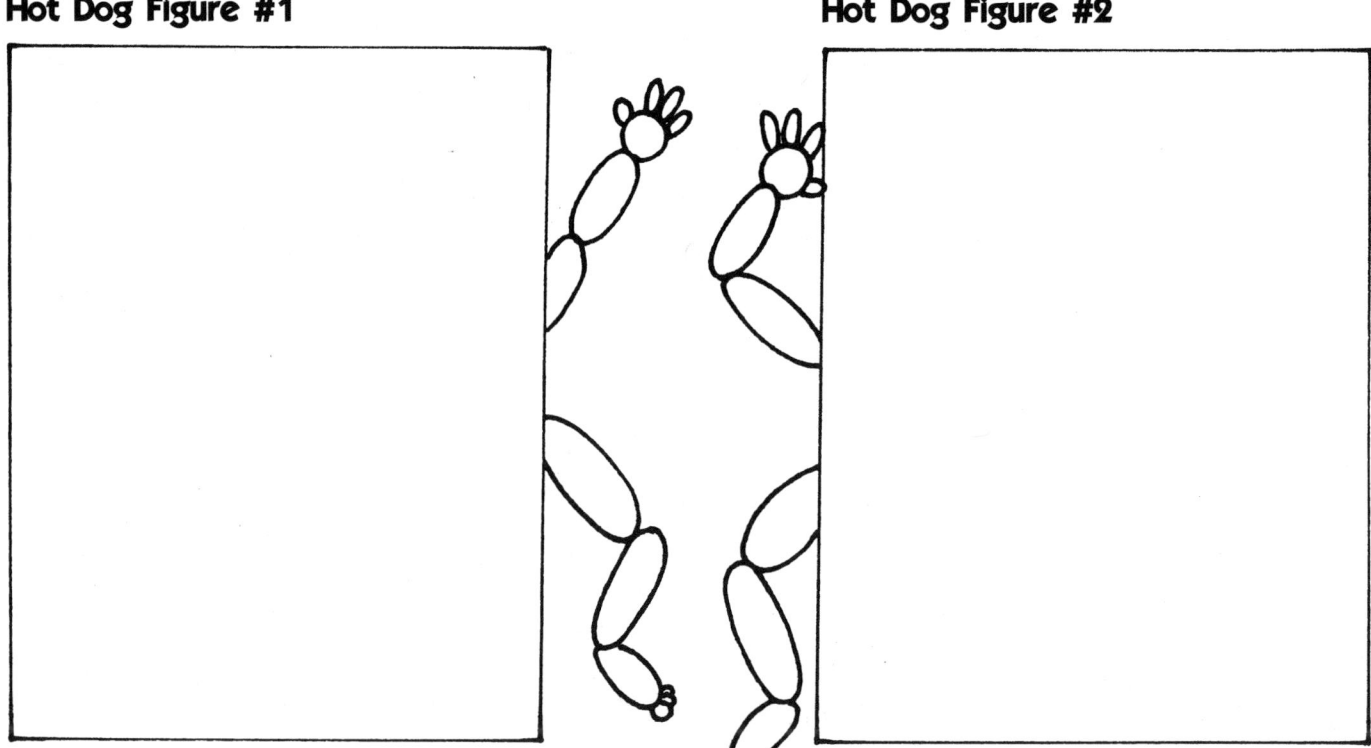

Lesson #48: *People With Pizazz.*

For today's assignment, find an old photograph of yourself or a picture from a magazine and cut out the head. Using your black pen, draw a picture of the body of someone you would like to be below and glue the picture of your face to the top of the body. You can be anyone you like: a ballerina, an artist, an athlete. When you are finished, color the picture with your colored pencils. Do you remember how to color a flesh tone?

Draw Your Figure Here

Lesson #49: *People & Places*

Now let's start putting people in places. Below are some scenes for you to place them in. Can you draw a farmer and some workers in the field (A), and some children playing in the park (B)? Draw your people with your black colored pencil and color with colored pencils when finished.

A. Farmer on the Farm

B. Children at the Park

Lesson #50: *Showing Depth*

There are many ways to show *depth*. (Depth means showing things that go back in the distance.) One way of showing depth is to color things that are closer to you with more color, and things further away with less color. Another way is to draw objects smaller the farther they are in the distance. Things that are closest to you are in the *foreground;* things that are far away are in the *background;* and things that are between the foreground and the background are in the *middle ground.* For this assignment, draw the trees and figures (A) in the figure box below (B) with your black pen. Can you add more to your picture like flowers, a sunshine and a barn? After you have finished, color everything with your colored pencils.

A. Background

Middle Ground

Foreground

B. My Picture with *Foreground, Middle Ground, and Background*

"...whether in the evening, or at midnight, or when the rooster crows, or at dawn."

Mark 13:35

Lesson #51: *Coloring a Crowing Rooster*

Color the rooster below with a burst of warm colors. Do you remember what the warm colors are? They are yellow, red, and orange. You can make many other warm colors by mixing these colors together and also by using other warm colors. See how many warm colors you can mix in the circles below (A). Then color the rooster with yellow, red, orange, yellow/orange, and red/orange as he crows in the bright morning sun (B).

A. ◯ ◯ ◯ ◯ ◯ ◯ ◯ ◯ ◯ ◯ ◯

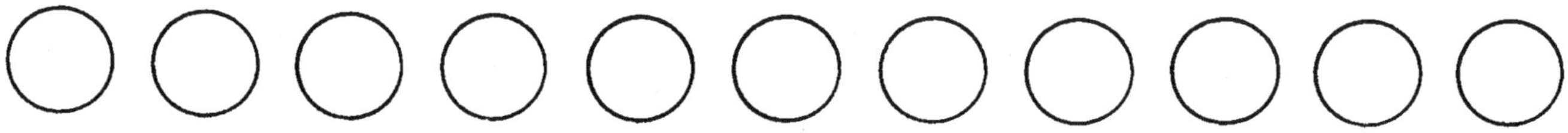

B.

Lesson #52: Can you draw a sheep? Start by drawing a cloud shape and adding the legs and head. Draw some sheep and a farm scene on the next page. Color with your colored pencils when finished.

Ol' MacDonald Had a Sheep Farm

"Far away, there in the sunshine, are my highest aspirations. I may not reach them, but I can look up and see their beauty, believe in them, and try to follow where they lead."

Louisa May Alcott

Lesson #53: An Array of Colors

Let's color with an array of colors! Use all the colors in your pack with the exception of brown and black. Color the picture of the clown floating above the earth, coloring the balloons, the clown and his clothing with a bouquet of vibrant colors. Use line to color and blending to make other colors. Try cross-hatching in some areas. Practice mixing your colors in the balloons before coloring your picture.

94

Lesson #54:   *Still Life with Fruit*

Do you know what a *still life* is? It is a picture of objects that do not move. None of the objects are alive and they are motionless. Do you remember drawing a bowl of fruit? You overlapped fruit and filled two bowls. Let's do the same thing, but this time the fruit will not be in a bowl. Place some fruit in front of you in a pleasing arrangement. You may want to place an apple slightly in front of some grapes and a pear behind them (A). Use your orange pencil to draw everything in the figure box (B.) Make sure to draw large. Color your assortment of fruit with bright colors when you are finished.

A.

B. ──────────── **My Fruit Still Life** ────────────

"There are two worlds: the world that we can measure with line and rule, and the world that we feel with our hearts and imagination."

Leigh Hunt

Lesson #55: *Coloring the Cover*

Notice that the cover of *"I Can Do All Things"* has a lot of bright colors. For this lesson, color in the copy of the cover on this page. This is similar to Lesson #44 in which you colored the grass and trees yellow before adding other colors. Color the sky a very light blue with your light blue pencil and then blending your white pencil over it. Color a light green over the grass and a darker green over the distant trees. Make the one tree in the background a different color green than the grass and the distant trees. (You may want to check Lesson #44 to find the right green.) Color each balloon a bright color using vertical lines, (like the lines on the distant trees). Can you color the little boy's flesh with a nice flesh color? Color the bunny a light brown and the bird a very light blue. Finally, add a splash of color to each of the little puddles of color on the palette.

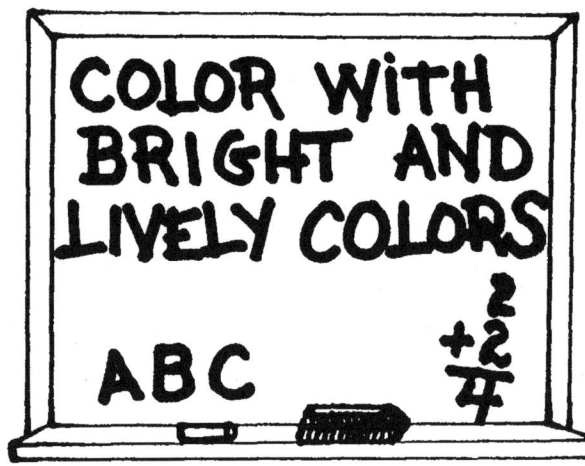

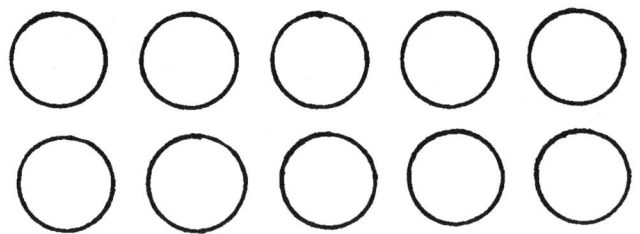

Practice your colors in the circles above, making sure you like them before coloring the picture. Take your time making your picture bright and colorful.

Lesson #56:   *Squares, Triangles & Circles*

Do you know another name for squares, triangles, circles, and rectangles? They are called *geometric shapes.* Let's create some geometric shapes, overlapping some of them (A). Practice drawing these shapes *freehand* (without the use of a ruler or compass). You have already learned how to make a circle and how to draw a straight line. Therefore, drawing geometric shapes should be easy to do. Use your orange pencil and fill the figure box (B) with overlapping, geometric shapes. Let's add some funny characters hiding behind the shapes, playing peek-a-boo. When you are finished, color in everything using vertical, horizontal, and diagonal lines.

B.

Lesson #57: *Coloring with One Color*

Have you ever tried to color something with one color? Most of the time it looks like a great big blob? You don't want to color an apple just one tone of red, or a frog just one tone of green, or a fish just one tone of blue. Students should learn how to make more colors, or tones, by simply using a wide range of one color. A picture that has variations of one color is called a *monochromatic* picture. When we color an apple with different tones of red, it will look much better than with just one tone of red. For this assignment, color one fish green, another fish blue and the seahorse red. However, use at least three different tones of the same color. Notice that lines have been added to help separate the different tones of color. If you are going to color the seahorse red, color some areas a light red by adding yellow and white, and others a dark red by adding blue and violet. Practice coloring the two fish and seahorse on the bottom of the page with your colored pencils. Before beginning, color in the circles to make sure you like the colors. Finally, see if you can draw the fish and seahorse in the figure box (A), adding at least three different tones of the same color for each fish.

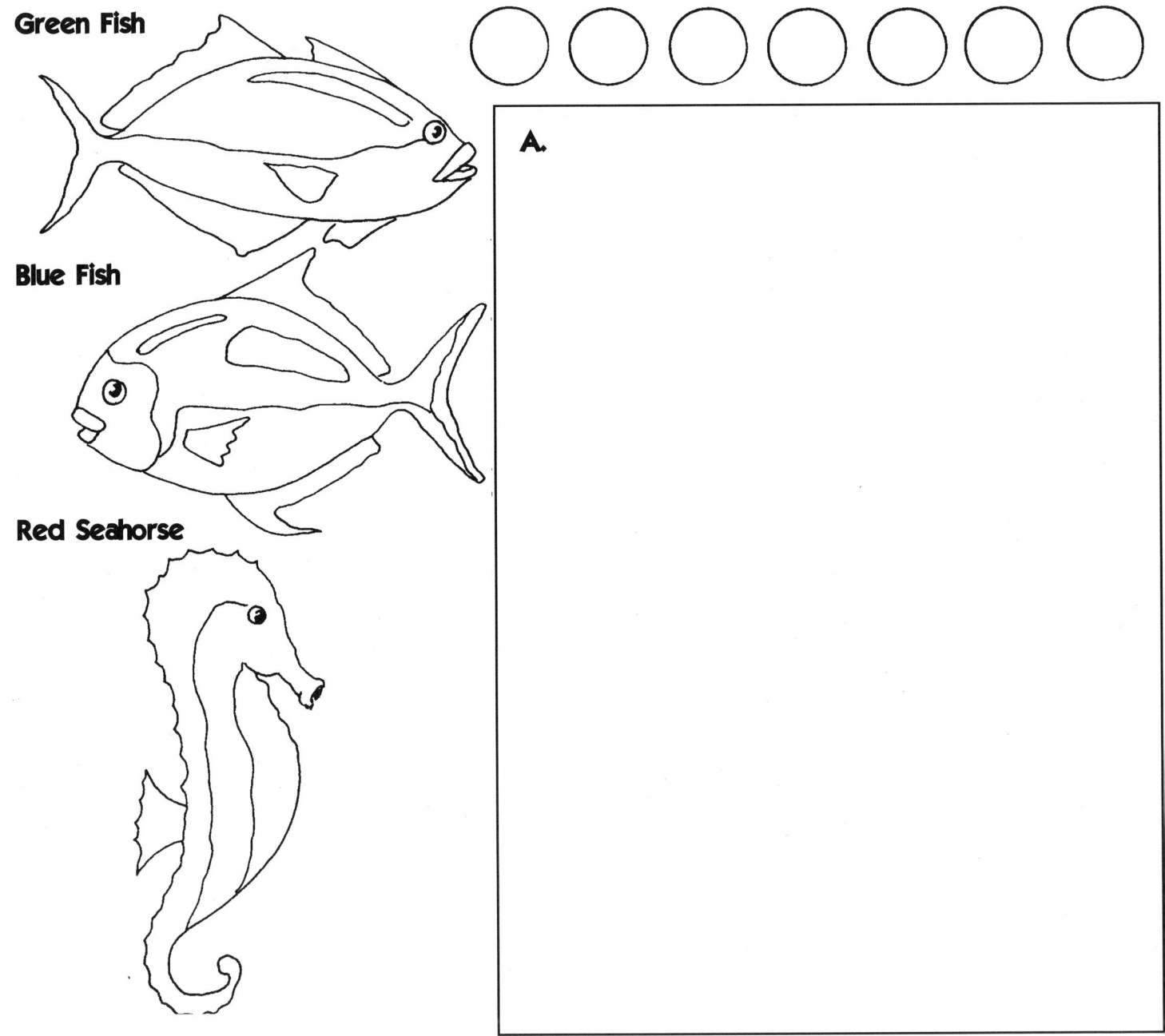

Green Fish

Blue Fish

Red Seahorse

A.

Lesson #58: *Fish in the Aquarium*

  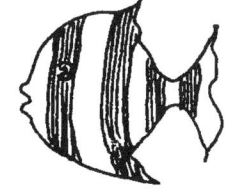

Let's draw an aquarium! We already know how to draw a box, so let's now draw a large glass box below. Dots have been drawn for the four corners of your aquarium. See if you can draw all your lines *freehand,* that is, without the use of a ruler. Then fill it with fish! You can copy the seahorse from page 98 and the other fish from this page. Draw with your black pen and then use your colored pencils to color your wonderful assortment of fish.

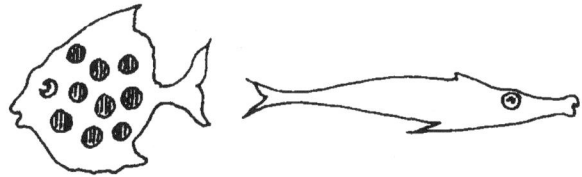  

Lesson #59: Curly-cues

How many things can you draw with curly-cues? Take a look at the objects above. You can draw a cloud, a tree, sheep, collars, and cuffs. You can even draw people's hair with curly-cues. When you are thinking, you can also wrap your thoughts around a big, puffy curly-cue! Draw each of the objects above with curly-cues. Can you think of any other things that can be drawn with curly-cues?

Lesson #60: *Drawing a Cartoon Character*

Do you know how to draw a cartoon character? In the chapter on drawing we learned many of the basic shapes for drawing a simple figure. Likewise, when drawing a cartoon figure, try to keep it simple. It is also good to give a dark outline with a fine black pen. Fill the bottom of the page with your cartoon characters. Be simple and creative!

Lesson #61: *Creating a Cartoon Strip*

Let's do a cartoon story with Wally the Worm! Do you remember what he looks like? I will tell you the beginning of the story. Then, finish it and draw the pictures that go with the story, or cartoon strip. "Once upon a time Wally the Worm decided to go to a baseball game. He really wanted to take his son, Wally Jr., with him because Jr. had never gone to a baseball game before. Well, as they were on their way to the ballpark, they saw a giant fish hook!" Complete the story below. Write each part of the story beneath your pictures with your black pen and color with your colored pencils when finished.

.... once upon a time Wally the Worm decided that he was going to go to a baseball game.

Lesson #62: *Clowning Around*

Can you complete the clown below? Can you add the rest of the stripes to his shirt? Can you draw another suspender and a shoe? Can you place three large, round balloons in his hand? Can you draw a hand going around the flower? Can you add more polka dots to his pants? Can you complete his clown face? Can you give him ears, hair, and eyes? Can you give him a hat? Can you draw a ball on the tip of the seal's nose? Finally, can you give your clown a name? When you are finished, color everything with bright colors.

My Clown's Name Is: _____

Lesson #63: *Fun Time!*

Here's a fun lesson that is from a home schooled student in New Mexico. See if you can draw it with your black pen, in the space below.

"Once there was a man."

"He had eight puppies."

"And they lived in a cave."

"One day two of the puppies died and they buried them with gravestones."

"They were also buried in the cave."

"After they buried the puppies, the other puppies ran down the hill."

"And then they ran back up again."

Submitted by:
Hannah Pierce (Age 8) New Mexico

Lesson #64: *Daniel and the Lion's Den*

For this lesson, see if you can illustrate this scene from the book of Daniel in the Bible: "At the first light of dawn, the king got up and hurried to the lions' den. When he came near the den, he called to Daniel in an anguished voice, 'Daniel, servant of the living God, has your God, whom you serve continually, been able to rescue you from the lions?' Daniel answered, 'O king, live forever! My God sent his angel, and he shut the mouths of the lions. They have not hurt me, because I was found innocent in His sight. Nor have I ever done any wrong before you, O king.' The king was overjoyed and gave orders to lift Daniel out of the den. And when Daniel was lifted from the den, no wound was found on him, because he had trusted in his God." Daniel 6:19-23. You can make your lion's with curly-cues too! Draw a lion like a cat with big paws and a long tail. Then put curly-cues around his head! Do your illustration of the story above and color it when finished.

Lesson #65: *Journal Time!*

Let's do another day in our art journal. Remember, draw things around you that are part of your day. Also, write about your experiences, what you are learning, what you like to do, etc. You can tape a leaf or a cut flower in your journal. If you went to the theater or on a trip, you can tape your tickets in your journal. However, the most important thing to do is draw what's around you. For example, you can draw your cat, a tree, some tools, a chair, some books, or anything else that you would like to fill the page with. Use your black pen and your colored pencils.

_____
_____
_____
_____
_____
_____
_____
_____
_____
_____
_____
_____
_____
_____

Colored Markers

"I want to recapture the freshness of vision which is characteristic of extreme youth when all the world is new."
Henri Matisse

Colored Markers

Colored markers are great for children to use and can provide wonderful results. Some basic things that students should know are:

1. Markers offer certain effects and techniques that cannot be obtained with colored pencils or paints.
2. They are great for assignments like lettering, making a poster, or doing bright, simple illustrations.
3. They work best on certain surfaces, like white poster board.

Rules for Beginning with Colored Markers

1. **Keep Your Materials Organized:** It's important to keep your markers together. When cleaning up your work area, place them back in their box or in another container. It is difficult to do a colorful picture when markers are misplaced.

2. **Draw Your Picture in Pencil First:** Before you begin to color your picture, draw it in pencil or with your yellow marker. This will help you draw everything correctly before the bolder markers are added.

3. **Use a Suitable Surface:** Colored markers, as every other medium in art, work best on certain surfaces. With watercolors, it is best to work on watercolor paper. With colored pencils, drawing paper is best. However, a heavy paperstock is an ideal surface for markers. It is thicker and will not allow the colors to seep through to the other side.

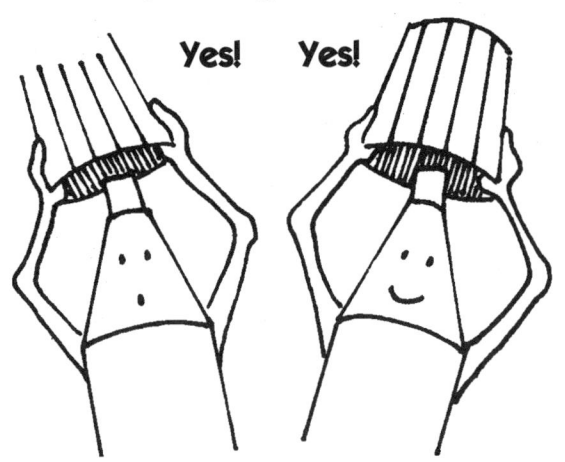

Yes!   Yes!

4. **Work From Light To Dark Colors:** Start with lighter colors, like yellow or orange. Then complete your picture with darker colors.

5. **Place Tops Back On Your Markers:** Markers will dry out quickly. Be in the habit of placing tops back on the markers as soon as you're finished using them. This preserves the colors and your markers will last much longer.

6. **There Are No White Markers:** Since there are no white markers, leave white areas on your paper to be your white.

7. **Work with Strokes, Lines, or Dots:** Often beginning students use markers like crayons, coloring in large areas, like a blue sky, with one color. This will not only use up the markers quickly, but most times the color is too dark. Students should learn to color with lines, strokes or dots just like with colored pencils.

> *"A picture is an unusual combination of lines and colors that set one another off."*
>
> Edgar Degas

8. **Materials:** Students can start with a basic set of *washable* markers. A simple set would consist of about eight colors and is reasonably priced. For our purpose, the bold tips are preferable. Washable markers are good to use. Most of the lessons in this section will be done on the *Marker Cards* provided with the text. However, we also recommend you obtain several sheets of white poster board (22" x 28") to be cut into various sizes for some of the assignments.

Materials Needed:

1. **One set of Eight** *Washable* **Markers**
2. **Several 22" x 28" Sheets of White Poster Board**
3. **One Medium Brush**

Note: For the "painting" assignments with washable markers, make sure the students do not use too much water or scrub the water into the marker cards. This will cause the cards to bubble. An ideal surface for painting with markers would be the shiny side of poster board.

"For precept must be upon precept...line upon line."   Isaiah 28:10

Lesson #66: *Line upon Line*

The number one principle that I like to start with is to *color with line*. When you learn to color with line, your pictures will be brighter and more colorful. This is different than coloring areas with one solid color, like coloring an apple entirely red. If you add orange lines, red lines, and even some violet lines, your apple will have more color and be more pleasing to the eye as illustrated in Lesson #45. Let's practice coloring with lines. Before beginning, color the flowers on the next page with colored pencils. *Try not to use markers in this text* because markers will bleed to the other side of the paper. Color the inside of each flower with yellow and orange dots (D).

A. Vertical Lines   **B. Diagonal Lines**   **C. Horizontal Lines**   **D.**

Always start by coloring with the lightest marker. Color between the yellow lines of the first flower with orange lines, between the yellow lines of the second flower with red lines, and between the red lines of the third flower with blue lines. *Take your time!* The more time you take, the better your flowers will look. On the bottom figure box of *Marker Card #1,* color the flowers with lines and bright colors. Use any bright colors you like for the flowers. For the petals and stems, use yellow, green and blue lines to make your greens colorful.

Lesson #67: Cut a piece of white poster board to 11" x 7" and fold it evenly to make a 5 1/2" x 7" card. Draw a large flower on it with a smiling face. Color it with colored markers and send it as a greeting card to a friend and brighten their day!

Note: Coloring with lines can be both tedious and frustrating in the beginning. The student may not like the results of coloring with line at first but, after several exercises, he should appreciate the results much more. Younger students may run out of patience with line   coloring. If they are starting to do careless work, have them take a break and return to it later with a fresh start.

Marker Card #1: *Coloring with Line*

Vertical Lines:
Yellow & Red

Diagonal Lines:
Yellow & Orange

Horizontal Lines:
Yellow & Violet

Color the flowers above with lines and lots of color!
For the green you may want to use yellow and light green.

Lesson #68:   Dot....Dot....Dot....

Another term for coloring with dots is *pointillism*. Coloring with dots can be a lot of fun to do with markers because the points of the markers are so fat. However, it takes patience to color. Remember, the more patience you have when it comes to coloring, the nicer your pictures will look. If you become tired while coloring with dots, take a break. You can even stop and go on to another assignment and finish it later. Then, when you are refreshed you will feel much better about adding more dots! See if you can color the pictures on the next page with your colored pencils and lots of colorful dots. Don't forget to keep your dots very close together!

Yes!   No!

Blue
Dots

When you are finished, take out *Marker Card #2*. First, practice coloring the fruit with dots in the middle of the card (A). Just like the last lesson, we will start with the lightest color. Color each of the fruit with yellow dots, making sure to place the dots close together. When you finish, nearly all the apple should be filled with dots (above). Add orange dots and a lot of red dots to your apple. Last, add some blue or purple dots to the shaded side of your apple. Then add green dots to the yellow dots on your pear, and orange dots to the yellow dots on your orange. Notice the two apples above. Make sure to keep your dots close together!

Next, color the three trees (B). Start by coloring them with yellow dots. Then add green dots to the first tree, blue dots to the second tree and green and blue dots to the third tree, keeping your dots close together. Which one do you like best?

In the third row color the pine trees with dots (C). Color the first three with any warm colors you like and the last three with any cool colors. Do you remember what the warm colors are? They are *yellow, red,* and *orange.* Cool colors are *blue, violet,* and *green.*

Color in the balloons on the bottom of the card (D). You can use any two colors of dots you like for each balloon. Try to make each balloon a different color by using various colors. Finally, color the picture on the bottom of the page with dots (E). Again, use any colors you like. Take your time. Coloring with dots takes longer to do but it can also create some pretty pictures.

Lesson #69: Cut a piece of white poster board to 11" x 7" and fold it evenly to make a 5 1/2" x 7" card. This is the size that will fit into a standard envelope. Lightly draw a picture of flowers on the card and color it with dots. Look at pictures done by George Seurat and Paul Signac to see how they used dots for color.

Marker Card #2: *Coloring with Dots....*

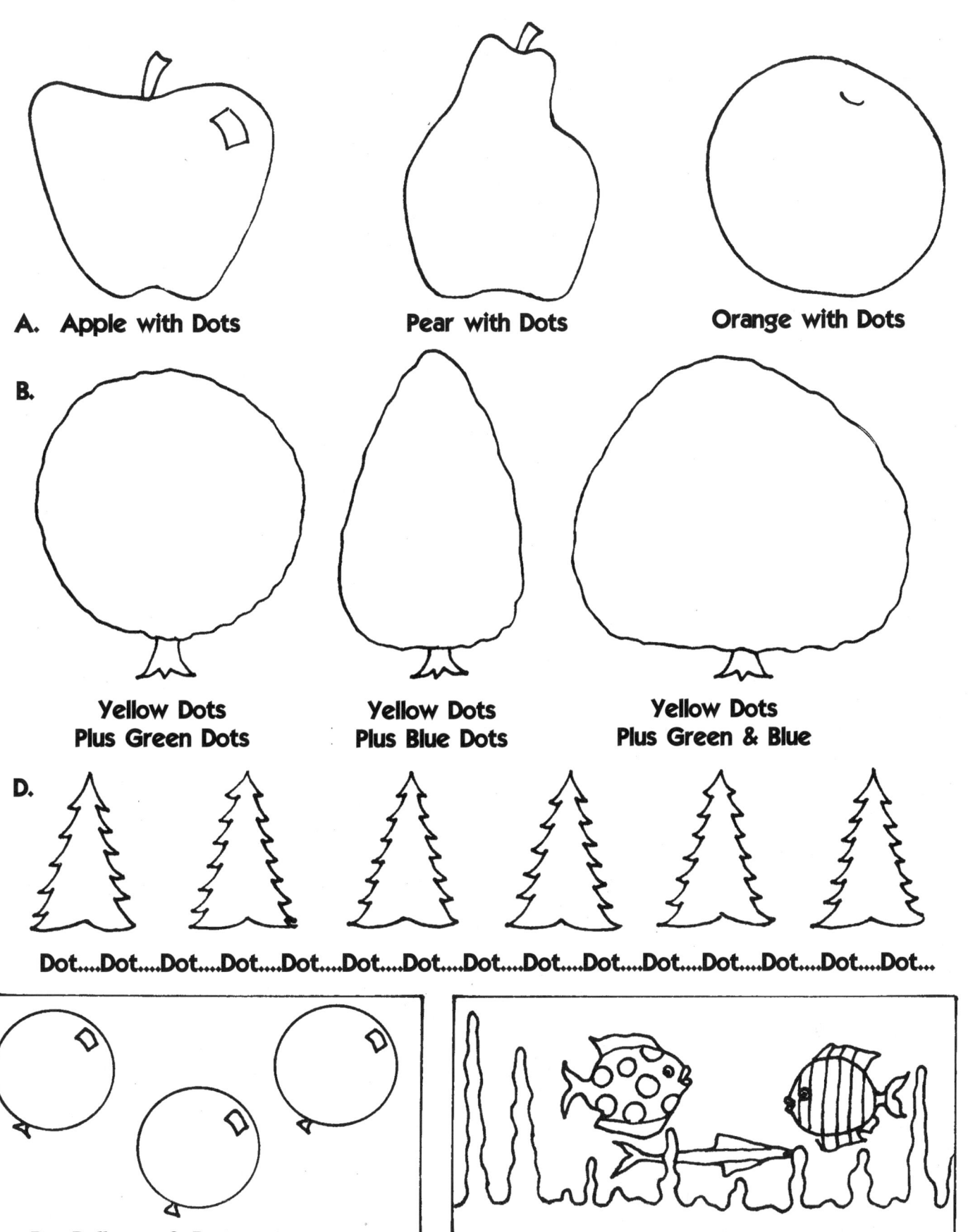

A. Apple with Dots

Pear with Dots

Orange with Dots

B.

Yellow Dots
Plus Green Dots

Yellow Dots
Plus Blue Dots

Yellow Dots
Plus Green & Blue

D.

Dot....Dot....Dot....Dot....Dot....Dot....Dot....Dot....Dot....Dot....Dot....Dot....Dot....Dot....Dot....Dot...

D. Balloons & Dots

E. Color the Picture With Dots of Color

Lesson #70: *Painting with Markers*

A.

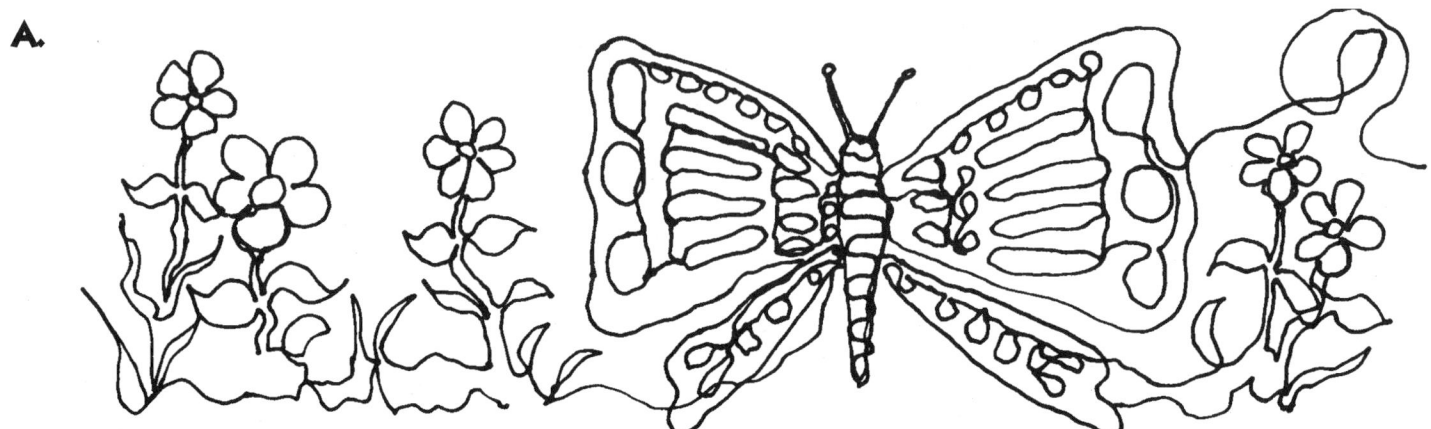

A *contour line* is a drawing done with one continuous line, not stopping from begin-ning to end (A). At first, drawing like this is difficult. However, the more you practice, the better you will become at doing contour drawings. Practice drawing two butterflies below with contour line, looking at the butterfly at the top of this page and on the next page. Remember, don't lift your pencil from beginning to end. Allow your line to go over and around. When you are finished, color your butterflies with a bouquet of beautiful colors. Then draw a design on the wing of the butterfly on the bottom of the next page with your black pen and color in the different shapes with lines using your colored pencils. Finally, color in the picture of the flowers on the next page with your colored pencils. Use your light colors first and color with line and dots.

Place *Marker Card #3* in front of you. Using your yellow and orange washable mark-ers, color some of the flowers on the top of the card with dots and some with lines. Then color sparingly with your darker colors. When you have finished, take your brush and dip it in clean water. Paint lightly with water over all the areas you colored with your washable markers. Watch the colors blend! How do you like the results?

Return to *Marker Card #3* and lightly draw the patterns in the other wing of the butterfly on the bottom of the card with your orange colored marker. When you are fin-ished, go over your butterfly with colored markers, using lots of colorful dots and lines. Wet your brush and blend the colors together.

—————— **Butterfly #1** ——————————— **Butterfly #2** ——————

Marker Card #3:   *Painting with Markers*

Color the Flowers with Lines & Dots and then Blend with Brush & Water.

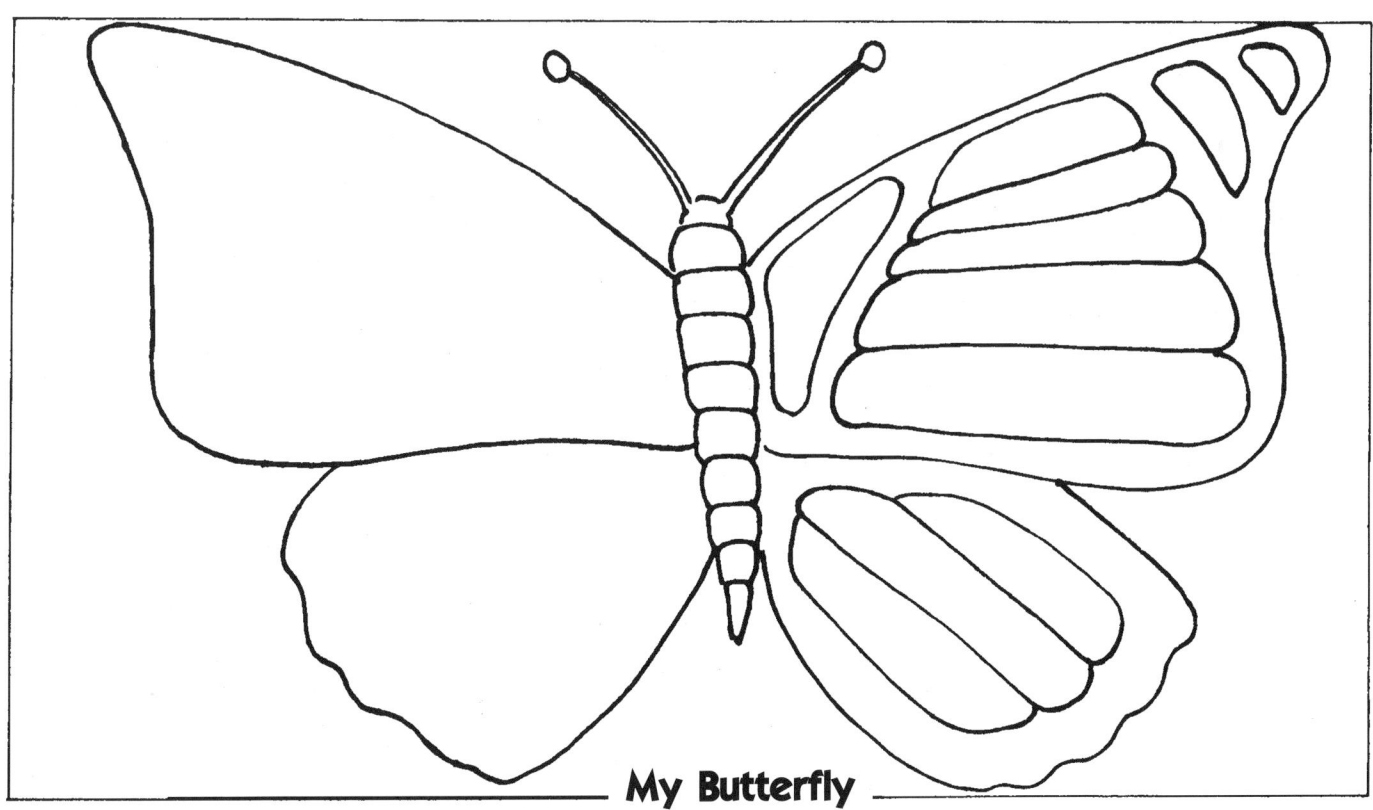

My Butterfly

Lesson #71: *Colorful Designs*

For this lesson we are going to color creative patterns. First, draw some designs and patterns that are floating around in the little girl's mind as she does her artwork (below). Some designs have already been drawn in. Can you draw some more around her? Outline your creative designs with a fine black marker and then use your colored pencils to color the entire picture.

Color the patterns and designs on the top of the next page with your colored pencils. Use lines and dots. On the bottom of the page, create some interesting patterns and designs and color them in with your colored pencils.

Take *Marker Card #4* and place it in front of you. First, color in the patterns on the top of your card with your washable markers using lots of dots, lines, and color! When finished, blend the colors with a wet brush. Finally, create your own patterns and designs on the bottom of the card. Draw them lightly with your orange pencil before coloring them with a bright array of washable marker colors.

Lesson #72: Draw some creative designs on two pieces of 5 ½" x 7" white poster board. Color one with the warm colors: yellow, red, and orange. Color the other with the cool colors: blue, violet, and green.

Colored Marker Card #4: *Colorful Designs*

Color with Lines, Dots, and a Wet Brush

Create Your Own Patterns & Designs Above

Lesson #73: *Frames & Patterns*

Did you know that when you draw a frame around your pictures, it can make your pictures look even better! Let's practice making frames for our pictures. Notice the frame around *Marker Card #5*. It was drawn with a ruler and its sides are all the same thickness. Nice patterns and designs can be added to make the frame even more appealing and to give it some harmony with the picture.

Take a ruler and your black pen and add a 1" border around the figure box below. Make sure to keep your lines straight. Draw and color a picture inside the frame with a bright array of colored pencils. Likewise, add some nice patterns and designs to the border of your frame to make your picture even nicer!

Color the picture on the next page with colored pencils. Add some designs and patterns to your frame. When you are finished, place *Marker Card #5* in front of you. Color in the sunset with your washable markers using orange and yellow for the sun and its reflection in the water. and blend the colors with a wet brush. Color the rest of the picture and add more creative designs to the border.

Let's

Make a

Frame

Lesson #74: Take a piece of 11" x 14" white poster board and place a 1" border around it with your pencil and ruler. Do a colorful picture inside the border and then add a colorful frame to complete the picture by gluing old puzzle pieces around the border. You will love the results!

118

Marker Card #5: Colorful Frames

"Those who sow in tears will reap with songs of joy. He who goes out weeping, carrying seed to sow, will return with rejoicing."

Psalm 126:5-6

Lesson #75: Warm & Cool Colors

We have already learned there are *warm* and *cool* colors. The warm colors are *yellow, red,* and *orange.* These colors actually look warm. When we color with warm colors they make everything seem cheerful and bright. The cool colors are *blue, violet,* and *green.* Cool colors are good to use to create a sad mood.

Let's draw a happy clown and a sad clown in the squares below (A & B). Just draw their faces. You may want to copy the clown's faces from page 55. Color the happy clown with warm colors. Can you make more warm colors besides yellow, red, and orange by mixing them together with dots or lines? Practice mixing some of the colors in the balloons above the clowns on the next page. Color in the clowns with colored pencils before coloring *Marker Card #6* with your markers. Remember, color the happy clown with warm colors and the sad clown with cool colors!

A. *Happy Face!*

B. *Sad Face*

Happy faces up! Draw the hair, smile, and everything else going up on the happy clown. The sad clown's hat, mouth, and even teardrop go down.

120

Marker Card #6: Warm & Cool Colors

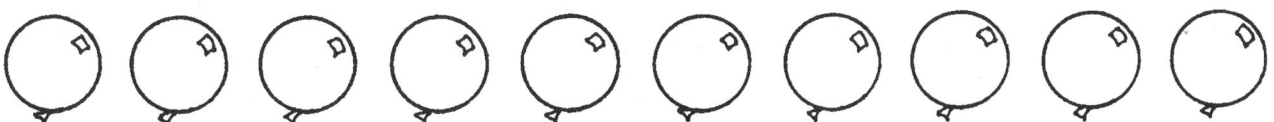

Warm Colors.....Warm Colors......Warm Colors.....Cool Colors.....Cool Colors.....Cool Colors.....

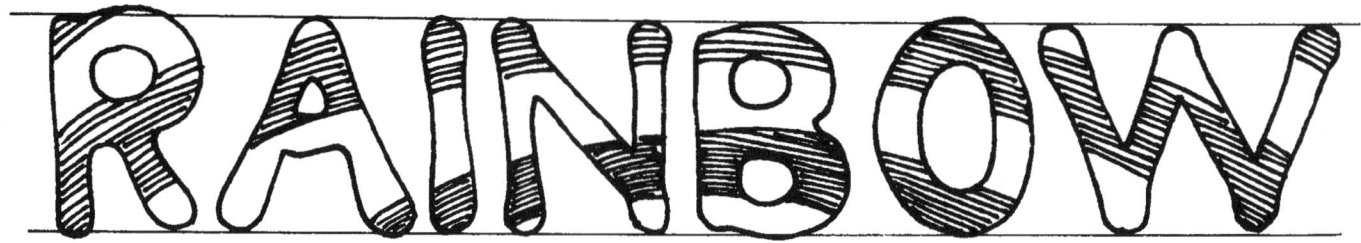

Lesson #76: *Bubble Letters*

Lettering should be learned by every student. Reports, signs, posters, and many other things we do in art require us to letter in a good manner. One of the first things to learn in lettering is how to use *guidelines*. Guidelines are light lines used to show where to place the top and bottom of each letter. This allows all the letters to be the same size and to be straight. First, practice lettering the word RAINBOW below without using guidelines (A). Do not use bubble letters yet. See if you can keep your word straight and all the letters the same size. Use your orange pencil.

A.

Letter the word RAINBOW again, using the guidelines provided on the top of the next page. Start to the far left to give you enough space for the entire word. Make sure all the letters are the same height, touching the top and bottom of the guidelines. Draw the letters in lightly with your yellow colored pencil before going over each with your colored pencils.

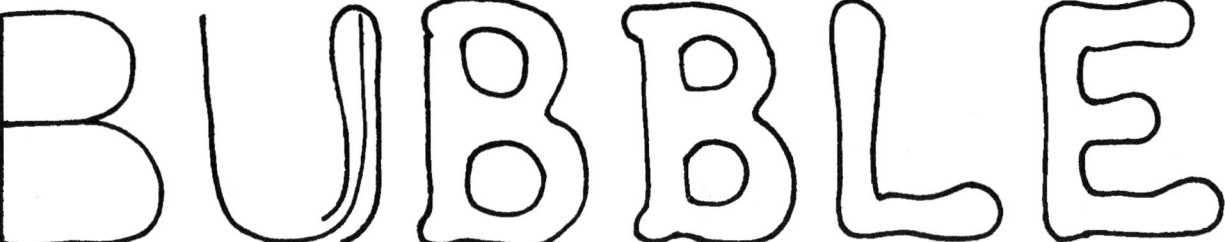

To make *bubble letters,* inflate the letters by putting air into them, making them round and fat in shape. Practice making bubble letters with your colored pencils by lightly going around the word RAINBOW you printed at the top of the next page. Then, outline and color them with a rainbow of colors. Next, add flowers and other colorful designs to the word *NATURE* with your black pen. Finally, fill the bottom of the card with any bubble letters you like floating on the page.

When you are finished, turn to *Marker Card #7* and do the assignment again. First, draw everything with colored pencils and then color with line, dots or blending, using your colored markers.

Marker Card #7: *Bubble Letters*

Letter the word *RAINBOW* above.

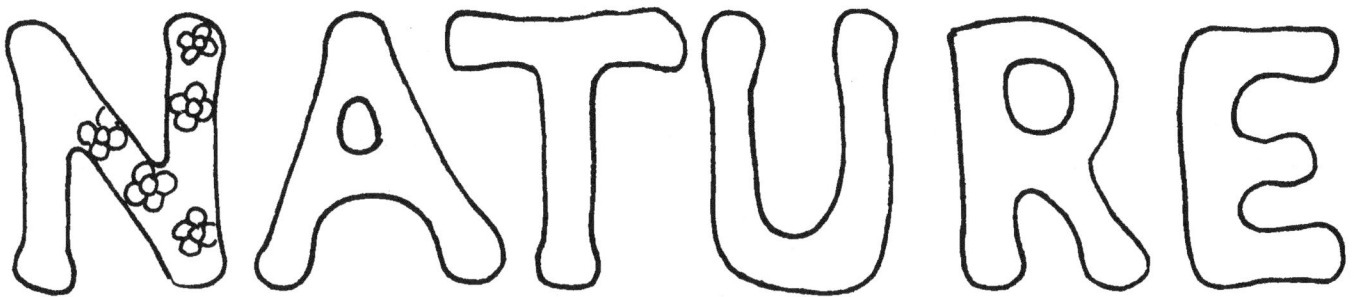

Place flowers and other designs in the word NATURE above.

Practice drawing and coloring bubble letters floating in the air above. Color with line, dots, or blending.

Lesson #77: *Designing a Cereal Box*

Let's design a cereal box. First, create a new name for your cereal and print it in the guidelines below (A). Then, create a new design for the shape of your cereal (B). It could be stars, "O"s, alphabets, etc. Design the cover of your box by making little sketches on the boxes below (C) with your black pen. Draw and color your final design on the cereal box on the next page. When you are finished, take out *Marker Card #8* and place it in front of you. Draw everything with colored pencils, and then color your cereal box with markers using lines, dots, or blending. Make sure to use guidelines for your

A. My Cereal Name Is: _____

B. My Cereal is Going to Look Like This:

C. Practice Your Cereal Box Design Below

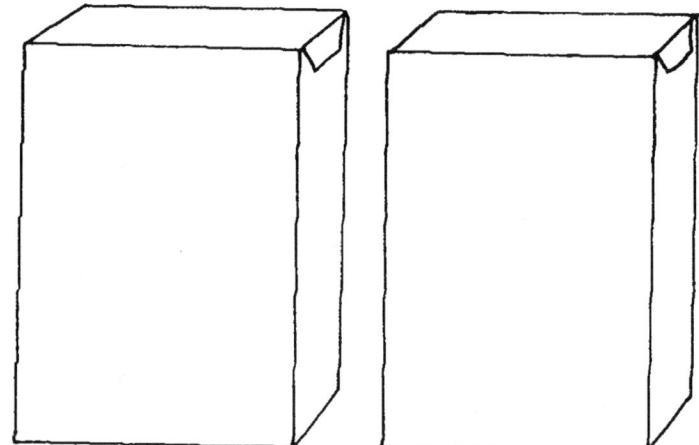

Lesson #78: On a piece of 11" x 14" white poster board, design a label for a new can of beans or soup. Draw your can large. Color it in with markers. Be creative!

124

Marker Card #8: Designing a Cereal Box

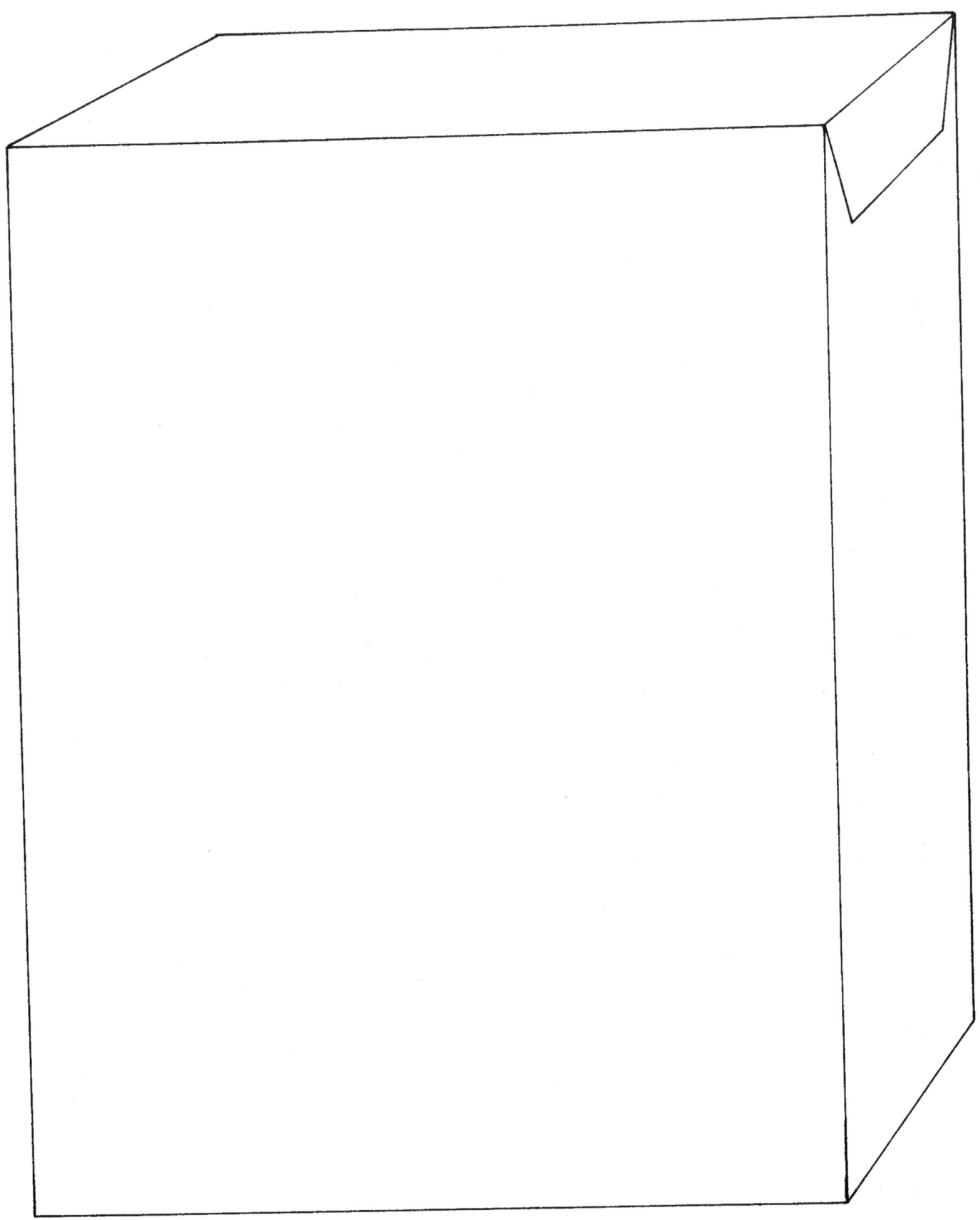

"A candle loses nothing of itself when lighting other candles." Thomas Jefferson

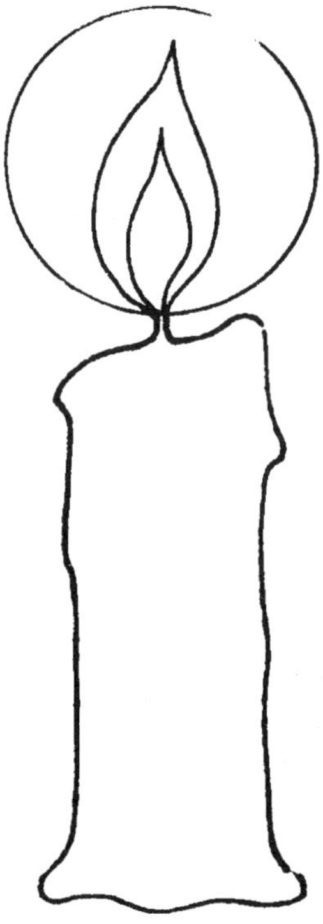

Lesson #79: *Creating a Warm Glow*

Have you ever looked at the color of a candle's flame or the fire in a fireplace? The colors seem brightest near the flame, going from an orange to a yellow/orange, to a yellow. Practice coloring the warm glow of a candle with your colored pencils by coloring the candles to the right and left. Make the center of your flame a red/orange, the next part a yellow/orange, and the round glow around the flame a bright yellow. You may even want to make your flames look brighter by adding a dark blue and violet background behind the candles. Don't forget to color with line.

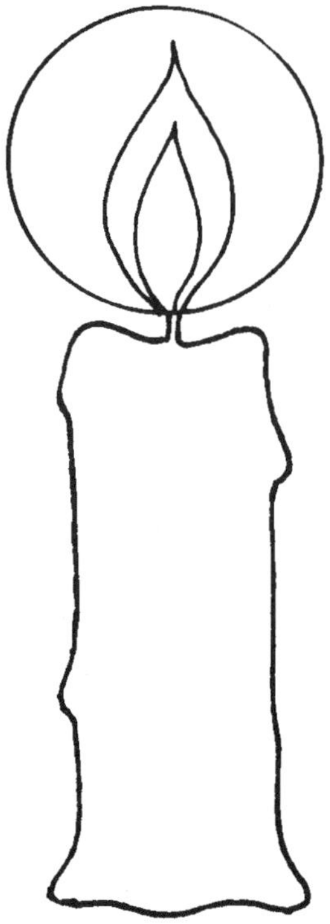

A.

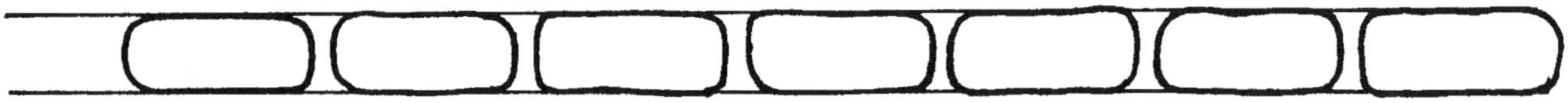

Do you know how to draw rows of bricks? First draw one row of bricks (A), trying to make them all the same size and in a straight line. You may want to use your ruler to make guidelines for the bricks, the same way you use guidelines for lettering.

The next layer of bricks will go on a line just above the first layer. However, each brick will start or end in the center of the brick below it (B). Then, the third layer of bricks will be just the same as the first layer.

B.

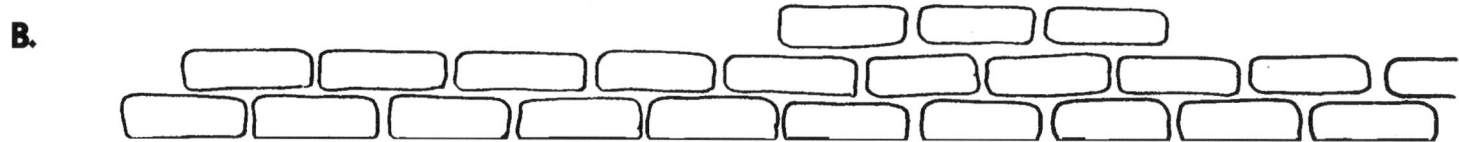

Practice adding some more bricks to the rows above (B) and then finish drawing the bricks above the mantle and around the fireplace on the next page. After you have drawn them correctly, go over each brick with your fine black marker and color them with red and orange pencils using vertical lines. Next, color in the flames just as you did above. Finally, place *Marker Card #9* in front of you and draw in the missing bricks. Color the candles and fireplace with your colored markers and blend the colors with a wet brush.

Lesson #80: On a piece of 11" x 14" white poster board, draw a brick house in the country with the sun setting behind it. Color everything with colored markers.

Marker Card #9: *Creating a Warm Glow*

Lesson #81: Making a Grocery List

Let's have some fun! Today we are going to draw and color a grocery list. Do you know how to draw all your groceries? In the space below, practice drawing some things you will need at the grocery store like apples, oranges, eggs, milk, bread, etc. Use your colored pencils to draw everything. Next, print your grocery list (A). When finished, draw and color all your groceries on the next page using your colored pencils. Place *Marker Card #10* in front of you. Draw and color your groceries again, this time with bright and colorful markers.

A. Grocery List:

_____
_____
_____
_____
_____
_____
_____
_____
_____
_____
_____
_____
_____
_____
_____
_____

Lesson #82: Take a piece of 11" x 14" white poster board and draw and color a garden filled with vegetables and fruit. Let's make them into cartoon characters. Can you give them faces, arms, and legs? Use your markers and bright colors!

128

Marker Card #10: Making a Grocery List

Lesson #83: *Yipes! Stripes!*

Let's draw and color some beach balls. Fill them with stripes, making some large and some small. Then, add a bright assortment of colors to them!

A.

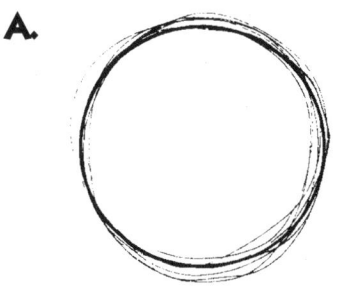

Do you remember how to draw a circle? You learned this in Lesson #9. Remember, go around and around with your pencil four or five times until you have the shape of a circle (A). Make sure to draw *lightly* until the circle is round. Practice drawing a ball in figure box B. Start with your yellow pencil, and then go to a darker pencil when it has been drawn correctly.

B.

D.

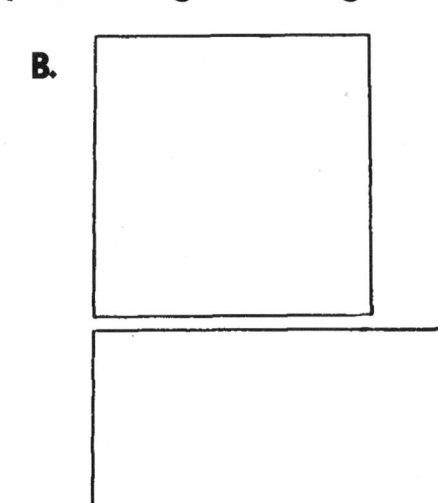

C.

After you have drawn the ball, add stripes to make a beach ball. Don't forget that stripes go *around* a ball, so draw them going around (C). Draw your beach ball with stripes that go around in the figure box above (D). Notice all the different designs on the beach balls below. Can you add some designs to the beach balls on the next page? Also, draw three beach balls in the empty spaces on the shelves. Put designs on them using lots of stripes. Then color all the beach balls with your colored pencils. Make sure to color with lots of color.

When you are finished, place *Marker Card #11* in front of you. Draw three more beach balls in the empty spaces with your yellow marker, giving each a nice design. Color all the beach balls with plenty of lines and stripes. Remember, everything is to be drawn and colored with lines. *Yipes! Stripes!*

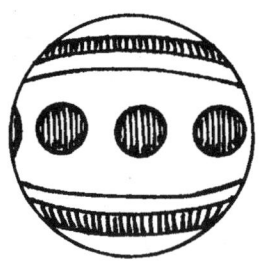
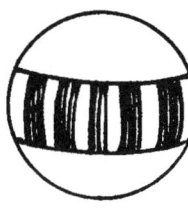

Lesson #84:
On a large sheet of 22" x 28" white poster board, draw and color some hot air balloons. You may want to go to the library to find some nice designs.

Marker Card #11: *Yipes! Stripes!*

Lesson #85: *Stickers*

Let's make some stickers! All you have to do is create some nice designs, color them with bright colors, cut them out and glue them to something. Draw creative designs in the shapes below with your orange colored pencil. Then, color them with bright colors. Finally, color all the little sticker drawings on the next page with your colored pencils.

When you are finished, place *Marker Card #12* in front of you and color all the stickers with your bright colored markers! Can you be creative? Color some with stripes, some with dots, and some by blending. You may want to take a fine black marker and outline your drawings to make them stand out. Then, all you need to do is cut them out and glue them to your letters and cards. A glue stick works well with stickers!

Lesson #86:
Build your collections of colorful stickers. Take a piece of 11" x 14" white poster board and draw some of your own sticker characters. Color them with your markers, cut them out, and stick them on your letters with a glue stick.

133

Lesson #87: *Coloring Baby Lambs*

How would you color a white lamb with colored markers? It's really difficult to do, since there is no white color in your marker set. One way to do this is to leave some areas uncolored to allow the white of the paper to be your white. Sometimes by coloring everything in, our pictures become too dark. For today's assignment leave some areas white and color around them to make them look brighter.

Let's start by coloring backgrounds behind the baby lambs below, allowing the lambs to remain white. Use your colored pencils for this. In figure box A, color rich greens behind the lamb to bring out the color of his white wool. See how many different greens you can make. In figure box B, color bright, colorful flowers around the lamb. In figure box C, color the blue pond behind the baby lamb.

In D, draw some baby lambs in the field with your black pen. Color everything except the lambs and see if this makes the wool look white. Next, color a background for the baby lambs on the top of the opposite page. Finally, color the bouquet of flowers behind the baby lamb in the basket.

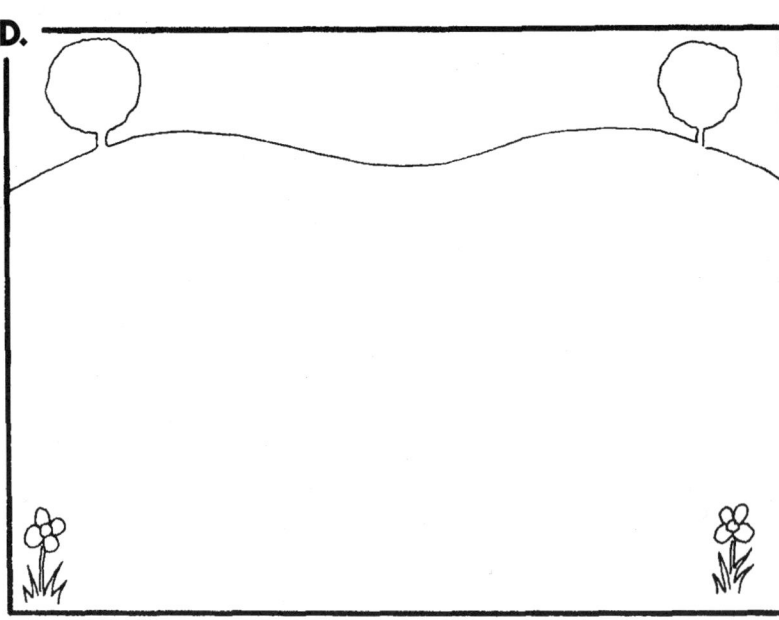

Place *Marker Card #13* in front of you. First, color the backgrounds behind the three baby lambs at the top of the card with your colored markers. Use a deep green to bring out the white of the first lamb, mixing green and blue together, color the flowers with bright, warm colors to bring out the white of the second lamb; and a deep blue pond to bring out the white of the third lamb. Then, color the flowers and background behind the baby lamb in the basket. Can you make a nice yellow/orange to color the basket?

Marker Card #13: *Coloring Baby Lambs*

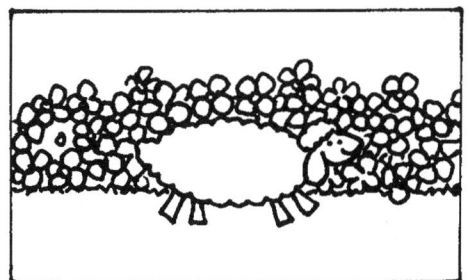

135

Lesson #88: *Coloring Like an Impressionist*

Have you ever seen paintings by the *Impressionists?* They are very colorful. The Impressionists were more concerned with *strokes* and *color* than they were with being realistic. Coloring like an impressionist can be fun. Your artwork will be bright and colorful, and you will learn much about color. Two things to keep in mind when coloring like this are:

A.

B.

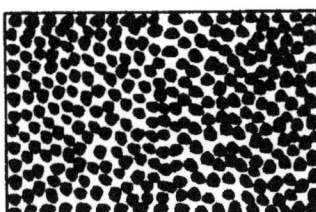

1. *Learn how to place one color next to another.*
2. *Use lots of strokes to apply your color.*

Colored markers work well when coloring like an impressionist because they make bold, colorful strokes. Notice the flower above (A). Strokes of color can be applied like this. Try to apply one series of colorful strokes next to another. You should be very good at doing this by now because of all the drawing and color assignments you have done with *lines.* However, you are now going to use bolder and shorter strokes. Look at the balloon above (B). This was done with dots, or pointillism. It is another wonderful way to color.

Color the sunflower on the next page with your colored pencils. Try to use a lot of bold strokes of color. You can use your orange, yellow, and green pencils for the inner circle and yellow and orange for the larger circle. Use a bright yellow for the petals. Can you pick a nice color to color the background?

C. Short Strokes

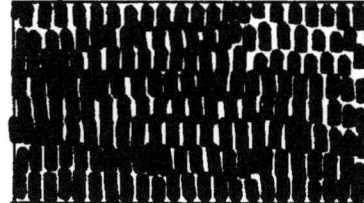

D. Circular Strokes

E. Pointillism

Place *Marker Card #14* in front of you. Practice making colorful, bold strokes in the figure boxes above the sunflower. In the first figure box, make short strokes (C). Use your yellow and orange markers for this. In the second figure box make circular strokes (D). This is a good way to color a sun or the inner core of a sunflower! Use yellow and a little orange. In the third figure box, practice coloring with dots (E). Use yellow and orange for this also. (You may want to add a little brown or red to show the texture of the seeds in a sunflower.) Finally, color the sunflower with lots of bold strokes. Color the inner circle yellow and orange; the outer circle yellow with a little orange; and the petals a bright yellow with bold strokes! Use light green, yellow, and blue strokes for the stem.

Marker Card #14: *Coloring Like an Impressionist*

Short Strokes   **Circular Strokes**   **Pointillism**

Lesson #89: *Noah's Ark*

Let's illustrate another story from the Bible. However, this time let's do some *thumbnail sketches* first. Thumbnail sketches are small, simple sketches done to create several ideas before starting on your final picture. Today, let's illustrate the story of Noah's Ark. First, draw three thumbnail sketches below of different parts of the story of Noah's Ark. Take your best sketch and draw it large in the figure box above, placing as much detail in it as you can. When you are finished, color it with colored pencils. Finally, cut a piece of 11" x 14" white poster board and draw your picture of Noah's ark larger and with more color using your washable markers!

"Then God said to Noah, 'Come out of the ark, you and your wife and your sons and their wives. Bring out every kind of living creature that is with you - the birds, the animals and all the creatures that move along the ground - so they can multiply on the earth and be fruitful and increase in number upon it.

So Noah came out, together with his sons and his wife and his sons' wives. All the animals and all the creatures that move along the ground and all the birds - everything that moves on the earth - came out of the ark, one kind after another."   Genesis 8:15-19

Thumbnail Sketches

More Colored Marker Lessons

Lesson #90: Tropical Colors! On a sheet of white card stock paper, lightly draw some colorful, tropical birds and color them with bright, colorful colors.

Lesson #91: A Pineapple Picture. Place a pineapple in front of you. Draw it first with colored pencils. Then draw and color it with your colored markers on a sheet of white card stock paper.

Lesson #92: Coloring Fruit with Dots. Take four sheets of white card stock paper and draw and color a piece of fruit on each with your colored markers. You may want to color an apple, an orange, a pear, and some grapes.

Lesson #93: A Bouquet of Flowers. Can you draw and color a bouquet of flowers? Find a picture of a bouquet of flowers and draw it on a sheet of white card stock paper with your yellow pencil before coloring the picture with markers.

Lesson #94: Cartoon Characters. Select three cartoon characters and copy each one of them on a sheet of white card stock paper. Color them with bold colors. You may want to outline them with a fine black marker.

Lesson #95: Illustrating a Children's Story. Write a children's story. Draw the pictures that go with the story on drawing paper and color with colored pencils. Then draw and color it on 8 1/2" x 11" white card stock paper with markers. Punch three holes to one side of each sheet and attach your story with colorful thread.

Lesson #96: Cuddly Greeting Cards: For this assignment, draw and color some of the cuddly stuffed animals you have in your home. First, draw them on drawing paper with colored pencils. Then take several sheets of white card stock paper and fold them in half. Place your cuddly companions on the front of each with markers to make nice greeting cards! You may want to practice mixing and blending different colors together before coloring them.

Lesson #97: Drawing a Still Life. For this assignment, set up a vase with flowers and some fruit in a pleasing composition. Do a color study of it on a sheet of white card stock paper.

Lesson #98: Coloring on a Bright Color. For this assignment, use a bright colored poster board, like yellow. Cut it into 5 1/2" x 7" pieces and color some fruit or flowers using horizontal, vertical, or diagonal lines. The yellow poster board will make a nice backdrop for reds and oranges.

Lesson #99: An Imaginary Scene. For this assignment, draw an imaginary scene on a piece of drawing paper. When you have drawn it exactly the way you like, then do it over again with colored markers on a sheet of white card stock paper.

Lesson #100: *Another Day in the Life of.....*

It's journal time! What did you do today that was interesting? What are you doing in art? What did you learn? What should you practice in art to become better? Remember, keeping an art journal requires that you write about your day and also draw about your day. Fill the page below with your thoughts and drawings. Don't forget to write the date. Use colored pencils and your black pen for this assignment.

Beginning Painting

"*Life is a great big canvas, and you should throw all the paint on it you can.*"

Danny Kaye

Beginning Painting

Drawing

Painting

Learning to paint is different than learning to draw. In many ways it is easier and more fun. More than anything, painting takes lots of patience. However, to grow as a painter, you must also improve your drawing skills. Drawing and painting go hand in hand and, like flowers, they both need lots of time to grow. Learning to mix paints and coloring with a brush can be a wonderful form of self-expression. Before we begin, take your colored pencils and color everything on this page using lots of color.

Three Things About Painting:

1. **Learn How To Mix Colors:** Your colors will be much nicer when you mix two or three colors together. Most beginning students simply squeeze paint out of the tube and begin painting. Learn to mix a few colors together before you paint.
2. **Learn How to Take Care of Your Materials:** You must learn to take care of your brushes and paints. Treat them with care and they will last longer. If you clean up and don't make a mess, it will encourage your parents to allow you to paint even more!
3. **Learn What to Paint:** Students need a broad curriculum so that they will have a lot of assignments to do with their paints.

Rules & Regulations

1. **Setting Up Your Painting Area:** You may want to place newspapers on the table before you begin. Put on old clothes and make sure to roll up your sleeves. You will need paints, brushes, two small jars for water, a large jar or container for your brushes, a plastic picnic plate for a palette, a rag to clean your brushes, and something to paint on (such as the painting cards provided with this text).

No!　　　Yes!

To set up your painting area, place the two water jars and a brush container above your picture. If you are right-handed, place your palette on the right side, up and away from the end of the table to prevent accidents. Placing the palette on the same side as your painting hand will make it easier to reach. Remember, if you are right-handed, the palette will go on the right. If you are left-handed, it should go to the left.

2. **Water Jars:** You will need two water containers - one for clean water and one for dirty water. Use the clean water container when you want to blend your colors. For example, to paint a blue sky, you'll need lots of color. Therefore, dipping your brush in the clean water and then into the paint will allow your paint to spread out further. The dirty water jar is for cleaning your brushes. Let's say you just painted a blue sky and now want to paint a white cloud. You would clean your brush in the dirty water container and then wipe your brush dry with a rag before dipping it into the white paint. It is important to have clean brushes to dip into your colors! Only fill the water jars half-way and don't be in a hurry or splash when cleaning your brushes. This will prevent making a mess.

Don't Splash!

3. **Store Your Brushes:** The best way to store your brushes is in a jar or other container with the *hairs up!* Learn to always put your brushes in your brush container and you will not make a mess. Remember, never lay your brushes down, but place them *hairs up* in your brush container.

4. **Paints:** We are using an acrylic paint. This is a permanent paint but will come out of clothing if it is washed right away with warm, soapy water. We are only going to use yellow, red, blue, and white. From these colors you can make every other color under the rainbow. If you use a liquid paint, make sure you shake it before squeezing some out. For most lessons you will only need a dab of paint about the size of a dime. When you are finished painting for the day, you can put your palette of paint in the freezer. The paints can be used again when they thaw out. Finally, before cleaning up, you may want to practice *dip painting* with the leftover paint (see *Paint Card #4*).

5. Mixing Paints: Use styrofoam, picnic plates for your palettes as they are excellent for this purpose and very practical. One of the most important things to teach students in beginning painting is how to mix paints. There are two basic rules for mixing paints:

A. Mix at Least 2 Colors

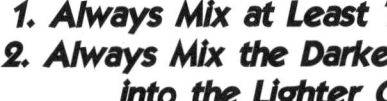

1. Always Mix at Least Two Colors
2. Always Mix the Darker Color
   into the Lighter Color

Mix Darker into Lighter

lighter   darker

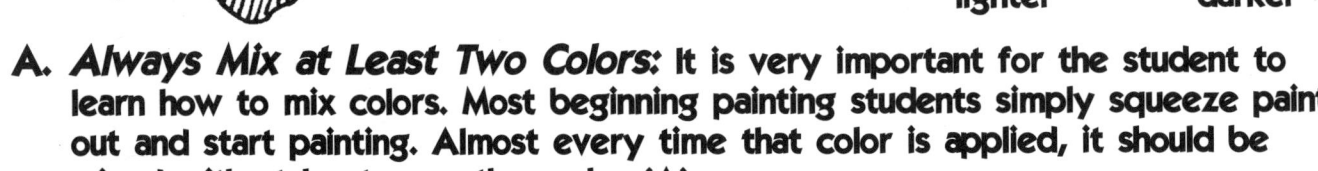

A. **Always Mix at Least Two Colors:** It is very important for the student to learn how to mix colors. Most beginning painting students simply squeeze paint out and start painting. Almost every time that color is applied, it should be mixed with at least one other color (A).

B. **Always Start with the Lighter Color and Mix Only a Little of the Darker Color Into It:** Just about every student paints with colors that are too dark! Learn to mix colors properly by starting with the lighter color and mixing only a little of the darker color into it (B). For instance, if you want to make pink, you would start with white and add just a touch of the darker color (red) into it. If you want to make a light blue, you would put just a speck of blue on the tip of your brush and mix it into the white. Mixing light colors takes practice. When students learn how to paint with light colors, they will make beautiful paintings. Tape a note in your work area to remind you to: *Always start with the lighter color and mix only a little of the darker color into the lighter color.*

7. Paint with Large Brushes: You should have at least three or four brushes: a large brush, a medium brush, and a small brush (we recommend a #1, #5, #7, and #9 round brush). Many students like to paint with their smallest brush. However, a general rule for painting is to paint with a larger brush. Use your larger brushes whenever possible and save your smaller brushes for details.

8. Allow Your Painting Time to Dry: When you are finished painting, your painting will still be wet. Place your picture in a place where it will be out of the way. If you place something on top of your painting before it is dry, it will stick to the surface and pull off some of the colors and also make a mess.

Have you ever painted with watercolors? You can see underneath the colors because watercolors are *transparent.* Acrylic paints are basically an *opaque* paint. Opaque means you cannot see through them. However, if you mix enough water into your acrylic paints, they will become thinner and more transparent. For the most part, everything we paint will look opaque, and the colors can be painted over when dry. For instance, after painting a bright green field, let it dry and then paint some colorful flowers over the green. If you want to paint a cloud in the sky, let the blue dry and then paint your white clouds right over the blue.

Don't Scrub Paint!

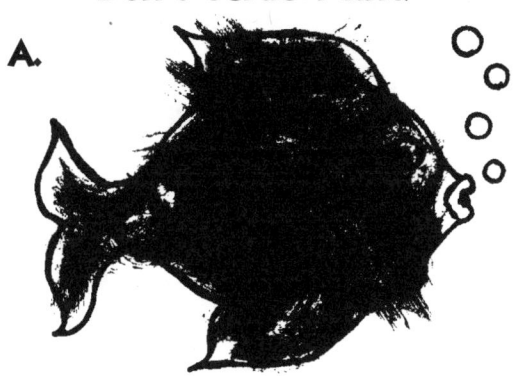

A.

9. Don't Scrub Paint! Scrub painting is when the paint is applied by scrubbing back and forth. Painting like this looks messy and will not create a nice painting. When painting, it is very important to *take your time!* Many students scrub paint because they are in a hurry to finish. Remember, there is no hurry or race to finish first. The painting assignments will turn out much nicer if the student takes his time, stays in the lines, and paints with control.

B.   **C.**

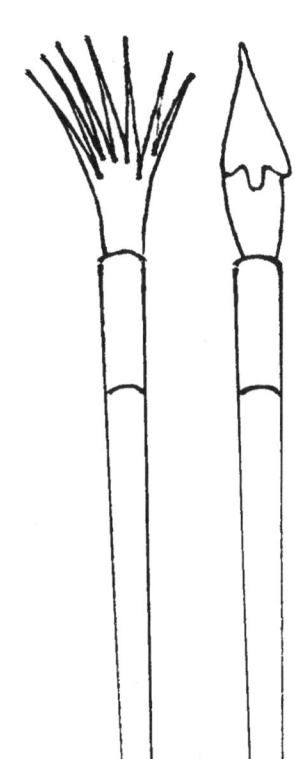

Another reason for scrub painting is not having enough paint on your brush. Your brush should always be *loaded* with paint. This means that the tip of the brush has a lot of paint on it. When you paint with a loaded brush, the colors go on with a better flow and you do not have to scrub them on. Notice the examples of the two brushes (B & C). The shape of the hairs will reveal the amount of paint you have on your brush. Without enough paint on your brush, the hairs will split and look scraggly (B). However, if you put a lot of paint on your brush, the hairs will have a nice point (C). Therefore, mix enough paint in your puddle to really load the hairs of your brush.

10. Clean Up Your Painting Area: Cleaning up is a big part of your painting class. If you do not clean up properly, a lot of your art materials may be ruined, and you may not be allowed to paint again. First, store your painting in a safe area to dry, making sure it is out of the way. Then, clean your brushes with warm, soapy water and dry them with a rag. Store your brushes with the hairs up in a container. Caring for your brushes will help them last a long time. If there is still paint on your palette, you can place it in the freezer and use it again. If there isn't much paint, throw your plastic palette away. Drain and clean your water jars. Fold the newspapers and store them if you can use them another day. Store your painting rags since they can also be used again and again.

DRAW ME

TAKE CARE OF YOUR ART SUPPLIES

ABC

$\begin{array}{r} 2 \\ +2 \\ \hline 4 \end{array}$

Lesson #101: *Primary Colors*

By now you should know that the primary colors are *red, yellow,* and *blue.* Color in the color wheel on the top of the next page with your colored pencils. Color one pie section with yellow vertical lines, another pie section with red horizontal lines and the last pie section with blue diagonal lines. This is a basic *color wheel.* In future lessons we are going to learn more about the color wheel.

Even though there are only three primary colors, you can make each color much lighter or darker. Do you know what color to add to red to make it lighter? If you add just white, your red will turn pink. You can make red lighter by adding a little yellow and a little white. If you add too much yellow, it will turn orange. (If you don't have white, then color gently with your red to make it light). Do you know how to make red darker? One way is by adding a little touch of blue (not too much or it will turn purple). Draw two more hearts by the heart below (A). Make one a light red, one a medium red, and one a dark red. Then, draw two more birds by the one below (B) and color one a light blue, one a medium blue and one a dark blue. You can make a blue darker by adding dark blue or a touch of red to it. Color the beaks and feet of each bird orange. Finally, draw two more half moons next to the one below (C) and color them with three different yellows: a light yellow with white, a medium yellow, and a dark yellow. Do you know what color to add to yellow to make it darker? Try adding a little violet. Then color the hearts, birds and moons on the next page with your colored pencils.

A. 3 Red Hearts

Color the three balloons on the next page with the primary colors using your colored pencils. Make your yellow and blue lighter by adding white or by coloring gently with your yellow and blue pencils.

Finally, draw a scene from your bedroom in the large figure box and color it with your pencils, using only the primary colors.

B. 3 Blue Birds

Take out *Paint Card #1.* Paint the color wheel on the top of the card with the primary colors. Can you make a lighter yellow, red, and blue? Color the hearts, birds, and moons. Paint one a light color, one a medium color, and one a dark color. Do you remember how to make a yellow darker? A red lighter? A blue darker? Next, paint the three balloons with the primary colors. See if you can paint them with a light yellow, a light red and a light blue. Finally, draw a scene from your bedroom in the figure box on the bottom of the paint card. Paint it by using only the primary colors, making your primary colors, making your colors lighter or darker.

C. 3 Yellow Moons

Paint Card #1: *Primary Colors*

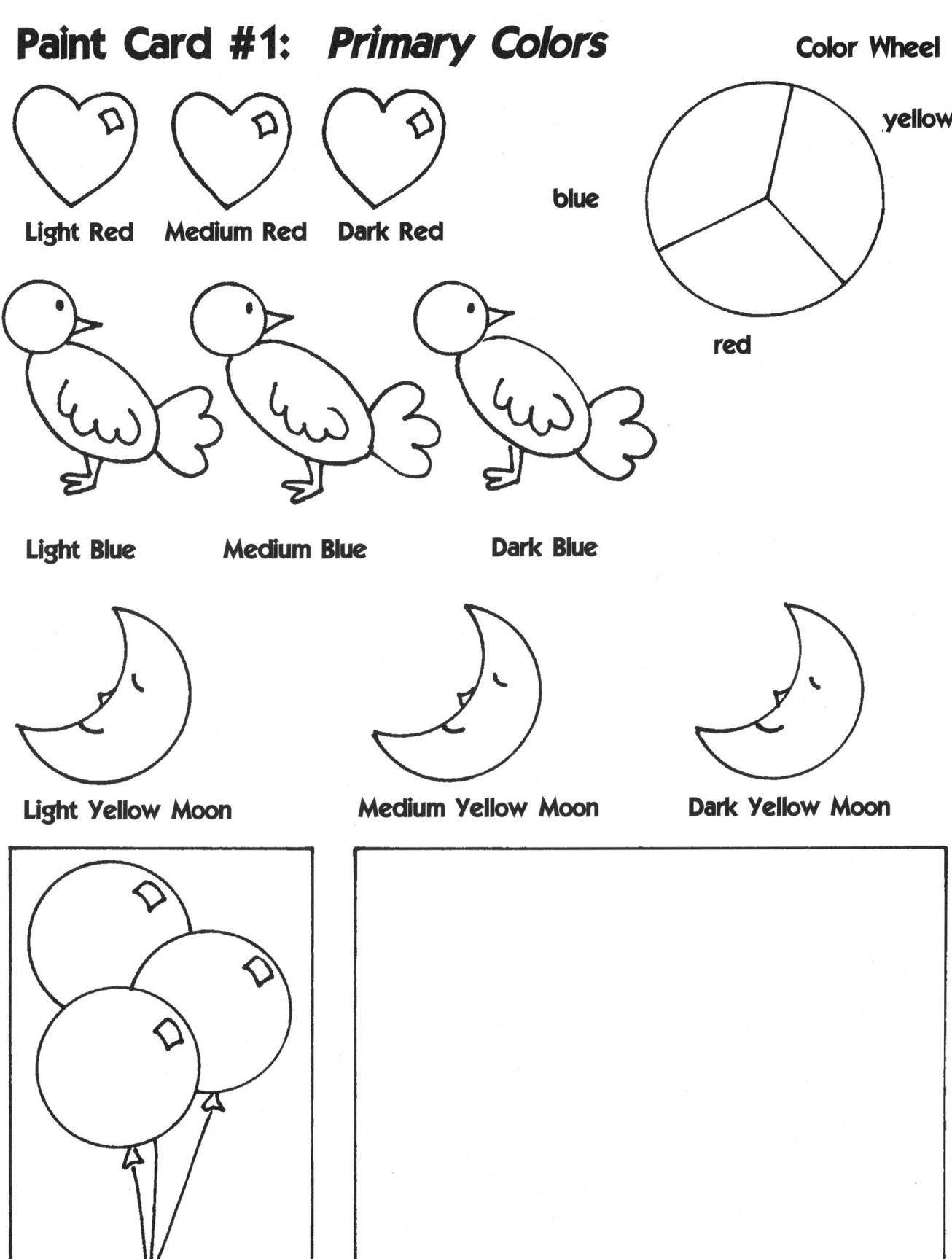

Color Wheel

yellow

blue

red

Light Red   Medium Red   Dark Red

Light Blue   Medium Blue   Dark Blue

Light Yellow Moon   Medium Yellow Moon   Dark Yellow Moon

Three Balloons   My Bedroom in Primary Colors

Lesson #102: *Secondary Colors*

Look at the color wheel on the top of the next page. There are six pie sections instead of three, with a *secondary* color between each of the primary colors to either side. *Secondary colors* are the colors made by mixing any two of the primary colors together. For instance, yellow and red make orange; red and blue make violet; and blue and yellow make green. Color in the color wheel with your colored pencils, using your red, blue, yellow, orange, violet and green pencils.

Color each of the balloons on the top of the page with a secondary color. This time, however, make the secondary colors. Using your colored pencils, blend yellow with red to make orange; red with blue to make violet; and blue and yellow to make green. In the balloons below, practice mixing orange, violet, and green with your colored pencils by mixing the colors together before coloring them on the following page.

Yellow & Red = ?
Red & Blue   = ?
Blue & Yellow = ?

Orange Balloon   Violet Balloon   Green Balloon

Next, color the fruit: three green limes, three orange oranges, and three violet plums. See if you can make a light, medium, and dark tone for each color. If you add just a little green to yellow you will make a bright green. White will make your violet a lighter and more pleasant color. Yellow or white will make a brighter orange. You can make green and violet darker by adding blue to them. Use orange with only a *tiny bit* of blue to make orange darker, or try adding a little red.

Color the three pictures of the green frog, the orange pumpkin, and the purple fish. See if you can color each with three different tones of the same color: three different greens for the frog, three different oranges for the pumpkin, and three different violets for the fish.

Place *Paint Card #2* in front of you and paint the entire color wheel. Make your orange, violet, and green by mixing two of the primary colors together. For a lighter green, add a touch of green to yellow. For a lighter violet, add a touch of violet to white. Remember, always add a touch of the darker color into the lighter color.

Next, paint each of the three balloons with a secondary color. Try to mix a light orange, violet, and green. Now paint the three limes, oranges, and plums. Paint the first lime a light green by adding yellow, the second lime a middle green, and the third lime a dark green by adding blue. Can you make your oranges and plums lighter and darker also?

Finally, paint the frog, pumpkin, and fish. See if you can paint a light green on the top of the frog, a medium green in the middle, and a dark green on the bottom.

148

Paint Card #2: *Secondary Colors*

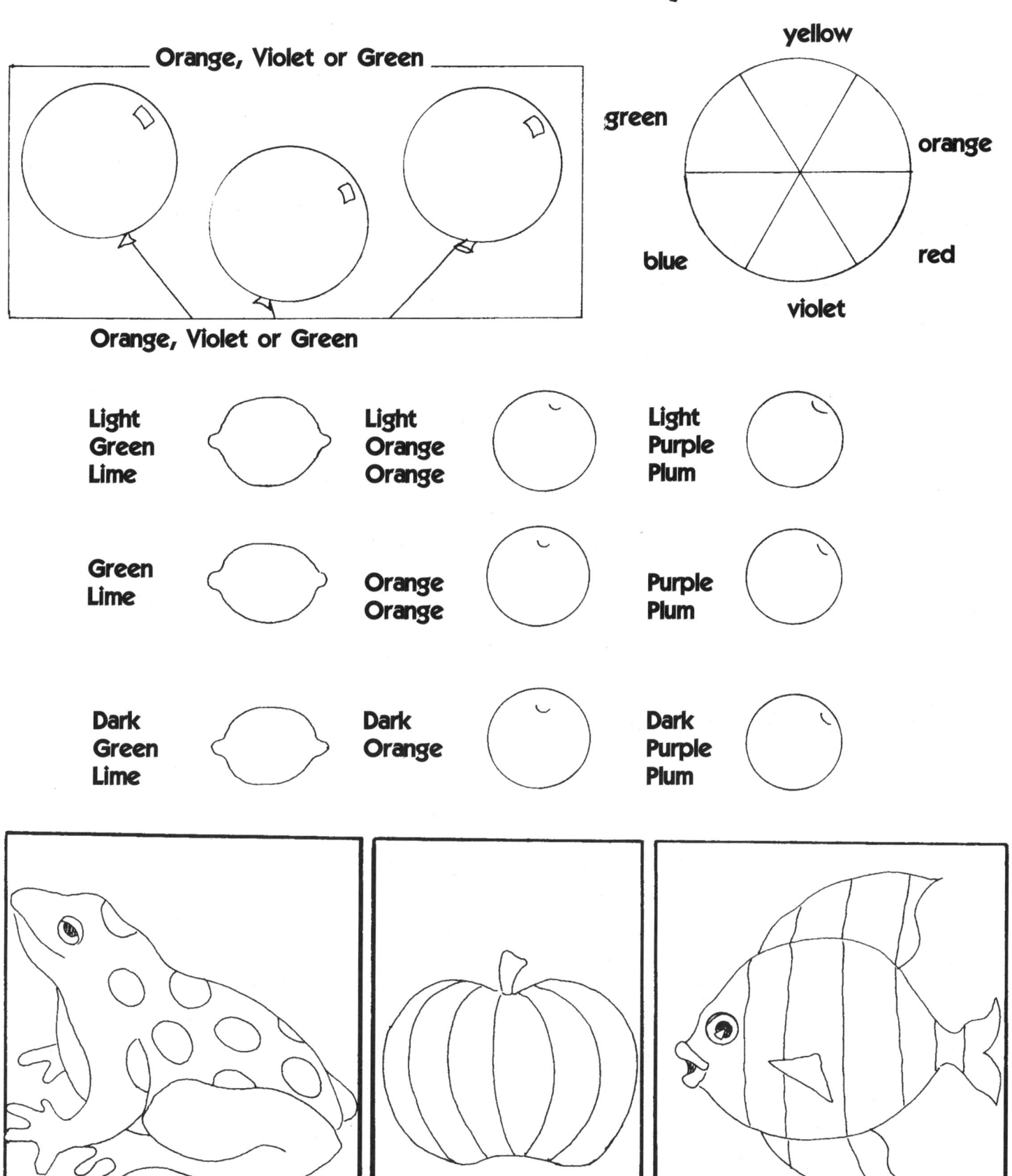

Orange, Violet or Green

yellow

green

orange

blue

red

violet

Orange, Violet or Green

Light Green Lime		**Light Orange Orange**		**Light Purple Plum**	
Green Lime		**Orange Orange**		**Purple Plum**	
Dark Green Lime		**Dark Orange**		**Dark Purple Plum**	

Green Frog

Orange Pumpkin

Purple Fish

149

Lesson #103: *Making a Color Chart*

Making a color chart can be enjoyable and very educational. A *color chart* is a chart of all the colors you have mixed together to make other enjoyable colors. If you have a good set of primary colors and white, you can make hundreds of different colors! Do you know how to make a pink? How about brown? Or a flesh tone? Let's see what colors you can make. After you have painted each circle with a new color, take your black pen and write the colors used to make that color. Start by writing the color you used most; then the next color you used next to the most; then the color you used least. Suppose you made a green with a lot of yellow, some blue, and a touch of white. You would print: Y + B + W; from the most to the least. A color chart is a reference chart to find the colors you want to use when doing a painting. You may want to do a picture in colored pencils and then do a painting of it on poster board. Before you begin your painting, you can look at the colors on your color chart and pick five or six beautiful colors to put in your painting! Place *Paint Card #3* in front of you and see how many colors you can create. Print under each color the colors you used to make each new color, starting with the color you used most to the color you used least.

Pink:	White plus a little red. (W+R)
Brown:	Yellow, red, and a touch of blue. (Y+R+B)
Black:	Blue, red, and a little yellow. (B+R+Y)
Flesh Tone:	White, a little red, and a touch of yellow. (W+R+Y)
Violet:	Red, blue, and some white. (R+B+W)

Lesson #104:
When you are finished with your color chart, take a large sheet of white poster board (22" x 28") and draw as many 1" squares on it as you can with your black pen. Make sure to use a ruler and keep all the squares in even rows. Then see how many colors you can mix! How many greens can you make? Can you make a light blue? A light violet? A light pink? How many browns can you mix? Be a scientist and see how many different colors you can create. Remember, print the colors you used underneath each new color.

Paint Card #3: *Color Chart*

Lesson #105: *Dip Painting & Flowers*

Dip painting is simply mixing the paints on your picture instead of on your palette. I recommend dip painting when you are finished painting for the day (with any painting assignment) because it is a good way to use up the extra paint on your palette. To dip paint, dip your brush in one color, then in another, then in another, and apply the paint to your picture with short brush strokes. You will see all three colors come off your brush at once, creating original, delightful colors! However, *do not paint back and forth with your brush.* The beauty of dip painting is the way the colors come off your brush on the first stroke. The only way the colors will stay nice is if you do not go over them again with your brush. Practice gently dipping your brush into three or four of your different paint puddles. You may want to dip in white first, then yellow, then red, or use any other color-ful combination. Remember, the darker the color, the less you dip into it.

Place *Paint Card #4* in front of you. Practice dip painting by filling the little squares above the flowers with different variations of color. Then select the colors you like best for your flowers. Make sure to paint each flower with at least a three layer coat of paint on your brush. Dip, one. Dip, two. Dip, three. You may want to paint the center of your flowers with orange, yellow, and white; and the stems and grass with blue, yellow, and white. Leave your sky white so all the colors will look nice and bright.

Dip

Dip

Dip

Dip

Dip

Dip

Dip

Dip

Paint Card #4: *Dip Painting*

Lesson #106: *Painting with Control*

Painting with *control* simply means commanding your brush to do what you want it to do. Taking your time is the first step in painting with control. Look at your first three paint card lessons:

1. *Did you stay in the lines?*
2. *Did you take your time painting?*
3. *Does your artwork look nice?*

Turn Your Card

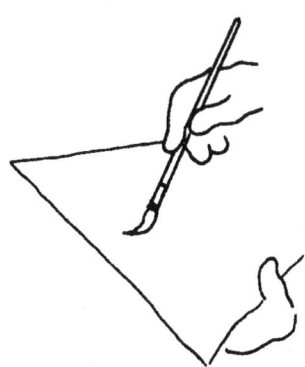

There is no reason why your artwork should not be pleasing to look at if you simply *take your time.* For today's assignment you are going to practice painting with control by staying in the lines. Learn to turn your card at different angles to give your hand and brush a better angle. This will greatly assist you in placing the paint in the area you desire. Use your medium size brush for this assignment.

Remember, to paint with control.
1. *Take your time!*
2. *Use a good brush.*
3. *Turn your card around.*

Place *Paint Card #5* in front of you and color in the shapes on the card. Make sure to use control and keep the paint within the lines. Look at your color chart and pick some nice colors. You may want to try a nice pink or light violet for the flowers. You may also want to experiment with dip painting. Be creative with your colors. Complete your paint card in a controlled and neat manner.

Lesson #107: On drawing paper, draw and color a picture of anything you like with colored pencils. Then, on a sheet of 11" x 14" white poster board, draw your picture again and paint it using your favorite colors from the color chart you made on *Paint Card #3.*

Paint Card #5: Painting with Control

Paint with Control!   Paint with Control!   Paint with Control!

Lesson #108: *Light Side & Shaded Side*

Tones are different shades of the same color; for instance, a light green and a dark green. We practiced tones on *Paint Card #1* by adding colors to make different reds, blues, and yellows. Today we are going to paint objects like balloons and pots that are in sunshine. Each object will have a light side and a shaded side. They will also have a middle tone (that is the color between the light side and the shaded side.) Look at the apple in the top row of *Paint Card #6*. Notice where the sun is and how it is shining on part of the apple. Lines have been drawn across the apple to show that the apple has a light side, a middle tone, and a shaded side. Paint the first row of objects: the pot, the apple, and the balloon with three different tones of red. Paint the second row: the pot, the banana, and the balloon with different tones of yellow. Finally, paint the last row: the pot, the box, and the balloon with different tones of blue. Here are some color combinations to help you mix the different tones:

1. *Add yellow and white to red to make it brighter:* As mentioned, if you add white to red, it will make pink. If you add too much yellow, you will make orange. Therefore, add yellow and white to lighten the red on the pot, apple, and balloon that are in sunshine.
2. *Add a little blue to red for the shaded side:* A little speck of blue will darken the red for a nice, shaded side. Don't add too much though, because it will turn a dark purple.
3. *Add a little violet to yellow for the shaded side:* If you add just a tiny bit of violet to yellow, it will make a dull yellow for the shaded side. Remember, all you have to add is a touch. If you add too much, it will look violet. If this happens, add some more yellow to it. Violet is red, plus blue, plus white.
4. *Add a little red to blue to make it darker:* Don't add too much red or it will also turn violet.

New Colors For Your Color Chart:

1. How do you make red lighter?
   (Add a little yellow and white.)
2. How do you make green lighter?
   (Try adding yellow or white.)
3. How do you make violet lighter?
   (Add some white.)

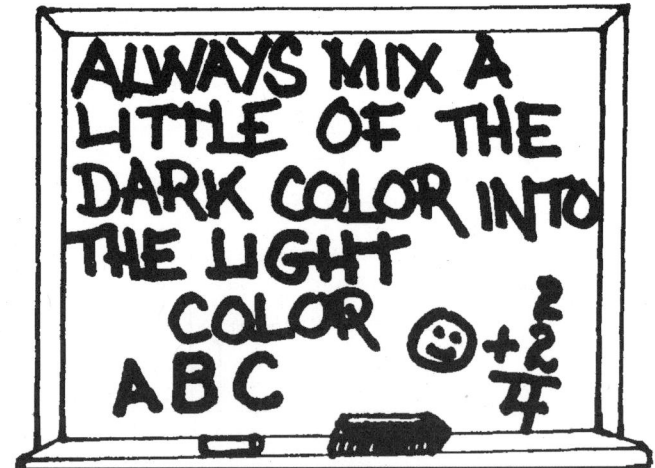

Color in the objects on the next page with your colored pencils, showing three different tones of the same color. Color the three circles on the side with three different tones of each color before beginning. Then place *Paint Card #6* in front of you and see if you can mix a light red, yellow, and blue; a medium red, yellow, and blue; and a dark red, yellow, and blue.

Paint Card #6: *Light Side & Shaded Side*

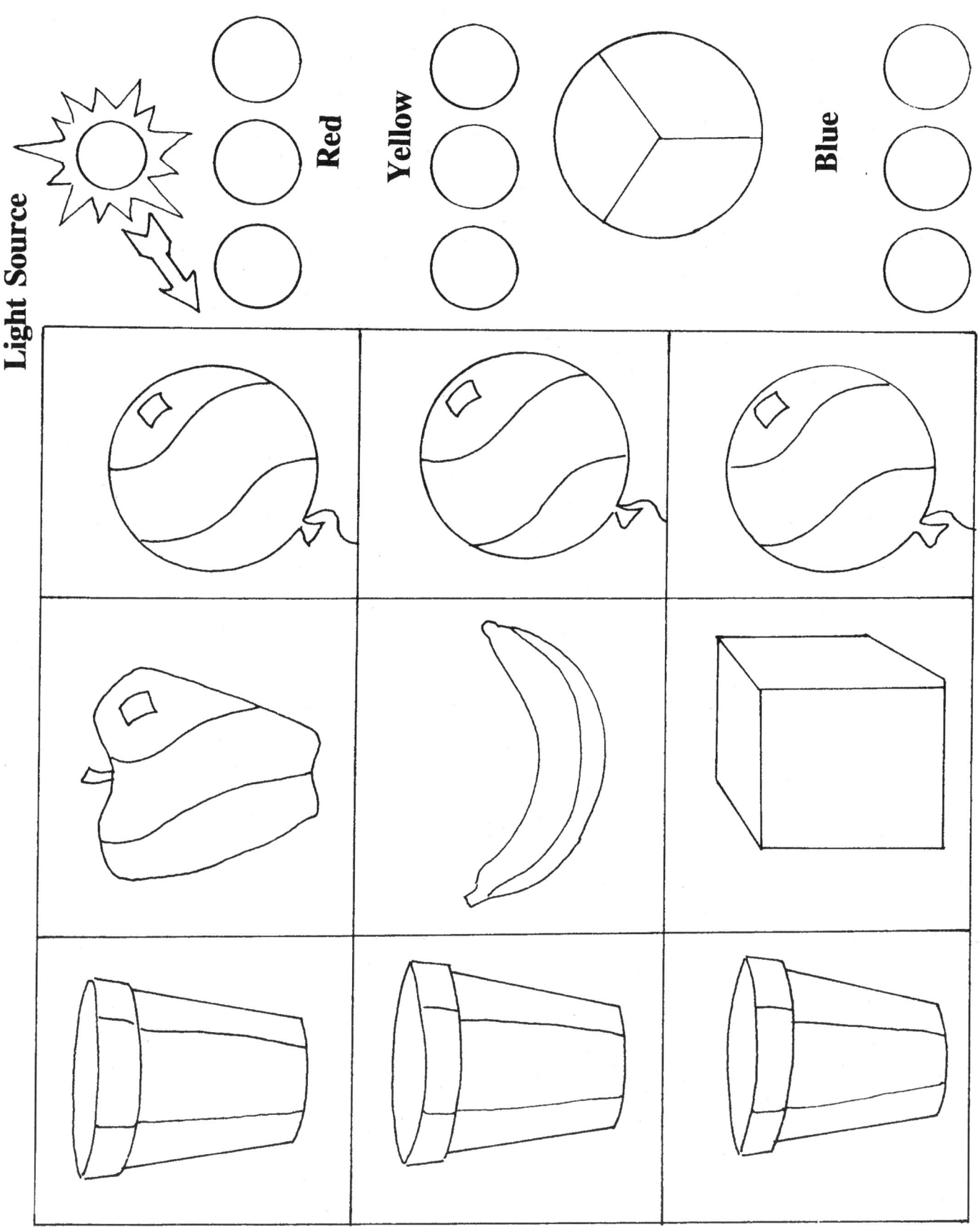

Light Source

Red

Yellow

Blue

"In those vernal seasons of the year, when the air is calm and pleasant, it were an injury and sullenness against nature not to go out."   John Milton

Lesson #109:   *Autumn Colors*

Did you ever notice all the different colors of leaves in autumn? Select some of the leaves from the next page and draw them with your black pen floating in the air around the little girl below. Color them with colored pencils creating *autumn colors*. Colors in autumn are bright and colorful. Some are also a rust color. Rust is a dull orange which you can make by adding a little blue and/or a little brown to orange. You can color some leaves yellow and orange, and others red with yellow and brown. Practice coloring differ-ent autumn leaves on the top of the next page before completing your picture below. Then select your two favorite autumn colors and color the large leaves on the next page. Can you draw two more leaves on the page and color them in also?

Place *Paint Card #7* in front of you. See if you can make some rust colors by adding a dull orange to yellow, red, and green. A dull orange is yellow plus red and a speck of blue. Color all of the small leaves on the top of the paint card with autumn colors, mixing some of your dull orange with red to make an autumn color, and mixing the dull orange with red to make another. Remember, mix at least two or three colors together to make a new color. Then draw two more leaves on the card and paint them with your favorite autumn colors!

Lesson #110: Fold a sheet of 11" x 14" white poster board to 5 1/2" x 7" and draw a large leaf on it. Paint it with autumn colors. Tape a small leaf on the inside of your card and mail it to a friend!

Paint Card #7: Autumn Colors

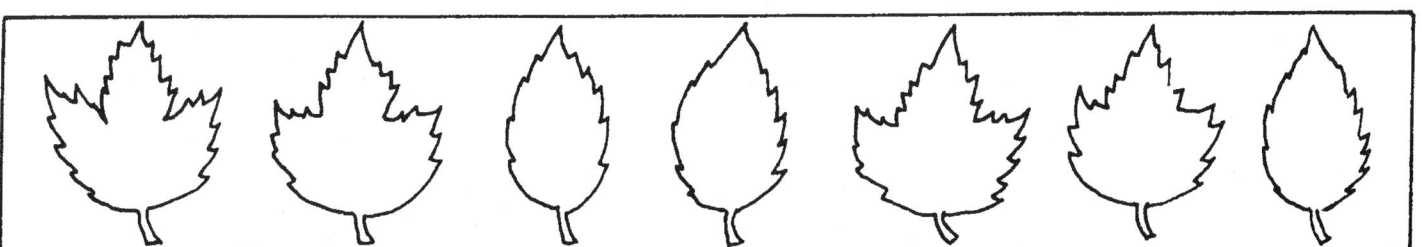

Lesson #111: *How Now Brown Cow?*

Brown is an easy color to mix. You should learn how to mix many different browns because there is so much brown around you. When you simply squeeze brown out of a tube and paint, all your colors seem to be the same. Let's see how many browns you can make with your colored pencils. To make some nice browns, try yellow, red, and a touch of blue. Any two secondary colors combined together also make a nice brown. You may want to try violet and orange; green and violet; and orange and green. Mix your light brown colored pencil in one or two of them also. Adding more yellow will make other variations of brown. See how many browns you can make. Practice mixing browns in the circles on the top of the next page and then color the four animals and bird. Can you draw another row of animals like those below (A)? Draw them with your black pen and color them with some of your new, colorful browns in the figure box below (B).

A.

B.

Place *Paint Card #8* in front of you. How many browns can you mix with your paints? First, check your color chart to see if you have already mixed some nice browns. Again, one way to make brown is with yellow, red, and a speck of blue. Add more yellow to see what happens. Add more orange to make brighter browns. After you have finished coloring all the circles with a variety of different browns, paint the pets with an assortment of colorful browns using your medium brush. Last of all, paint the whiskers and the straw in the cow's mouth using a small brush.

Lesson #112: Draw all the animals on the next page on a piece of drawing paper. Select your favorite one and draw it again *large* on white card stock paper. See how many tones of brown you can paint it. You may want to paint a spotted cow or a tabby cat.

Paint Card #8: *How Now Brown Cow*

Lesson #113: *Tropical Fish*

Let's color some tropical fish using *tropical colors*. Do you know what tropical colors are? They are light and bright. To make tropical colors, use lots of white. See how many light, tropical colors you can make by coloring the fish below with your colored pencils (A). Remember, blend lots of white in your colors to make them light, or simply place less pressure on your pencils to make lighter colors.

A.

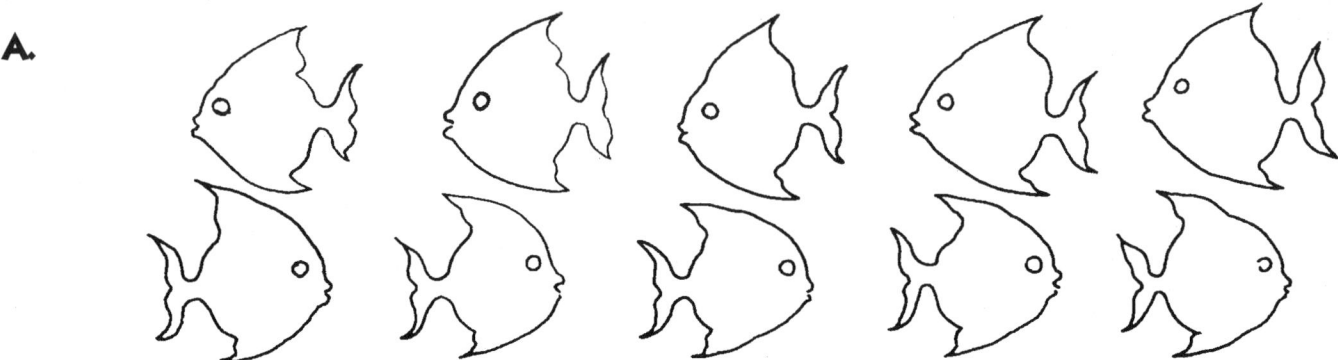

Color the two tropical fish on the next page with light colors. Notice there are stripes and lines separating different areas of the fish. Color in all the areas with different light colors using your colored pencils.

Lighter Color   **Darker Color**

Place *Paint Card #9* in front of you. Paint the fish with light pinks, oranges, yellows and violets. Paint the water a very light blue/green, mixing blue with yellow and a lot of white. The more white you add to a color, the lighter it becomes. Remember, always start with the lighter color and add just a little of the darker color into it.

Lesson #114: Find some pictures of tropical fish. On a large 22" x 28" white poster board, draw them with your colored pencils. Draw some of them large and some small. When finished, paint your fish with bright, tropical colors!

Paint Card #9: *Tropical Fish*

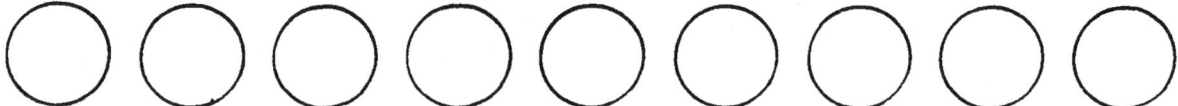

Lesson #115: *Signing Your Name*

Do you know how to sign your name to a painting? Many students sign their name with big, bold letters (A). Your name should be signed with small letters and a light color in the bottom right corner (B). An artist has two signatures: a regular signature (C), and one for signing his artwork. The latter is called his *artistic signature* (D). Notice the difference between my two signatures below (C & D). My artistic signature is more pleasing to look at and more simple. Observe signatures of some of the great artists throughout history. Look at the way Albrecht Durer signed his name by putting one initial inside another (E). Notice Vincent van Gogh's signature (F) and Claude Monet's (G). Practice your artistic signature in figure box H, signing your name in at least five different ways with your black pen. You can use your initials; your first initial and last name; or your first name and last initial (I). You can write or print your name. You can use fancy or simple letters. Remember, it should be pleasing to the eye. Keep it small and always use nice, light colors.

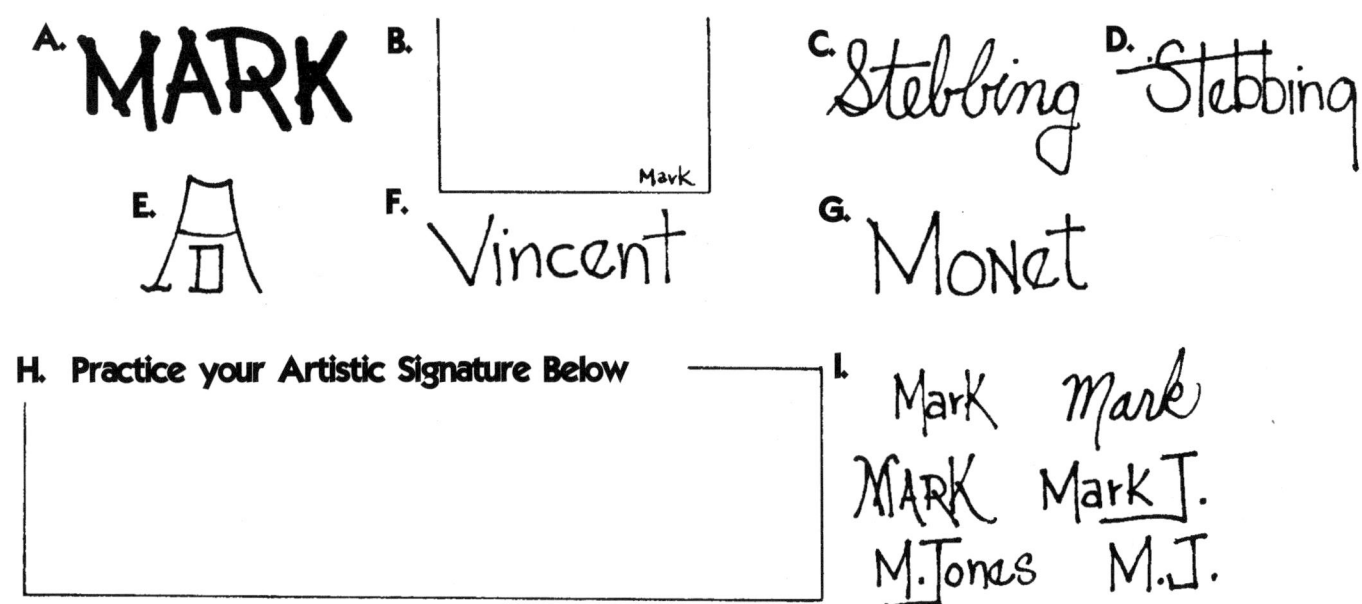

How many blues can you make? See if you can make enough different tones of blue to fill the circles above the porpoise. You can add white to make blue lighter or simply gently apply the color. Or a little red will make a darker blue. You can even make a blue/violet or a blue/green. Also, try adding a touch of orange to blue. See how many blues you can create. Color the porpoise, sky, and water with as many different blues as you can make with your colored pencils.

Place *Paint Cart #10* in front of you. Mix as many blues as you can on the top of the paint card. Paint the bottom of the porpoise a dark blue, and his fin and back a lighter blue. Keep your sky very light with a lot of white paint and a tiny speck of blue, and make your water a light blue/green.

Lesson #116: Take your smallest brush and mix a light blue color. Sign your painting with your artistic signature in the bottom right corner. Then, go back to all your previous painting assignments, and sign each with a nice soft color and your best artistic signature.

Paint Card #10: *Painting a Porpoise*

Lesson #117: *Green, Green, Green.....*

Look around you. Green is the most popular color in nature. How many different greens can you mix with your colored pencils? Color all the trees on the top of the next page with different tones of green. Try some of these combinations: yellow and blue; yellow and dark blue; yellow, blue, and green; yellow, blue, and dark green; green and yellow; dark green and yellow; green and blue; yellow, blue, and white; even green and a little bit of red!

In the last assignment we colored and painted a blue porpoise in a blue sea. Now let's color a green grasshopper. First, draw some grasshoppers jumping over the grass below (A) with your black pen. Let's make this a fun picture and give our grasshoppers cartoon looking faces and bodies. Color your picture with colored pencils when finished.

A.

Color the large grasshopper on the next page using a lot of different greens, like the greens used to color the trees on the top of the page. On the bottom of the page, color the four trees in sunlight. Notice where the sunshine is coming from. Make the top left of each tree a bright green, using a lot of yellow and a little green. Color the grass with this same bright yellow/green. Color the middle part of each tree a rich green with one of your green pencils. Then, color the shaded part of each tree and the cast shadow on the ground with your green and blue pencils to make a dark blue/green. See if you can color the background trees with another green. That's a lot of greens!

Let's see how many greens you can mix with paint! Place *Paint Card #11* in front of you. First, mix a variety greens and paint the trees on the top of the card. Then, paint the grasshopper with some nice, colorful greens. Finally, paint the picture on the bottom of the card. Use different greens for the sunny areas, shaded areas, and all the other areas in your picture. Remember, make a very light green by adding just a touch of green to yellow.

Paint Card #11: *Green, Green, Green....*

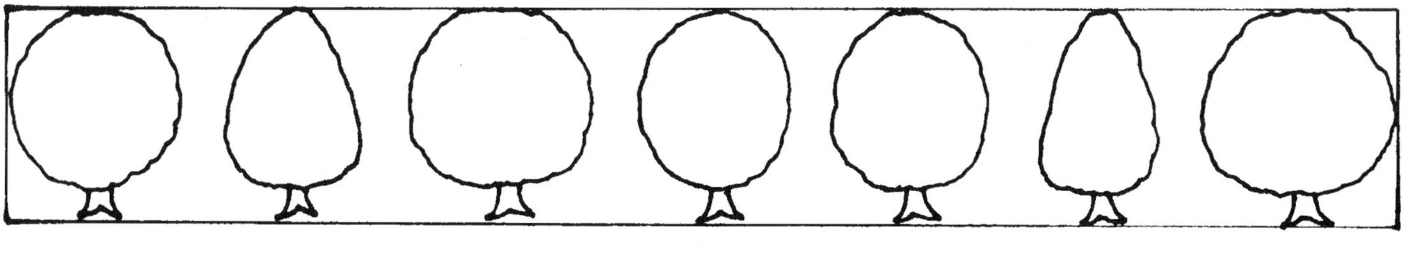

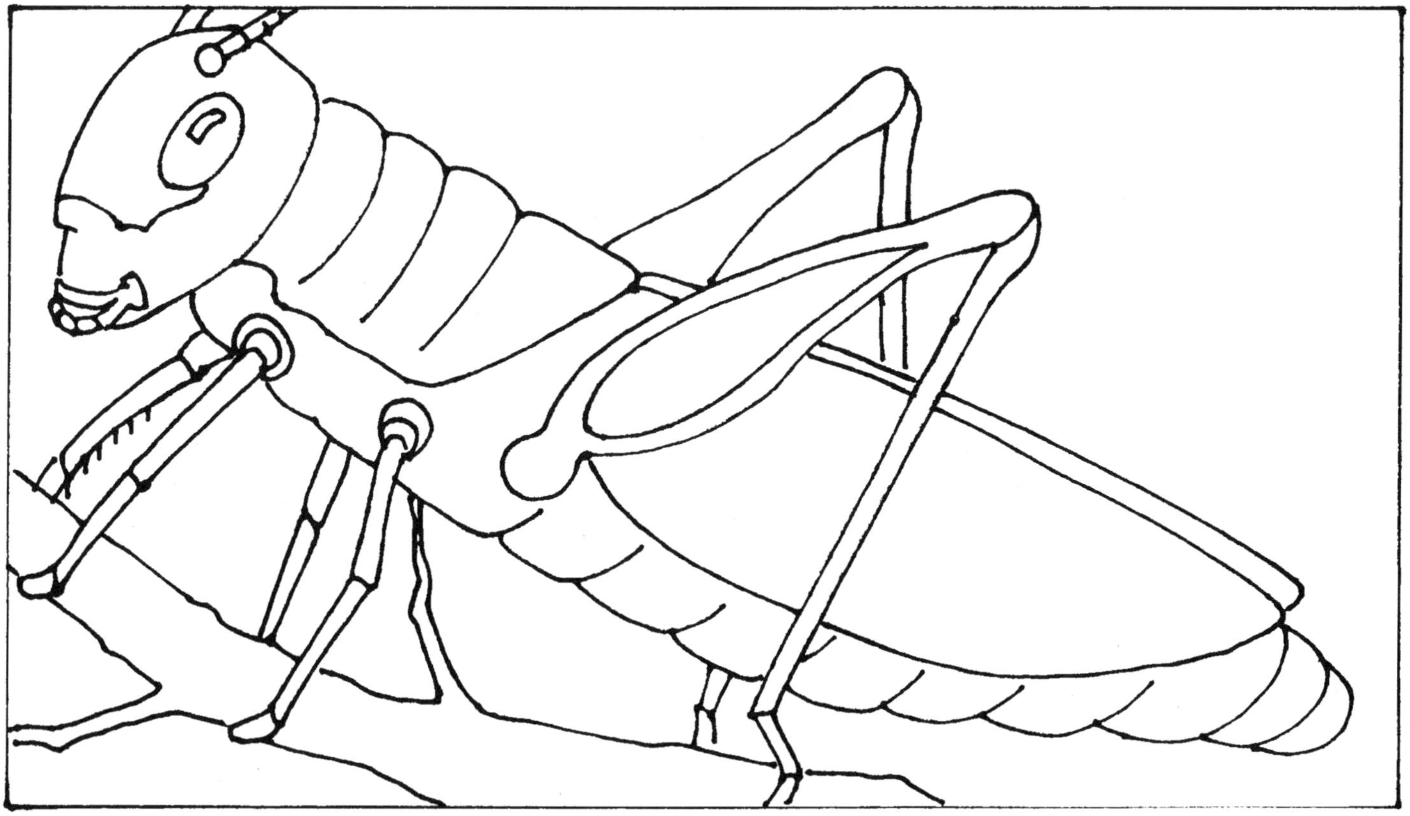

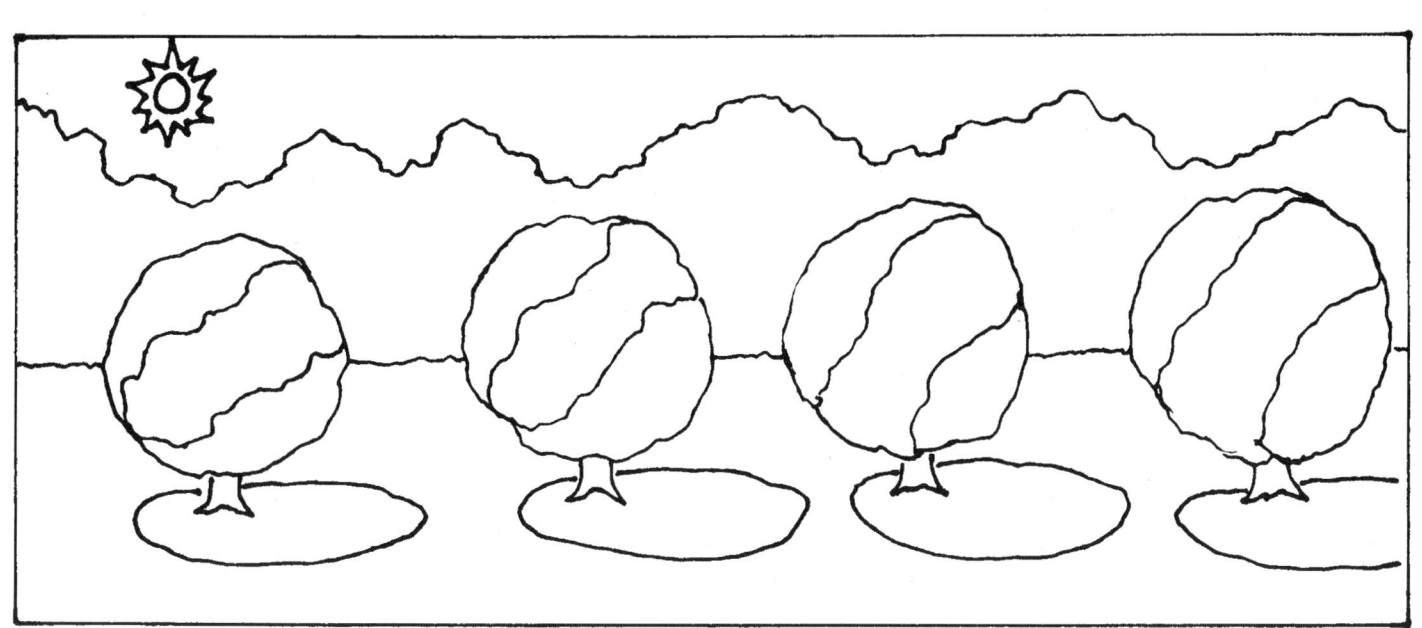

Lesson #118: Red Bucket By-the-Sea

A. **B.**

Do your know how to draw a bucket? It is drawn with two ellipses, one right under the other (A). Then all you need to do is connect the sides with two straight lines (B), and draw straight lines inside the bucket for shading.

Did you ever hear the saying, *"It's raining buckets?"* See if you can draw buckets raining down on the clown in the picture below (C). Draw your buckets in different positions like the ones shown. This will make them look like they are falling. Turning your picture around may help you see the buckets at different angles. Can you draw another clown with an umbrella next to the one below? Use your black pen and color your picture with your colored pencils when finished.

C. Raining Buckets

Next, color the picture on the next page with your colored pencils. Try a blue/green for your water, a light blue for your sky and a colorful red for your bucket. Notice where the sun is shining from. Can you color the part of your bucket in sunshine a different color than the rest of the bucket? Also, color the inside of your bucket with a darker red, adding a little blue to it. Use line for coloring. To make a light blue for the sky and a light red for your bucket, you may want to hold your forefinger out with your pencil underneath it and lightly color with the broad side of the point.

Place *Paint Card #12* in front of you. Before beginning, mix some different blues and put them in the circles on the bottom of the paint card. Try mixing blue with white, blue with green, blue with green and white, blue with violet, and blue with violet and white. Also, mix some reds for the bucket. Check your color chart to find a nice sandy color for your beach. A light flesh tone may be a good sand color for this.

Paint Card #12: *Red Bucket By-the-Sea*

Lesson #119: Colors with Harmony

Do you know how to create *harmony* with your colors? Harmony is like having all your colors singing together in perfect accord. One way of creating harmony is by using *analogous* colors. Analogous colors are colors next to each other on the color wheel.

On *Paint Card #1* we did a color wheel with the three primary colors: yellow, red and blue (A). On *Paint Card #2* we did a color wheel with the three primary colors and the three secondary colors: yellow, orange, red, violet, blue, and green (B). A secondary color goes between the two primary colors that make it. For example, orange goes in between yellow and red; violet goes in between red and blue; and green goes in between blue and yellow. Color the two small color wheels below (A & B), one with your primary colors and the other with your primary and secondary colors.

Next, let's color a color wheel with twelve pie shapes (C), putting a *tertiary color* between each primary and secondary color. A tertiary color is a color that goes between a primary and secondary color on the color wheel. The tertiary color between red and orange is red/orange; the tertiary color between yellow and orange is yellow/orange; the color between red and violet is red/violet, and so forth.

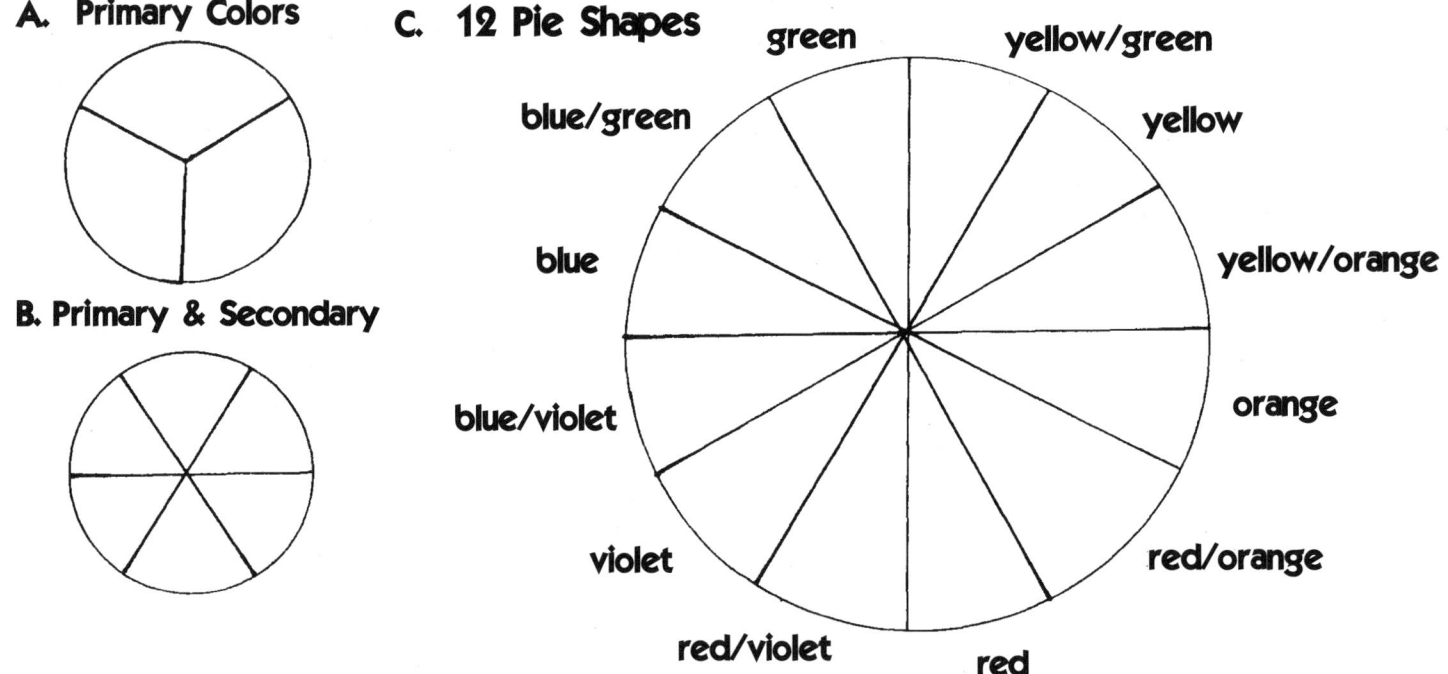

Color the color wheel above with your colored pencils. First, color the three primary colors: yellow, red and blue. Then color the three secondary colors between each primary color, skipping one pie section. Finally, color the tertiary colors between each secondary color. Now, color the color wheel on the next page. Also, color one of each of the colors on the palette below it. Finally, color the bird with any three colors next to each other on the color wheel (analogous colors) to give him harmony.

Place *Paint Card #13* in front of you and paint everything the way you did with colored pencils. Paint one of each color from the color wheel on the palette. (You may want to add a little white to some of the colors to lighten them.) Select any three colors next to each other on the color wheel to paint your bird, giving him harmony. Color his feet and beak a yellow/orange.

Paint Card #13: *Colors with Harmony*

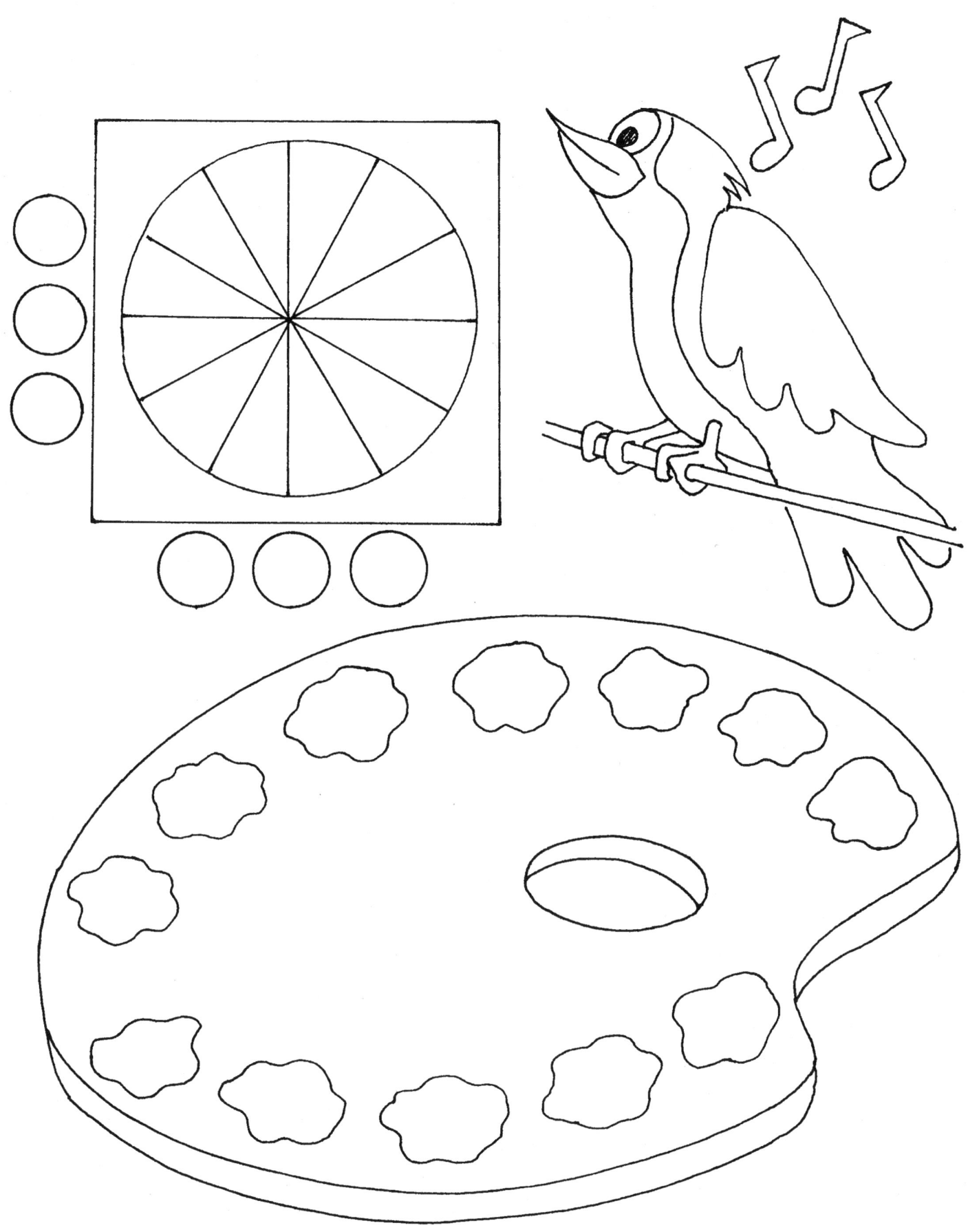

Lesson #120: *Painting a Blue Sky*

What flies in the sky? Can you draw a butterfly? A kite? A cloud? Some birds? Finish the picture below by drawing anything you like with your black pen along with some more trees on the earth. Color your picture when finished.

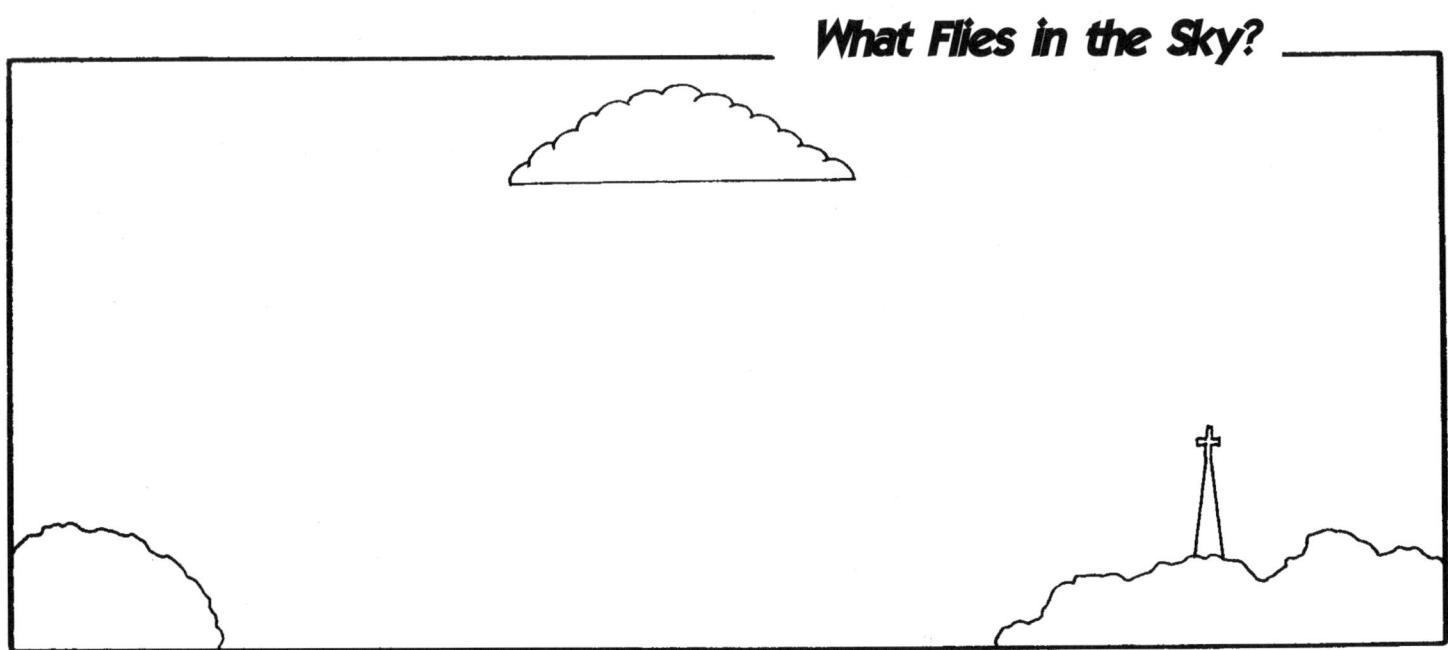

What Flies in the Sky?

Take your colored pencils and color the sky picture on the next page. Skies are always lightest near the horizon, and become bluer as they ascend, or go up. Color your skies softly and blend the blues with white. Or, gently color with the broad side of your blue pencil. (you can even erase your blue sky to make it lighter!) Color the two skies on the bottom of the page with four different blues. Place the lightest one near the horizon and make them a little darker as they ascend. Practice blending these colors in the circles on the middle of the page. Can you blend a nice brown to color the wooden piling and its reflection in the water?

Place *Paint Card #14* in front of you. One of the most difficult things to teach students is how to paint with *light* colors. Almost every student colors skies too dark. If you want to know if your sky is too dark, take your picture outside and hold it up to the sky and compare your blue to the sky. Remember the rule to mix a very light color: *always start with your lighter color and mix a tiny speck of the darker color into it.*

Use a large brush and paint your sky with long, horizontal strokes with a lot of white and a speck of blue. Paint it *flat* by going back and forth with your brush. Paint your sky light blue in A and allow it to dry. Next, draw the cloud in B on the dry blue surface in A. Paint your cloud with white and a little violet. In B, paint the sky but leave the area white where the cloud is. While the sky is still wet, paint the cloud white and blend the edges into the sky to soften it. In C, paint the sky with four different blues. Finally, paint the land and house. In D, paint the piling a nice brown after you have painted the sky and water. When the painting has dried, draw long lines on it with a pencil or your fine black marker pen to show the texture of the wood (see Lesson #27).

Paint Card #14: *Painting a Blue Sky*

Lesson #121: *Colors in the Sky*

Do you like to fly kites? They are very colorful and go far up in the sky. See if you can fill the border of the picture below with colorful kites. Use your black pen and give each one a different design. Select the two you like best and draw them way up in the sky, connecting them to the hands of the children with long strings. When you are finished, color your picture and frame with your colored pencils.

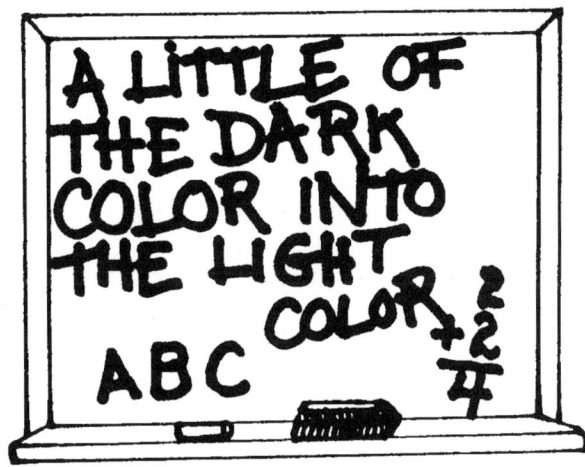

Color the kites on the next page with colors that have harmony. Look at the color wheel you painted on *Paint Card #13* and select any three colors next to each other to use to color your kites with harmony. Then, place *Paint Card #15* in front of you. First, paint your sky a very light blue using a lot of white and a tiny speck of blue. When your sky is dry, paint the cloud and seagulls white. Again, select any three colors next to each other on the color wheel and paint your kites with *harmonious* colors. Practice mixing your colors in the little kites on the top of the paint card before beginning. Try adding white to some of these colors to create lighter colors. Paint the tails of your kites and details with

174 your fine brush.

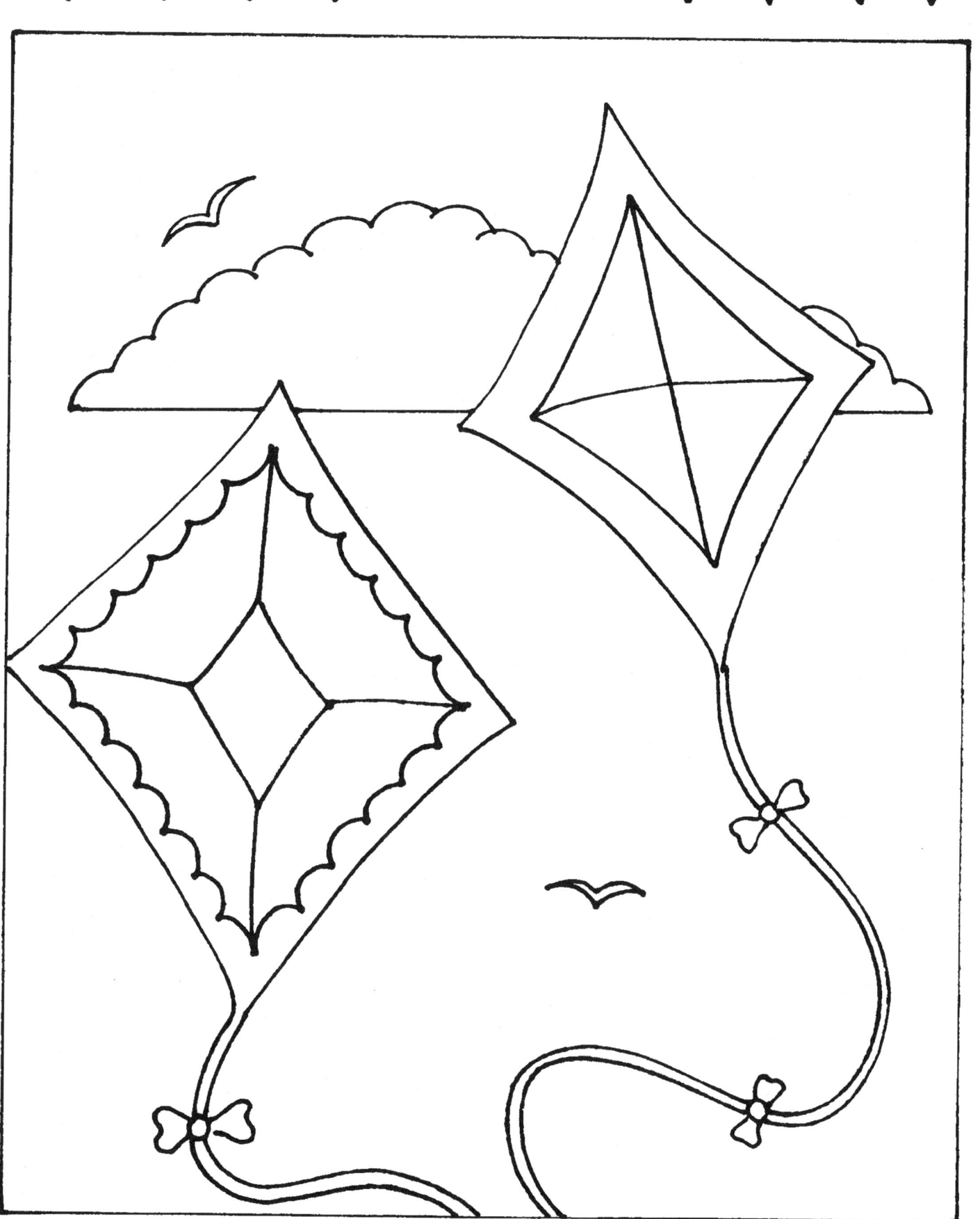

Lesson #122: *Sunsets & Rainbows*

Sunsets and rainbows are fun to draw and color. Do you know how to draw a rainbow? It is drawn with long half-circles that go all the way around and connect from one side of the horizon to the other. Using your yellow pencil, draw a rainbow above the sun in the figure box below (A) just as on p.177. What colors will your rainbow have? They are the same as the colors of your color wheel. Start with red in the circle closest to the sun, then orange, then yellow, then green, then violet. Save the blue to color your sky a very light blue and white. Color the sun and its reflection in the water a bright, yellow/orange. Finally, color your water a blue/violet with short, horizontal strokes. Horizontal strokes go straight across and will help show the flow of the water.

A.

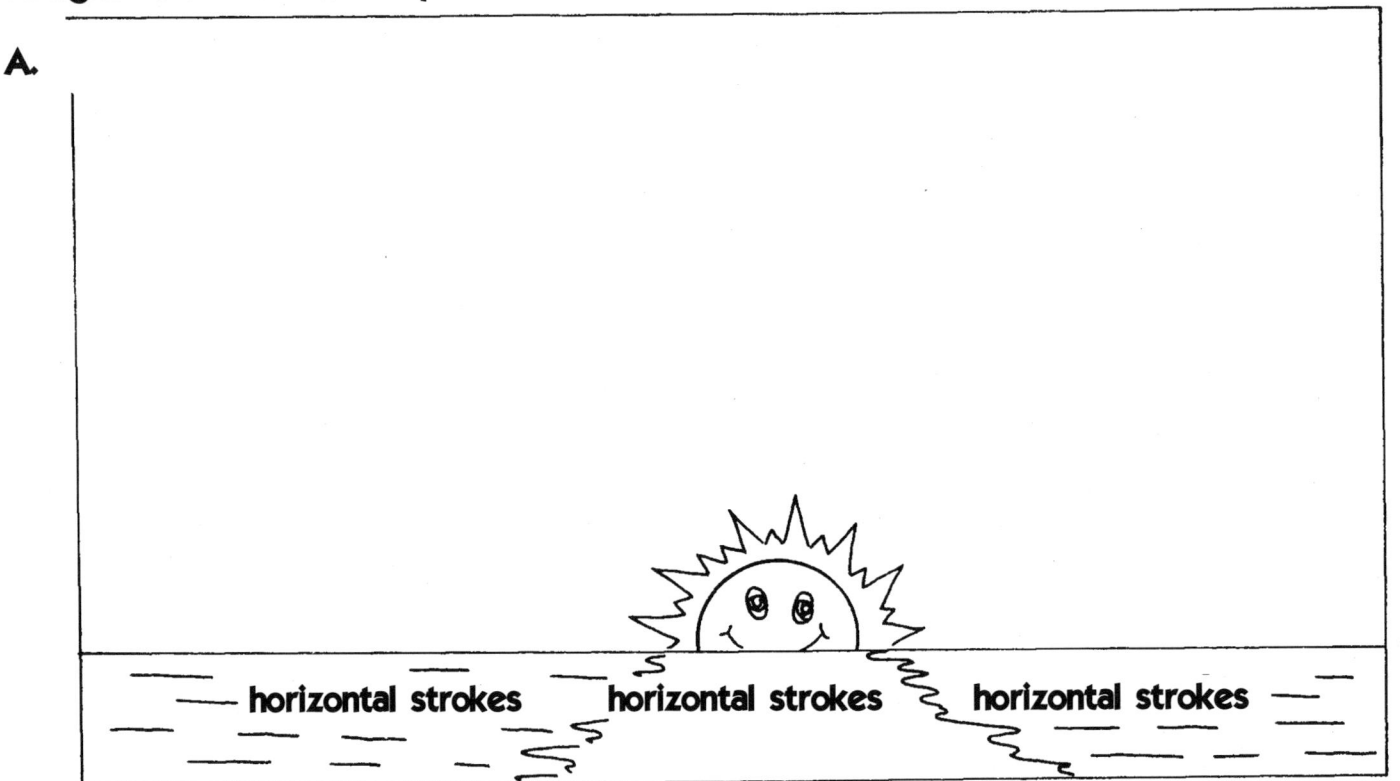

When you are finished with the picture above, color the picture of the sunset and rainbow on the next page with your colored pencils. Practice mixing your colors in the triangles below the picture before beginning.

Place *Paint Card #16* in front of you. Mix the colors for your sunset and rainbow in the triangles on the bottom of the card. Start by painting the sky a very light blue using lots of white and only a tiny speck of blue. Paint the water with horizontal strokes, and paint the seagulls white using your small brush. Are you going to sign your painting?

Lesson #123: Fold an 11" x 14" sheet of white poster board to 5 1/2" x 7" and draw a sunset and rainbow on the front of it. Paint it and write a scripture or verse inside and send it to a friend as a greeting card.

Paint Card #16: *Sunsets & Rainbows*

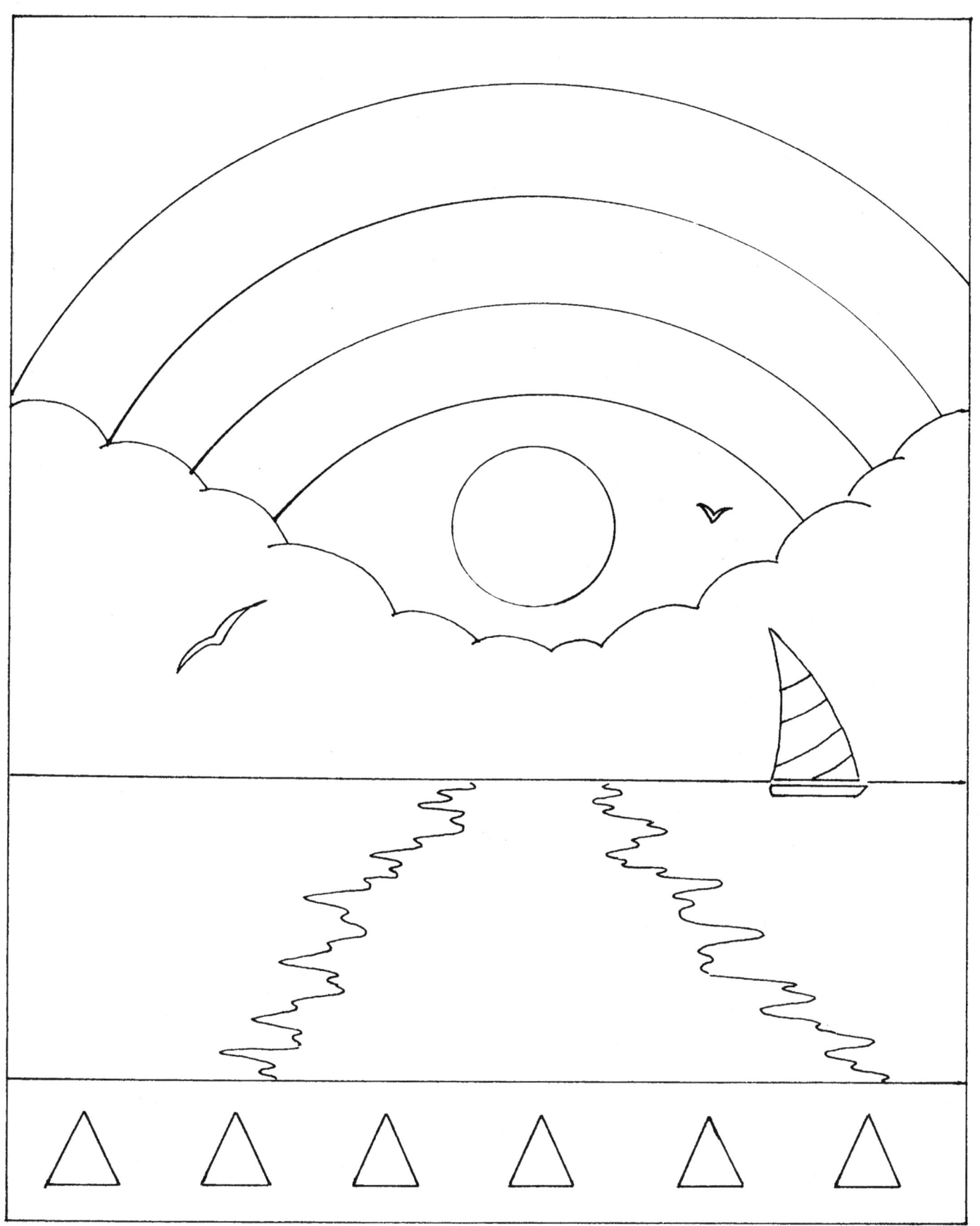

Lesson #124: *Painting Highlights*

Highlights are bright areas where light reflects the most on objects. Notice on the next page that all the highlights go *around,* following the shapes as the objects. See if you can draw the highlights on the objects below just like they are on the next page. When you are finished, color both pages with your colors pencils. Color some parts with line and some with blending. Color the pupil (the small circle) of the eye a dark color and the iris (the larger circle) a lighter color.

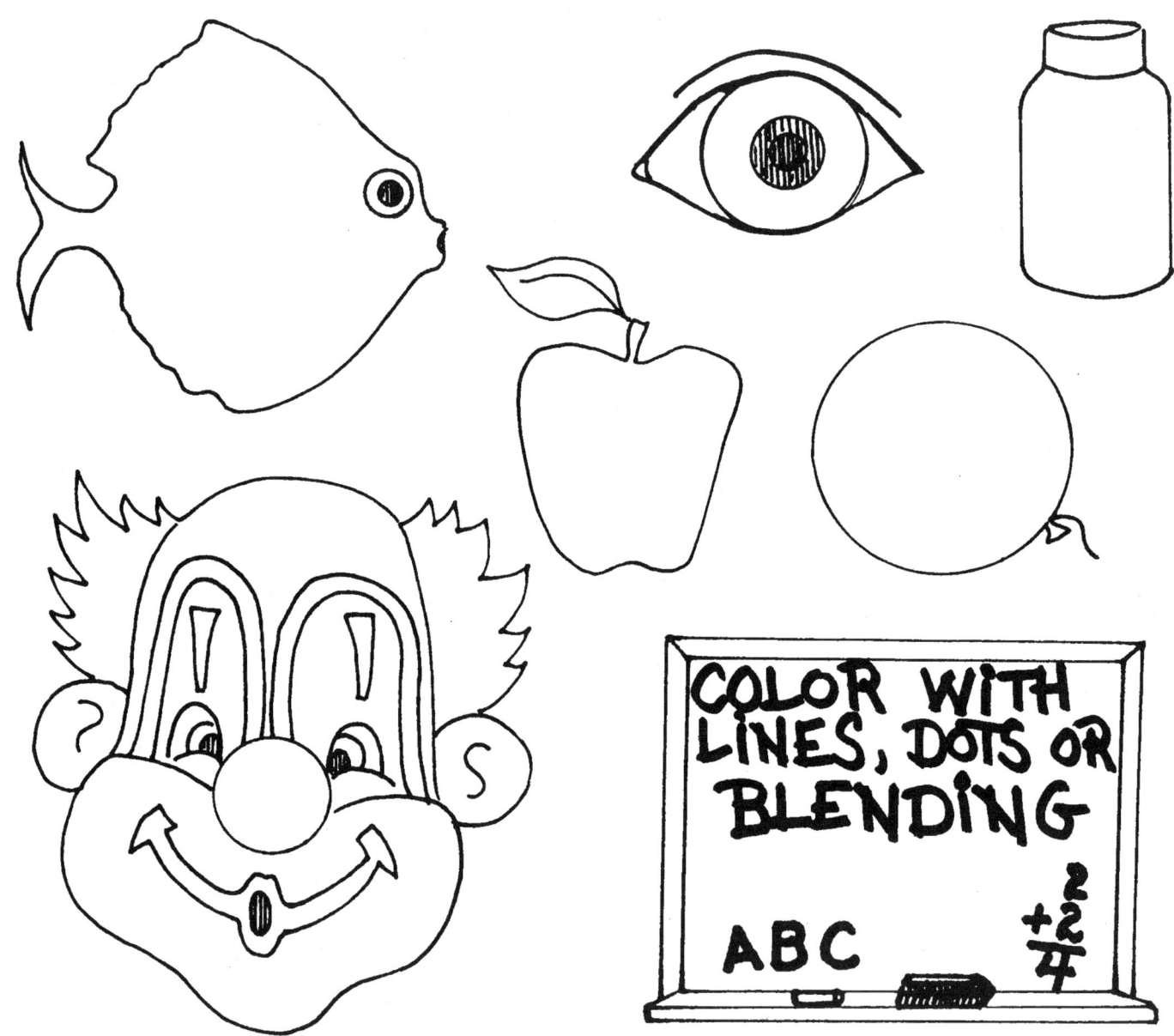

Place *Paint Card #17* in front of you. Paint everything with either a warm color or a cool color (as we learned in Lesson #69). Notice the lines that divide the light side of the jug, apple, and balloon. Try to paint each with a light side and a shaded side. Use another shade, or tone, of the same color between the two. After the entire object is painted, paint the highlight white with a small brush.

178

Paint Card #17: *Highlights*

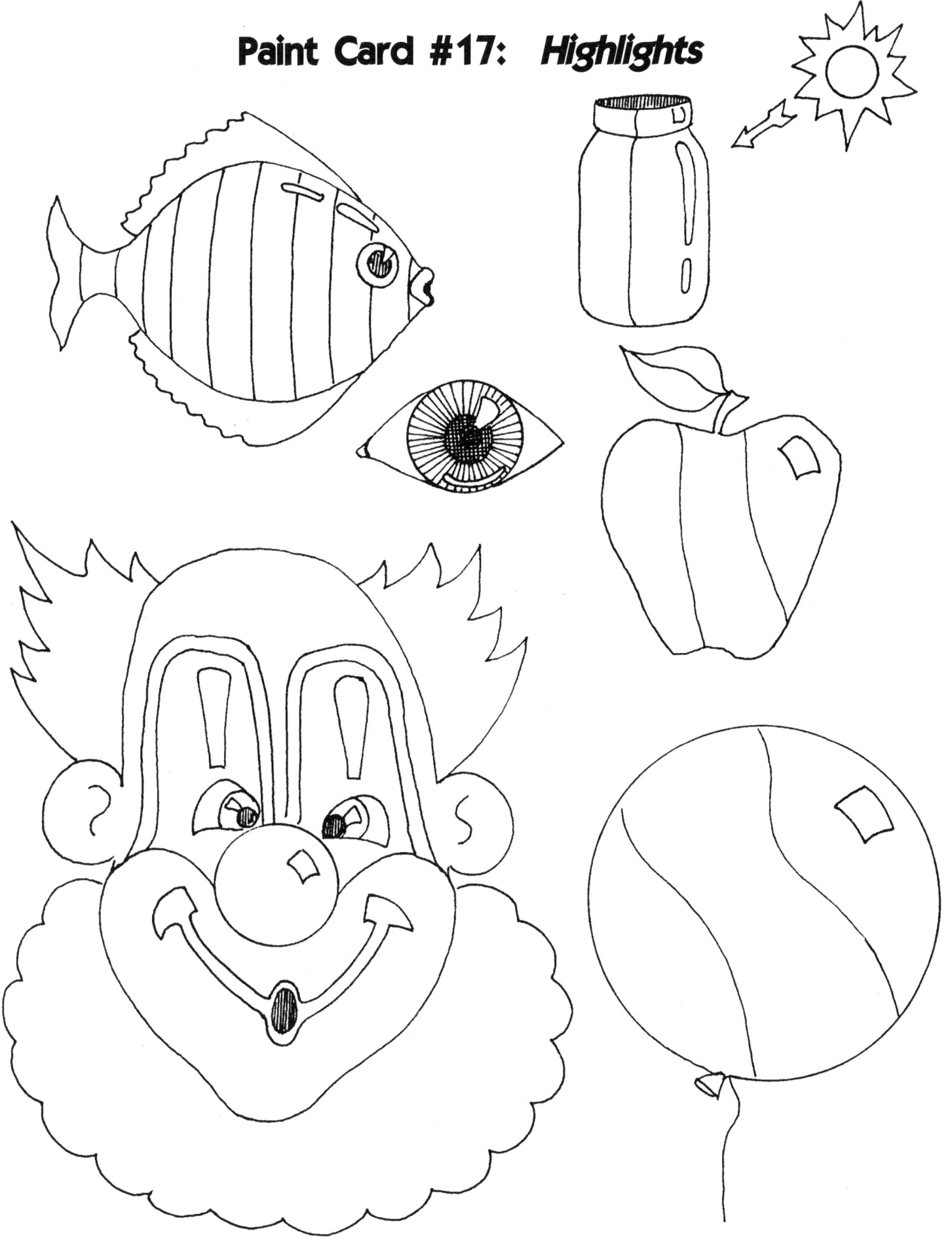

179:

Lesson #125: *Shadow Land*

Do you know what a *cast shadow* is? It is the shadow of an object that is cast upon the ground or other surface. Look at the drawing below (A). Do you know what direction the sun is coming from? See if you can draw another little figure in B like the one in A. Notice that you can see both of his hands in the cast shadow, but only one on his side. Color your shadows with cool colors, such as blues and violets.

A.

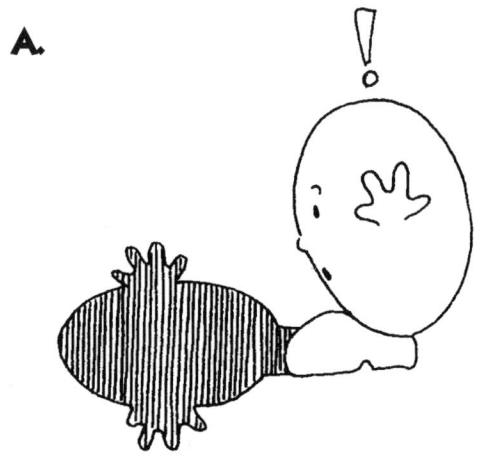

B. Draw Your Figure & Shadow Here

When you have finished, color the picture on the next page with colored pencils. First, fill the circles with the colors you want to use for the shadows, trees, road and sunshine. Then color the pictures. Try to show three different greens in your trees and color the cast shadows with cool colors. Let's color the road in the bottom picture with pink and the shaded part of the road with violet.

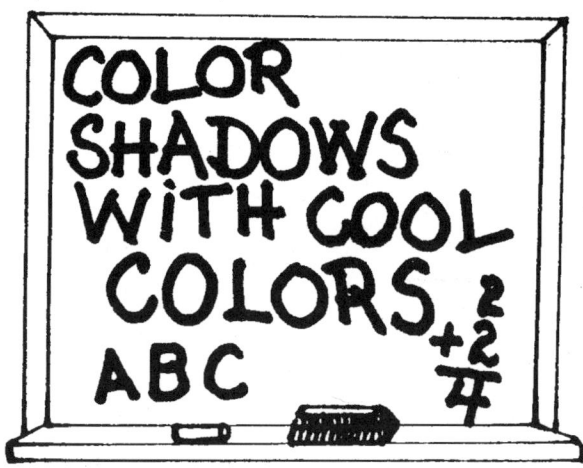

Turn to *Paint Card #18*. First, paint the circles to the left with the colors you want to use in the pictures. Paint everything the same as you did with the colored pencils. Whenever you paint a landscape, it is good to paint the background first (the sky), then the middle ground (the grass and road), and finally, the trees and shadows in the foreground.

Lesson #126: On a piece of 11" x 14" white poster board, copy some of the animals and people you have drawn or colored in previous lessons. Make sure to draw them large. Place the sun to the far left or right in your picture and then draw a cast shadow for all your figures. Take your time and paint them with your smaller brushes. Remember, all of your shadows are going to be painted with cool colors.

Paint Card #18: *Shadowland*

"I am the light of the world...." John 8:12

Lesson #127: *Sun Shine on Me!*

Did you know that sunshine is not the same color during different times of the day? Early morning sunshine is a pale yellow; afternoon sunshine is a bright yellow; and evening light is an orange/yellow. Let's draw and color a morning, afternoon, and evening sun. First, draw a circle just as you learned in Lessons #9, lightly going around four or five times (A). Draw the sunbeams coming out of the sun. Start with the longest ones: the top, bottom and two sides (B), and then add the rest of the points or sunbeams (C). Use your yellow pencil to draw a sunshine in D, and a red pencil to draw a face on your sun. Then color all three suns (B, C & D). The morning sun is a light yellow with white (B), the afternoon sun is a bright yellow (C) and the evening sun is a yellow/orange (D).

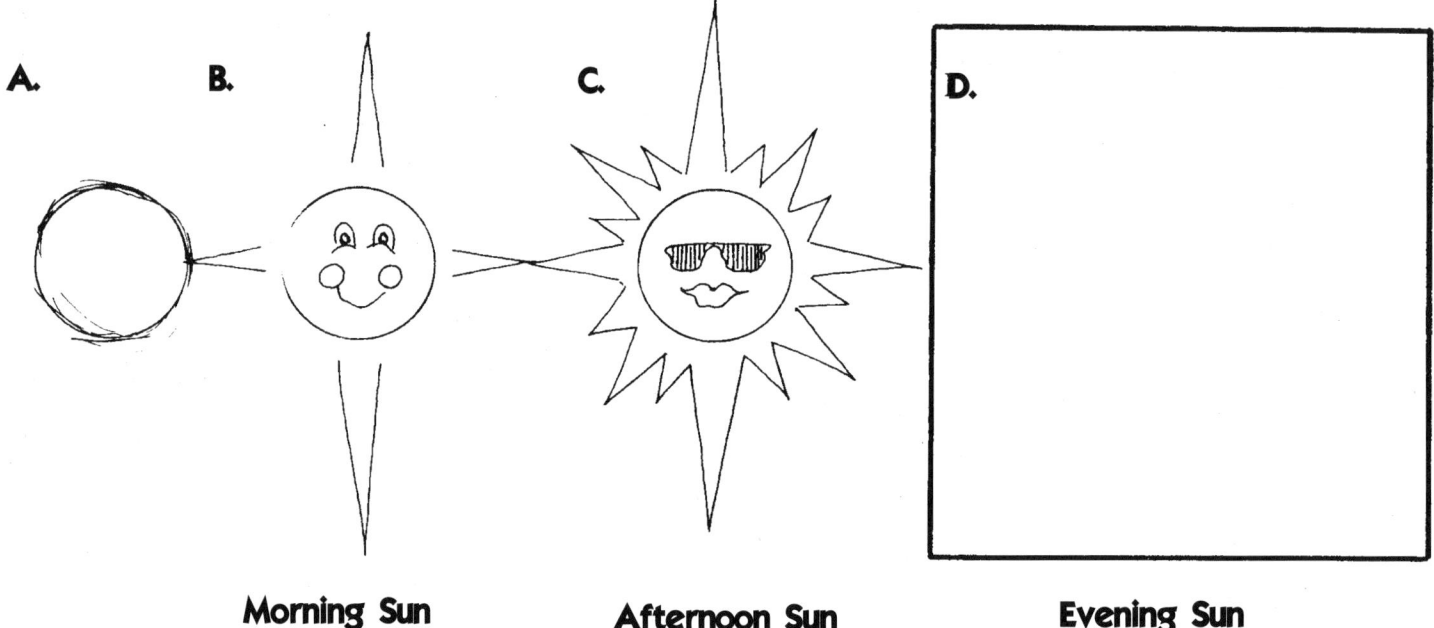

Morning Sun   Afternoon Sun   Evening Sun

Color the sunrise and sunset on the next page with your colored pencils. Use a light yellow with white for the morning sun, and a yellow/orange for the evening sun. Color the sun's reflection in the water with the same color as the sun and finish coloring the rest of each picture. Next, color the barn on the bottom of the page. Can you show that part of the barn and tree are in sunlight? Practice your colors in the circles in the middle of the card before beginning.

Place *Paint Card #19* in front of you. First, mix yellows in the small circles to see if you can find the colors for a morning, afternoon, and evening sun. The circles at the top of the paint card illustrate the three different brush strokes you can use to paint a sun. Practice painting a colorful sun in each using lots of brush strokes. Put plenty of paint on your brush and use the arrows to show the direction of the strokes. Do you like the effect of painting a sun using brush strokes?

Finally, paint the sunrise, sunset, and farm scene with the same colors used with colored pencils. In the farm scene, try to show the color of the sunlight reflecting on part of the barn and tree. Use bright colors!

182

Paint Card #19: *Sun Shine on Me!*

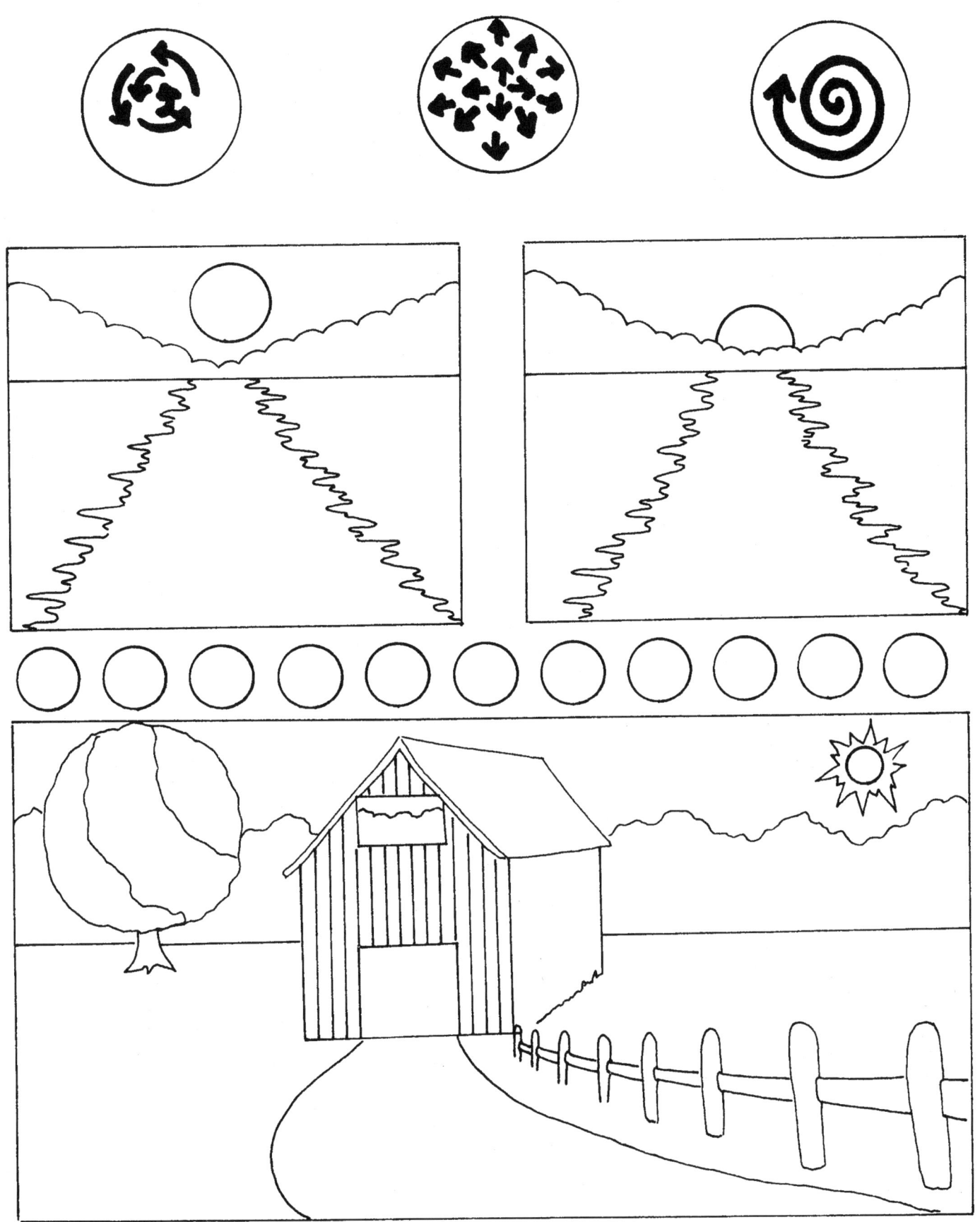

Lesson #128: *Painting a Parrot*

Parrots are bright and colorful! Can you draw and color Polly (A) in the figure box (C)? First, draw a parrot with your yellow pencil, making sure to start with the basic shapes (B). When you have drawn everything correctly outline all the details with your black pen and color it with a bright assortment of colors!

A. Drawing Polly

C. Draw Your Parrot Below

red/orange

yellow/white

black

yellow

light blue

red

B.

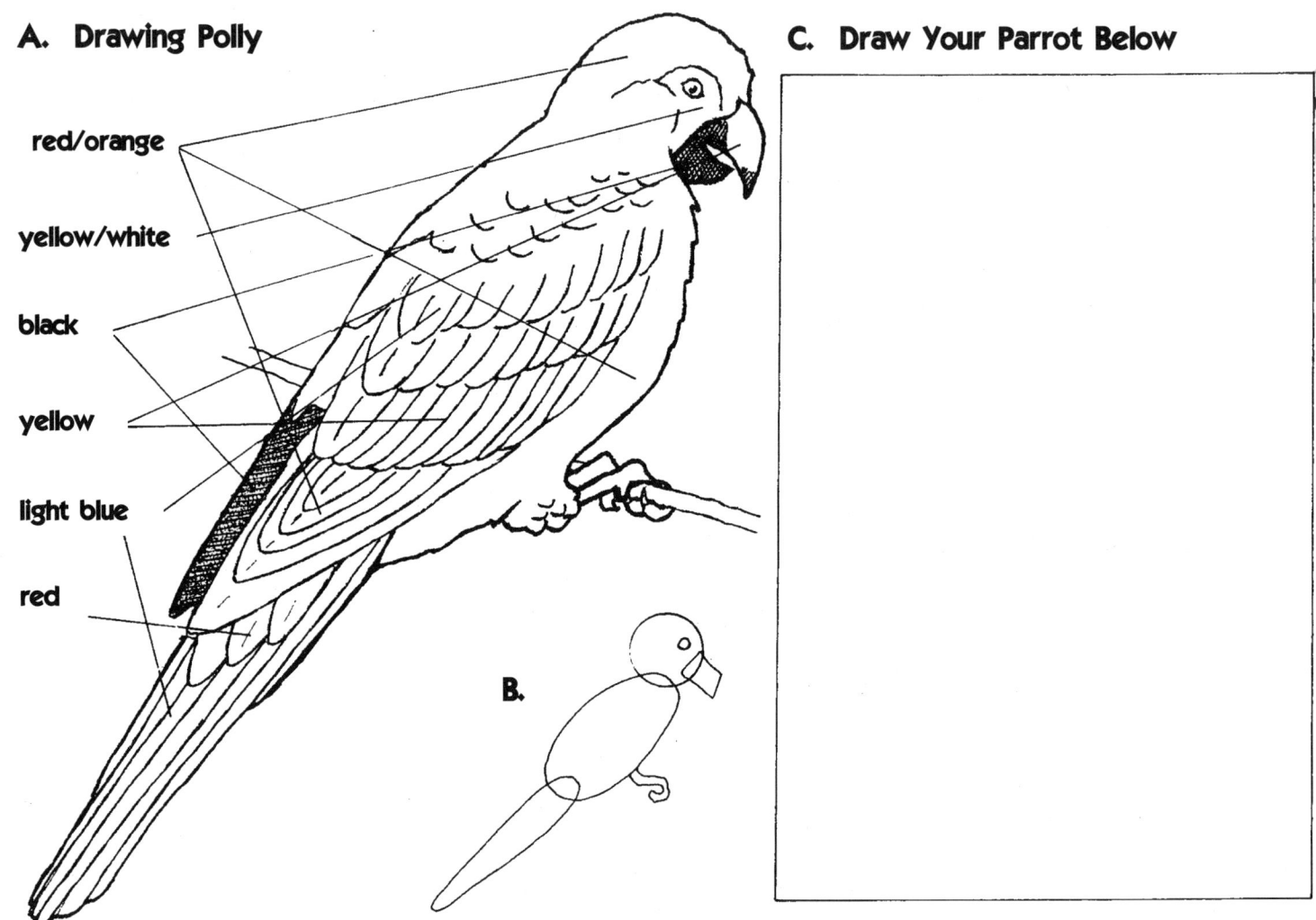

When you have finished your parrot, color the large parrot on the next page with your colored pencils. Practice blending some of your colors together in the feathers on the bottom of the page before beginning to make other interesting and bright colors for your parrot.

Place *Paint Card #20* in front of you. Paint the parrot with the colors suggested. Again, practice mixing your paints in the feathers on the bottom of the page before beginning. Remember, generally mix at least two colors together. Never paint with the red or blue straight out of the tube, but learn to mix a little of another color into each. For your red feathers, you may want to add a little yellow and white to make them lighter. For your blues and violets, add some white to make them lighter. Finally, paint your background with a very light color.

184

Paint Card #20: *Painting a Parrot*

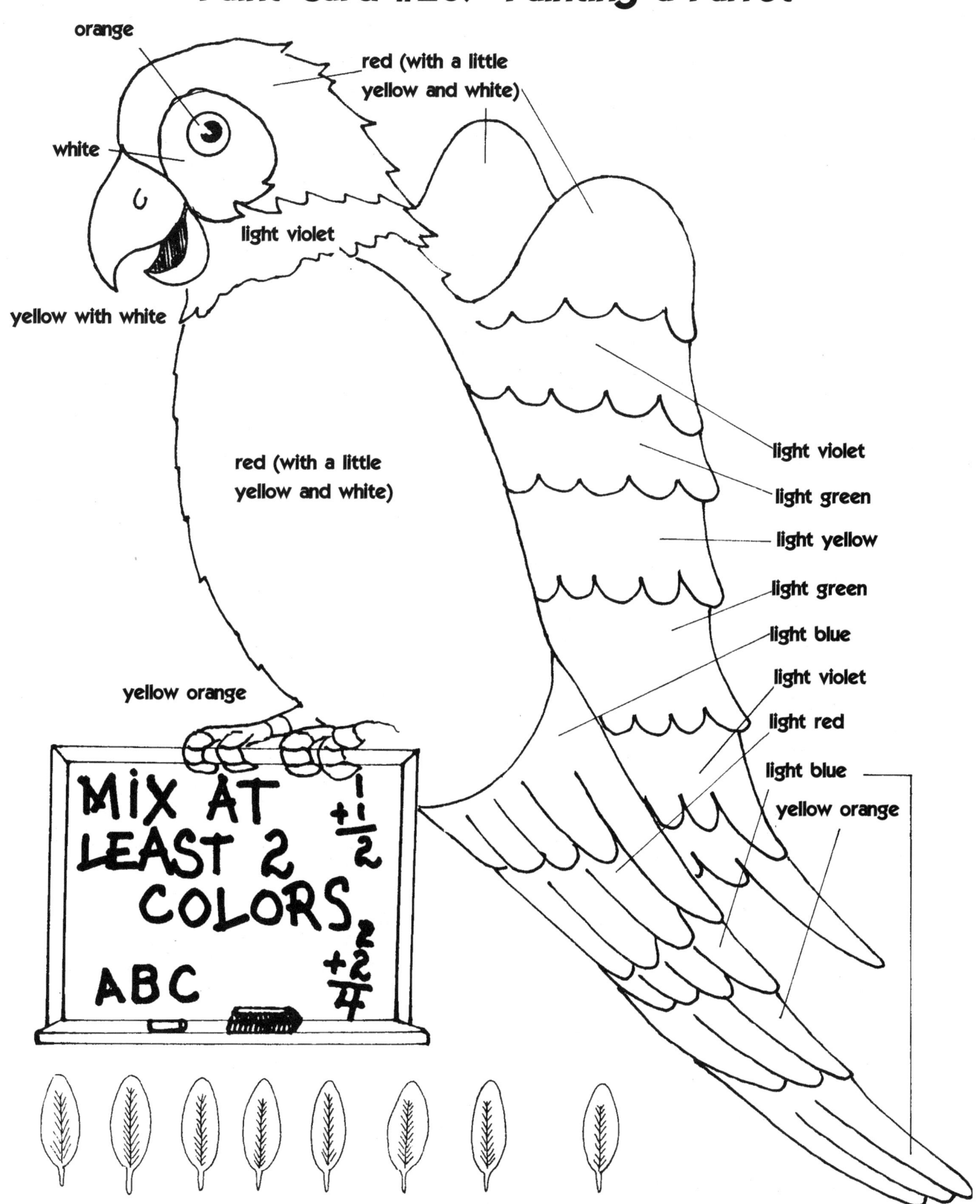

orange

red (with a little yellow and white)

white

light violet

yellow with white

light violet

light green

light yellow

light green

light blue

light violet

light red

light blue

yellow orange

red (with a little yellow and white)

yellow orange

MIX AT LEAST 2 COLORS ABC

$+1\frac{1}{2}$

$+2\frac{2}{4}$

Lesson #129: *Coloring a Landscape*

A landscape is a scene from nature. It may be distant hills, green trees, a blue river and a golden meadow or anything else that is out of doors. We can even learn to use *texture* in our landscape! As mentioned in Lesson #27, texture can be the grain on a piece of wood, the fur of an animal, or even the grass growing on the ground. There are many ways to draw and paint things to give a sense of texture. For grass, you can make short, yellow strokes, (pushing up) with your colored pencil (A) and then add short, green strokes. Practice in C.

A. Short Yellow Strokes

B. Short Green Strokes

C. Practice Here

D. Circular Strokes

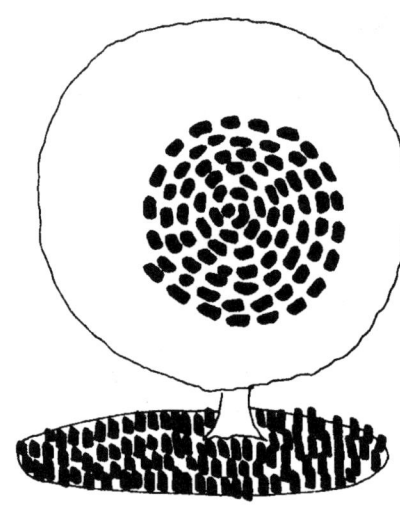

Now let's practice drawing and coloring a tree with colored pencils using short strokes. Start with your yellow colored pencil and make all your strokes go around in a circle. Then add short, circular, green strokes in between the yellow strokes (D). Finally, use short, vertical, blue and green strokes to shade under your tree. Practice drawing and coloring your tree in the figure box (E).

E.

Finally, color some flowers using dots or pointillism. Use at least two different colors of dots and color your flowers as shown in F. Color the circle inside your flower with yellow and orange dots. You may want to use red and blue dots for your petals. Next, color the landscape on p.187 using the colors suggested and strokes or dots whenever possible. Practice with your colored pencils in figure box G.

When you are finished, place *Paint Card #21* in front of you and paint everything with either short strokes, or dots! Can you paint the grass with short, vertical strokes, the trees with circular strokes and the flowers with dots?

F.

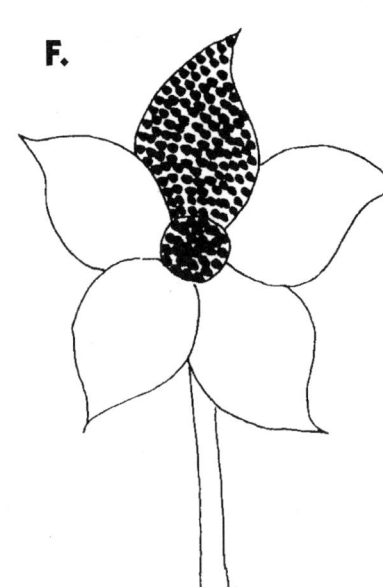

G.

Paint Card #21: *Painting a Landscape*

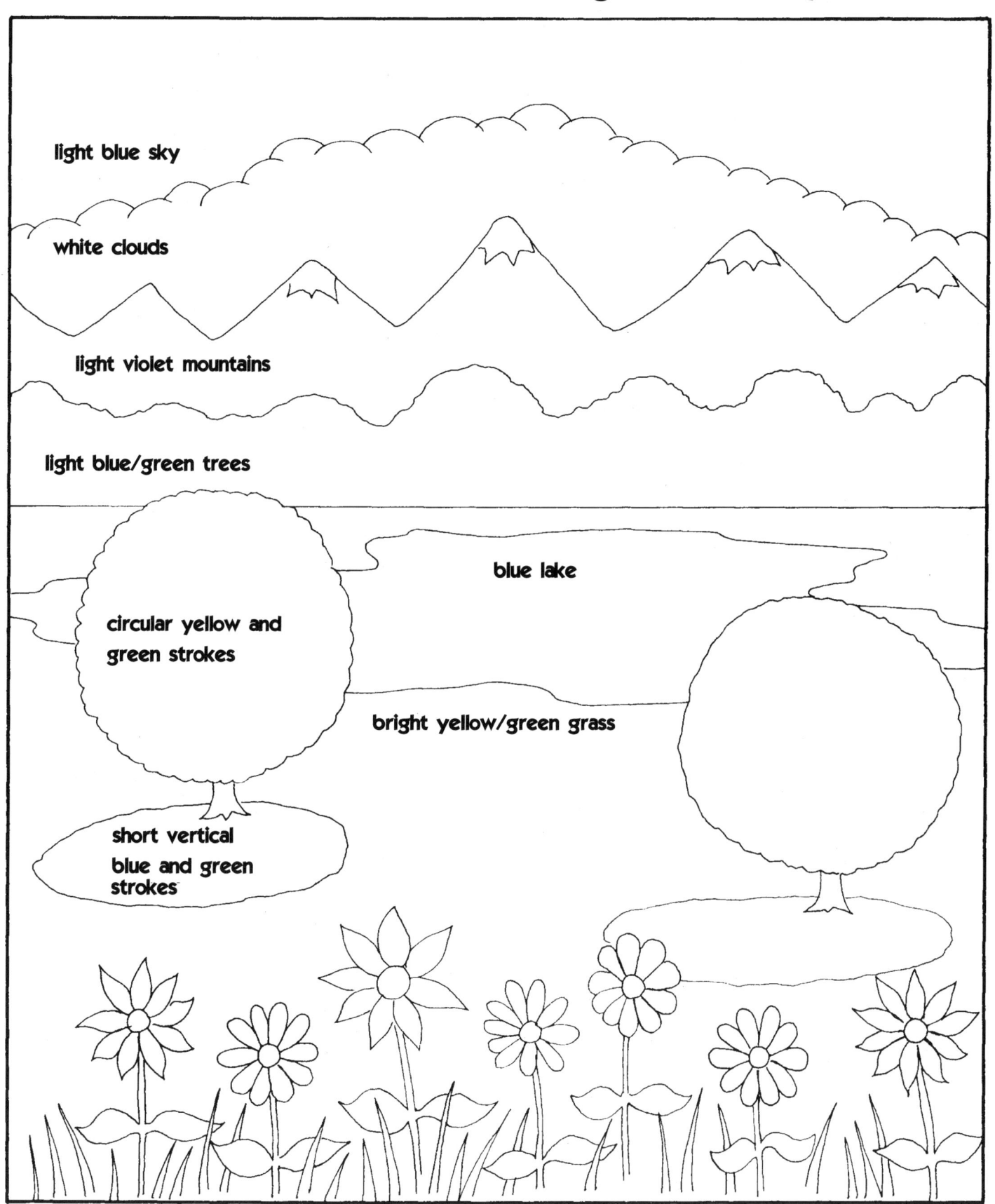

light blue sky

white clouds

light violet mountains

light blue/green trees

blue lake

circular yellow and green strokes

bright yellow/green grass

short vertical blue and green strokes

Use brighter colors in the foreground and duller colors in the background.

187

"I will not follow where the path may lead, but I will go where there is no path, and I will leave a trail."
Muriel Strode

Lesson #130: *Pin the Tail on the Horse*

Let's complete the horse below by looking at the horse's body on the next page. I have already drawn the head, the tail, and the hooves for you. All you have to do is complete the horse. Use your light yellow pencil to start with, and go over your horse with another color when you have completed the drawing. Can you blend some nice browns with your colored pencils? See how many browns you can blend in the circles on the next page. Try blending yellow with a little red, orange, and blue. You can even add violet and white. Experiment with these colors and others to see what colorful browns you can make! Refer back to the color chart of Lesson #103 and see if there are other nice browns you can use.

Finally, color in the horse on the next page. Color the entire picture with different browns: a light brown for his mane and tail, different browns for parts of his body, brown for the fence, and brown for the rope around his nose! Select some nice colors for the ground, distant hills, and sky.

Place *Paint Card #22* in front of you. See how many browns you can mix with your paints in the circles on the side of your paint card. Then paint your picture with a variety of different browns, some dark and some light. What do you think of your painting with many different browns?

Paint Card #22: *A Horse is a Horse*

Lesson #131: *Painting Flesh Tones*

Can you color some flesh tones? To make a skin color, mix a little yellow with a tiny bit of red and blend them with white, or lightly erase the color. Practice mixing flesh tones in the baby figure below (E).

Let's draw a little baby. First, draw a circle for the head (A), drawing the head fairly large. Next, draw a wide oval for the body (B). Add little round hot dog shapes for the arms and legs (C). Place circles on the end of the arms and plump hot dog shapes on the end of the legs (D). Give the baby some toes and fingers, draw a diaper, and give him or her some facial features (E). Is it a boy or a girl? If it is a boy, color the diaper blue. If it is a girl, color the diaper pink. Draw your baby in the figure box below (F), first with your yellow pencil and then with your black pen. Finally, color with your colored pencils.

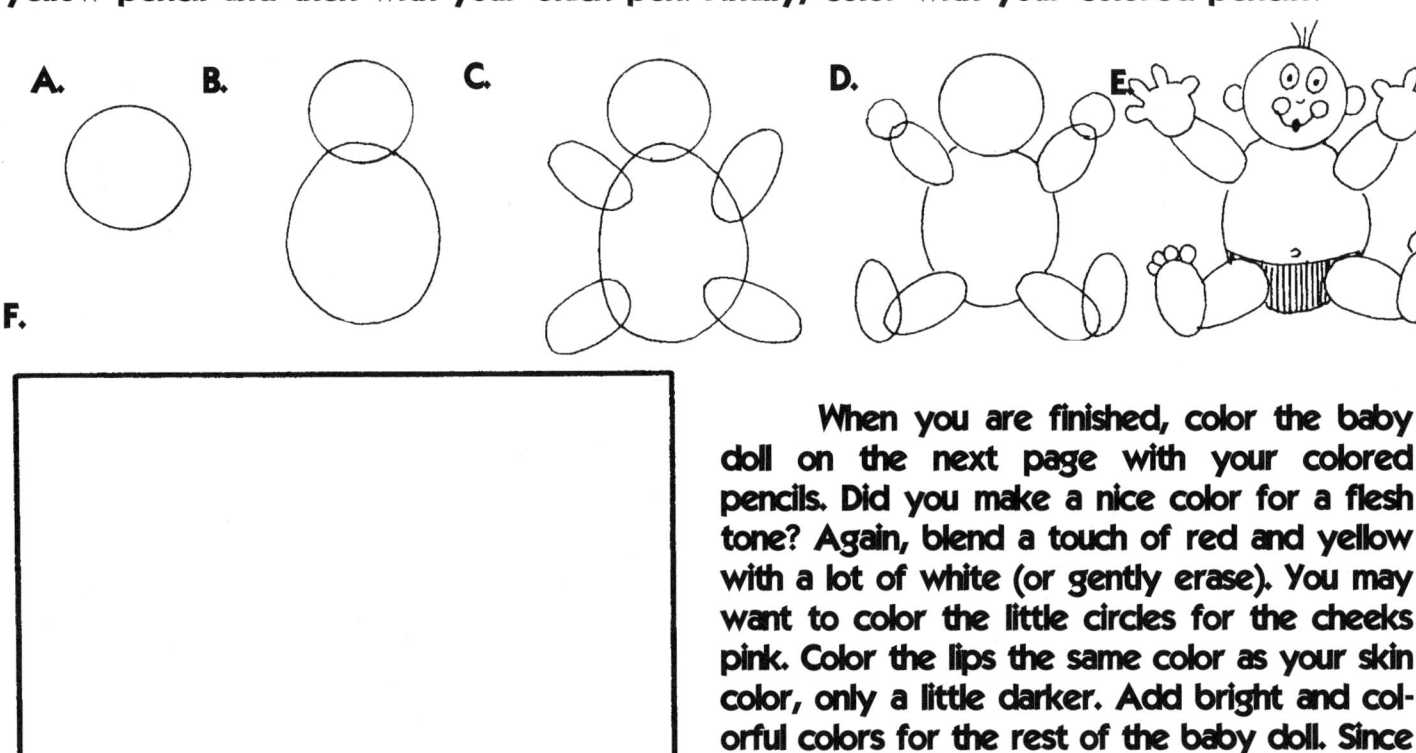

F.

When you are finished, color the baby doll on the next page with your colored pencils. Did you make a nice color for a flesh tone? Again, blend a touch of red and yellow with a lot of white (or gently erase). You may want to color the little circles for the cheeks pink. Color the lips the same color as your skin color, only a little darker. Add bright and colorful colors for the rest of the baby doll. Since it is a girl, you may want to use pinks and other light colors for her clothing and bows.

Place *Paint Card #23* in front of you. See if you can make flesh tones with your paints by mixing white with a little yellow and a touch of red, or make a light orange and add just a little of it to white. Before beginning, practice these colors in the circles on the bottom of the paint card, along with the colors you want to use for the clothing. Remember, lips are not red but a slightly darker flesh tone. Color the circles on her cheeks the same color as the lips.

Lesson #132: Let's have some fun! Look in a mirror and draw your face on a piece of white card stock paper. When you are finished, paint it with flesh colors. Find nice colors for your hair, lips and eyes. This is going to be funny looking, but don't worry, it's your first painted portrait!

Paint Card #23: Painting Flesh Tones

"Go not abroad for happiness. For see, it is a flower that blossoms at thy door."

Minot J. Savage

Lesson #133: *Painting a Season*

Do you like to color the seasons of the year? What colors would you color winter, summer, autumn and spring? What things remind you of the four seasons? Draw the four seasons in the figure boxes below: Summer (A), Autumn (B), Winter (C) and Spring (D). You may want to draw something that reminds you of those seasons from around your home or neighborhood, or you can copy pictures that represent the seasons. Whatever you like, express the seasons in a creative and colorful way, using colors that express the time of year. Finally, let's pretend we are making a calendar. Select your best drawing and color it in the large figure box on the next page. Neatly print the month of the year above the picture.

A. Summer

B. Autumn

C. Winter

D. Spring

Place *Paint Card #24* in front of you. Lightly draw your calendar month in the figure box with a light colored pencil. Select beautiful colors from your color chart of Lesson #103. Practice mixing your colors on another piece of paper before painting your picture. When you are finished, neatly letter the month of the year above your picture using one of your colored markers.

Paint Card #24: *Painting a Season*

Month: _____

More Painting Lessons

Lesson #134: *Copy the Masters.* Find a pretty picture by Claude Monet or Vincent van Gogh and copy it on a sheet of white card stock paper. First, draw it lightly with a colored pencil. Use plenty of bold brush strokes to paint your picture.

Lesson #135: *Painting Fish.* Use four sheets of colorful poster board for this assignment. You may want to select blue, yellow, orange, or red poster board. Cut each to 11" x 14". Find pictures of colorful, tropical fish and draw one large fish on each and paint them. How do you like painting on different colored surfaces?

Lesson #136: *Nature Studies.* Find three small rocks and bring them inside. Draw them large on a sheet of white card stock paper. How many colors do you see in the rocks besides black and brown? Try to mix these colors and paint your picture of the rocks. When finished, you may want to paint a nice design on one of the rocks!

Lesson #137: *Painting a Boot.* Sketch a large boot or other brown shoe on a piece of drawing paper for practice. Then, draw it on a sheet of white card stock paper, or even orange poster board. See how many brown colors you can paint in the brown boot, making a painting of colorful browns!

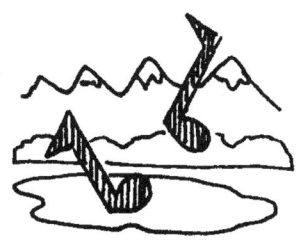

Lesson #138: *Painting to Inspirational Music.* Play a selection of classical music that you like. Close your eyes and listen to it. What do you see? What about colors? Draw what you have imagined on a sheet of drawing paper. Try to draw everything large. Use your colored pencils and put in as much detail as possible. Then, on a sheet of white card stock paper or colored poster board, do a painting of what you see in the music.

Lesson #139: *What's in the Kitchen?* Find some colorful grocery containers and do a drawing of them with your colored pencils. You may want to draw a can of soup, a box of tissues, a box of cereal or a combination of several grocery containers. Then, do a painting of it on a sheet of card stock paper or poster board.

Lesson #140: *A Zoo Animal.* Do a large drawing of any zoo animal. Then on a sheet of poster board do a large painting of it.

Lesson #141: *Shadrach, Meshach, and Abednego*

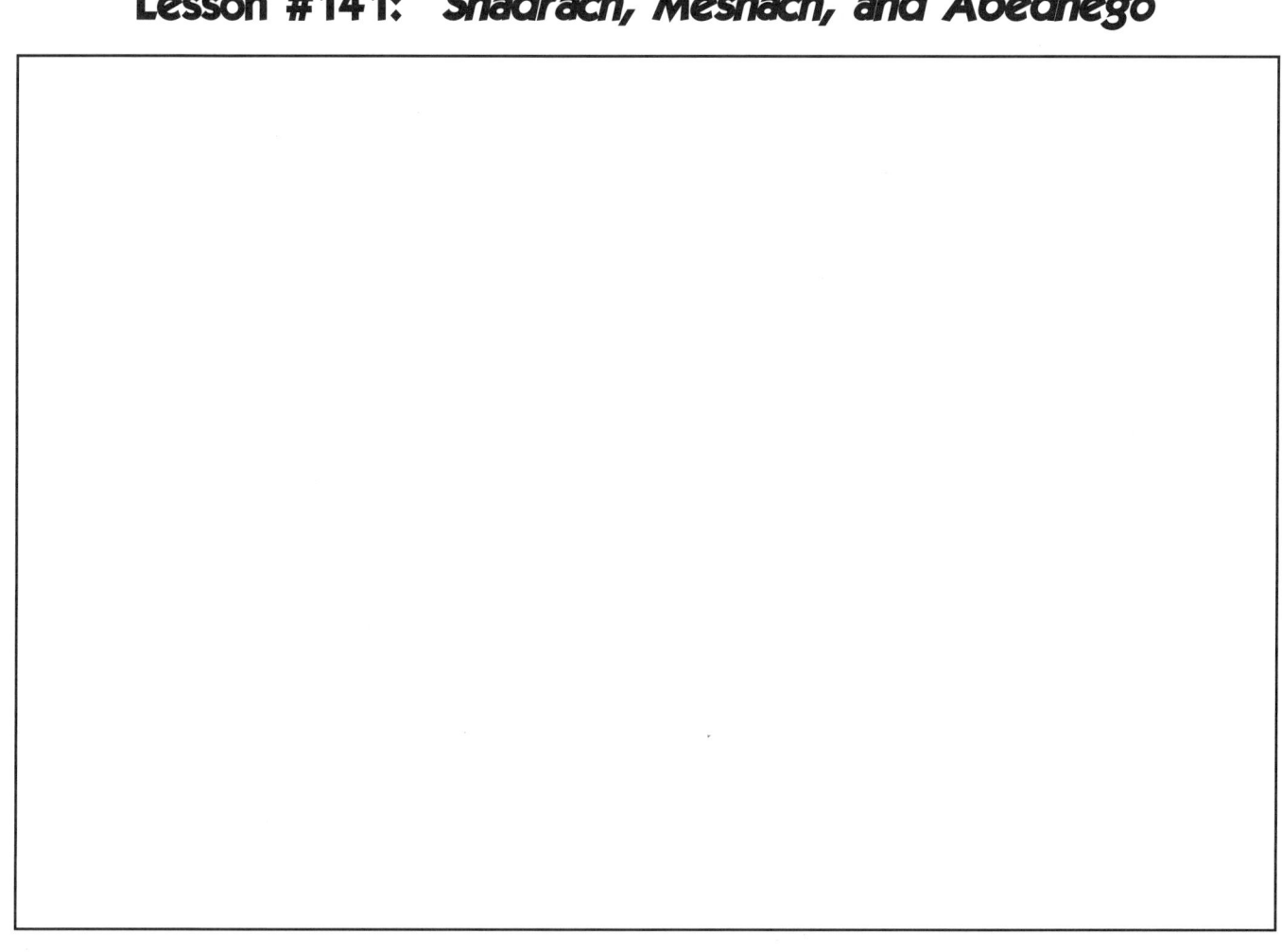

Let's do another illustration of a story from the Bible. Today's story will be about Shadrach, Meshach, and Abednego. Read the story below and do an illustration with colored pencils in the figure box above. Then, on a sheet of white card stock paper, do a painting of your picture. Use nice colors from your color chart. Make sure to work big! When you are finished, see if someone can identify the story.

"Then Nebuchadnezzar was furious with Shadrach, Meshach, and Abednego, and his attitude toward them changed. He ordered the furnace heated seven times hotter than usual and commanded some of the strongest soldiers in his army to tie up Shadrach, Meshach, and Abednego and throw them into the blazing furnace. So these men, wearing their robes, trousers, turbans and other clothes, were bound and thrown into the blazing furnace. The king's command was so urgent and the furnace so hot that the flames of the fire killed the soldiers who took up Shadrach, Meschach, and Abednego, and these three men, firmly tied, fell into the blazing furnace.

Then King Nebuchadnezzar leaped to his feet in amazement and asked his advisers, 'Weren't there three men that we tied up and threw into the fire?'

They replied, 'Certainly, O king.'

He said, 'Look! I see four men walking around in the fire, unbound and unharmed, and the fourth looks like a son of the gods.'"

Daniel 3:19-25

Lesson #142: *Journal Time*

It's time to do another entry in your art journal. Do you know what you are going to write about and what you are going to draw? What did you like about painting? What do you still have to learn? Did you do any paintings that you really liked? Write about your day and what you have learned below. Make sure to draw things around you that are part of your day. You may want to draw your paints and brushes or do little pictures of some of your paintings. Don't forget to date your paper.

_____

_____

_____

_____

_____

_____

_____

_____

_____

_____

_____

_____

_____

_____

_____

_____

Studying the Masters

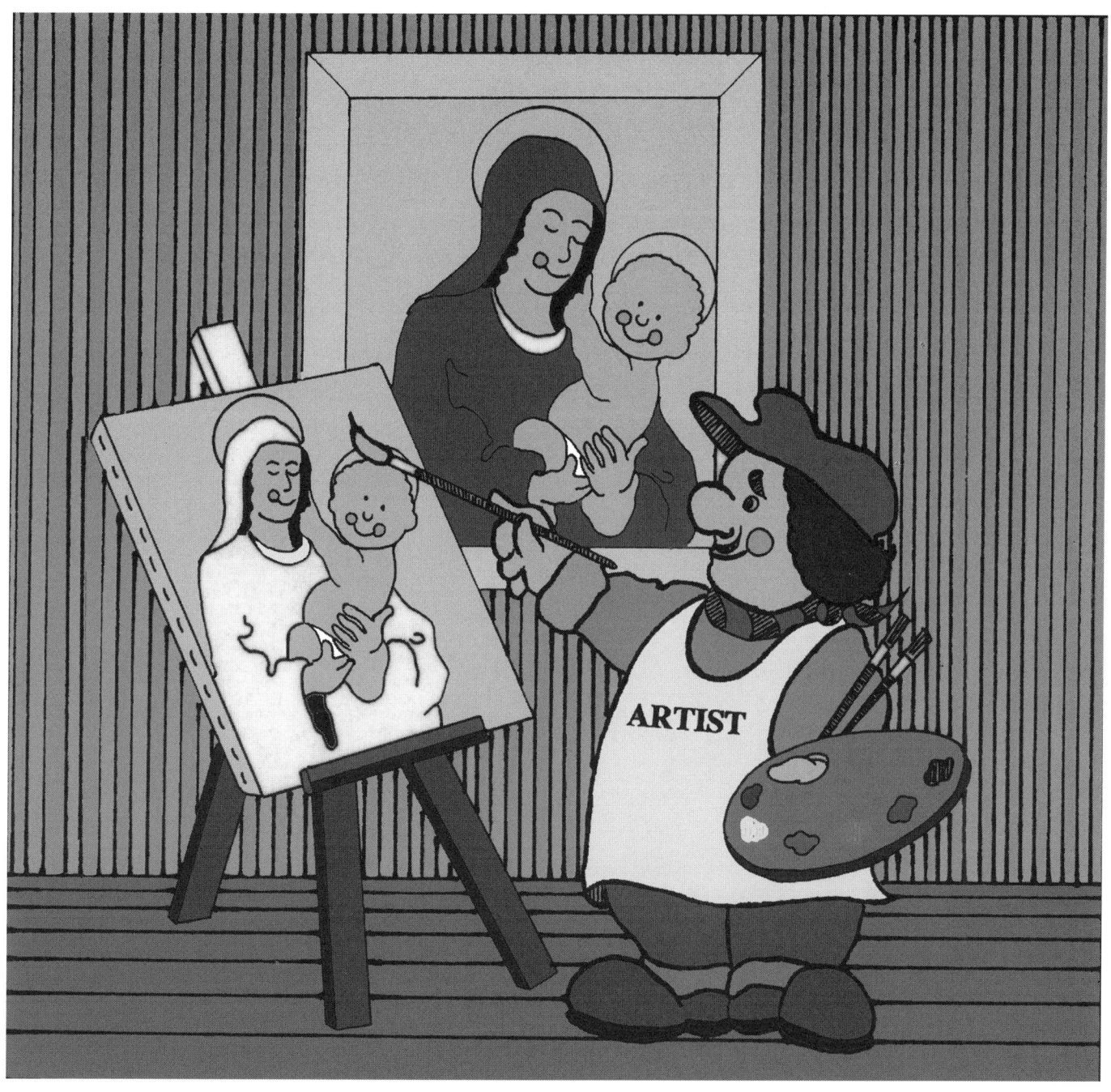

"Copy and re-copy the masters."   Edgar Degas

Studying the Masters

Have you ever studied the *masters?* Masters are great artists from the past and present. It is good to study their artwork because they can teach you much about art. Studying the masters can also be a lot of fun, especially if you love art! Understanding art from the past is as much a part of your art education as learning to draw and paint. Listed below are the names of some of the great artists for you to study. You can look them up in the encyclopedia, the internet, or simply go to the library to see many of their pictures in large art books. If the library does not have any books on the artists you want to study, make a request and they will send away for the books.

Great Artists

Michelangelo	Leonardo da Vinci	Raphael
Albrecht Durer	Peter Paul Rubens	Millet
Vermeer	Rembrandt van Rijn	Bernini
Jacques Louis David	Ingres	El Greco
Fra Angelica	Corot	Thomas Eakins
Edgar Degas	Claude Monet	Pissaro
Thomas Gainsborough	Vincent van Gogh	Holman Hunt
Georges Rouault	Carl Bloch	Winslow Homer
John Singer Sargeant	William Mallard Turner	John Constable
Charles Russell	Frederick Remington	Norman Rockwell

"Master-Q"

"Master Q" is a fun game that will teach you about some famous artists in history and great pieces of artwork. On the next several pages is information about artwork throughout history and the great masters. First, write the name of each artist or period of art three times to help you learn their names. Then, read about the artwork and see if you can answer the questions below:

1. What is the name of the artist?
2. How do you pronounce and spell his name?
3. What is the title of the piece of artwork?
4. During what period of time did he live, or what style of art is it?
5. Be able to discuss something about the artist's life or the artwork.

Next, neatly cut out each of the large pictures on pages 207 through 212. Glue, tape or paste each picture on a small sturdy surface like cardboard, posterboard or large index cards. Make sure not to include the number, title, or artist that are next to each picture when you cut them out.

After you have studied each artist and have affixed all the pictures on a sturdy surface, have someone sit across from you with the cards and "I Can Do All Things." Then have them hold up one card at a time, and ask you the questions that go with each. See how many you can answer correctly. Have a "Master Q" with the entire family and find out who knows the most about each artist! An art lesson is also included with each picture for you to do on your own.

#1 Ancient Egypt 2,000 B. C. to 1,000 B. C.   Ancient Egyptian Art

Many years ago, during the times of Moses in the Old Testament, Egypt was a powerful nation. Thousands of years ago, the ancient Egyptians placed artwork on the walls of their pharaohs tombs. The pictures told stories of the pharaoh and how the people lived. Back then artists did not try to make people look realistic, but showed them in profile (side view). The ancient Egyptians had many gods and goddesses which they also made large idols out of stone for. This style of artwork remained the same for a long time, as it was considered honorable to stick to tradition. Many years ago artists were like anyone else, the butcher, the baker, or the candlestick maker. Since artists back then were not considered famous, we do not know any of their names.

Ancient Egyptian Art

Questions:
1. How do you spell Egypt?
2. What famous Biblical character was living during the time of ancient Egypt?
3. What can you say about the style of artwork they did?

Lesson #143: *Amazing Maze* Draw a large pyramid. Place a hidden treasure and an entrance into your pyramid and then draw an intricate series of pathways with only one path leading to the treasure. Then, when you are finished, see if your friends can find their way through the pyramid to the secret riches.

#2 Ancient Greece 432 B.C.   The Parthenon

Another great civilization arose about 500 years before the birth of Christ. This was the civilization of ancient Greece. The artwork that came out of Greece during this time has been some of the greatest that man has ever created. They were not only great at painting and sculpting but also in the magnificent design of their buildings, or *architecture*. Below is a picture of the *"Parthenon"* (par-the-non), which was built in the city-state of Athens to honor one of their many gods and goddesses, *"Athena."* It was built in 432 B.C. and is located high on a hill called *Acropolis*. Greek architecture is noted for its use of beautiful columns that adorned the sides of many of their buildings. The ancient Greeks were famous for three styles of columns: *Doric, Corinthian,* and *Ionic* (i-on-ic). The Parthenon is still standing in Greece after nearly 2,500 years.

Questions:
1. How do you spell *Parthenon*?
2. When was the Parthenon built?
3. Where is it located?
4. What are the three main types of columns used by the Greeks?

The Parthenon

Lesson #144: *Greek Geography* For this assignment, go to a world atlas and find where Greece is located. Draw the country and locate the city of Athens. Then, do a drawing of the *Parthenon* inside your map of Greece.

#3 Ancient Rome 82 A.D.   The Colosseum

The Roman Empire followed soon after the glorious days of the ancient Greek civilization. The Romans were not great artists and borrowed artists and the style of art from Greece. However, along with being a great military empire, the Romans were also excellent builders, constructing many roads, aqueducts, and monuments that are still standing. One of their innovations was the creation of the *arch* in architecture. The *Colosseum* was created in Rome as an amphitheater, or open arena, for many events that were performed at the time. The Colosseum is a model for our modern stadiums. Notice all the arches that the Romans put in this design and how different it is from the Greek design of the Parthenon.

Questions:
1. What is the name of this building (right)?
2. How do you spell *Colosseum*?
3. When was it built?
4. What was its purpose?
5. What Roman innovation is included in the Colosseum?

The Colosseum

Lesson #145: *Drawing an Old Stone Arch* Draw an old stone building and put an arch in it. A good way to draw stones is to place them in rows. However, make them all different shapes. Color your stones with a nice mixture of violet, orange, blue, and red to make colorful stones.

The Roman Empire split into two empires around the fourth century after Christ. Part of it was in the East. Its capital was called Byzantium, or Constantinople. Today, this city is called Istanbul and is located in Turkey. However, during that time it became a Christian empire, starting with the Roman emperor, Constantine. He was so committed to Christianity that he made it the national religion. Constantine began building many glorious churches and filled them with beautiful pictures of Jesus and His disciples. This is a picture of *"Madonna and Child"* (Mary holding the baby Jesus). The art from this time and place has come to be known as *Byzantine Art.* The figures seem very long and not realistic, but the colors were beautiful. These pictures were intended to be simple and spiritual. Byzantine art is best known for its *mosaics* (moze-a-icks) which were small, colorful, cut stone or glass pieces that were glued together to form a colorful, puzzle-like picture.

Byzantine Art

Question:
1. What style of art is the picture?
2. How do you spell *Byzantine?*
3. When was the Byzantine period?
4. Where was Byzantium, or Constantinople, located?
5. What are mosaics?

Lesson #146: *Bright & Colorful Bible Stories* Copy the picture of the *"Madonna and Child"* that was done during the Byzantine period. Use your orange colored pencil to draw it and then place a lot of colors in it the way the Byzantine artists did. The more pressure you place on your pencils, the richer the colors will be.

#5 The Early Renaissance   Fra Angelica   "The Annunciation"

Renaissance means *"rebirth."* During the fourteenth century, Europe was experiencing a rebirth in art, especially in Italy. The Dark Ages had loomed over the land for many centuries and it was now a time of prosperity and encouragement in the arts. Many great artists lived during this period of time. *Fra Angelica* was a monk who lived in Florence, Italy and was committed to serving Christ. *"Fra"* means *"brother"* and *"Angelica"* means *"the angelic one."* He was born in a small town outside of Florence in 1400 A.D. and committed his life to God at the age of 20. Fra Angelica only painted when he was ordered to do so by the church authorities and would fast and pray before beginning each painting. It is said that he often wept when he painted Jesus on the cross. This painting is called, *"The Annunciation"* and shows the angel Gabriel telling Mary that she is going to be with child.

"The Annunciation"

Questions:
1. Who painted the picture and what is its title?
2. How do you spell *Fra Angelica?*
3. When and where did he live?
4. What does *Renaissance* mean?

Lesson #147: *"The Annunciation"* Draw a picture of the angel visiting Mary and bringing her the good news.

#6 Leonardo da Vinci (1452-1519)   "The Last Supper"

There were many great artists who lived during the *Renaissance,* but Leonardo da Vinci (vin-she) was one of the greatest. Leonardo was born in Florence, Italy in 1452. He was not only an artist, but an architect, scientist, inventor, and musician. The term *"Renaissance Man"* derives from Leonardo because he was talented in doing many things. He is best-known for his paintings, *"Mona Lisa"* and *"The Last Supper."* His *"Last Supper"* is considered to be one of the greatest paintings ever created. However, it has greatly deteriorated over the years and is now only a faint image of what it looked like when it was completed in 1498. The painting shows Jesus and His disciples at the moment He has stated, *"One of you shall betray me."* The painting is a beautiful composition that seems to capture so many different expressions by His followers after He has made this statement.

"The Last Supper"

Questions:
1. What is the name and title of this picture?
2. *What does "Renaissance Man" mean?*
3. What moment does the painting show?
4. When and where did Leonardo live?

Lesson #148: *"The Last Supper"* For this assignment, do your own drawing of *"The Last Supper."* Try to show different expressions on the disciples faces the way da Vinci has done.

#7 Renaissance Michelangelo   (1475-1564)   "The Pieta"

Michelangelo Buonarroti (bone-are-rot-tee) was born in Caprese, Italy in 1475. Michelangelo was both a great sculptor and a great painter. He painted the ceiling of the Sistine Chapel in the Vatican in Rome, Italy. This painting was a large undertaking as the ceiling is 10,000 square feet, or about the size of half a football field. It took him four years to complete the painting, which is filled with many scenes from the Old Testament. One of the great pieces of sculpture he created was the *"Pieta,"* meaning *"pity."* It is a large piece of sculpture and shows Mary holding Jesus after He was taken off the cross. Michelangelo sculpted out of stone and did it so realistically that one can almost feel the robe of Mary and the flesh of Jesus. He was only 23 years old when he completed this beautiful masterpiece.

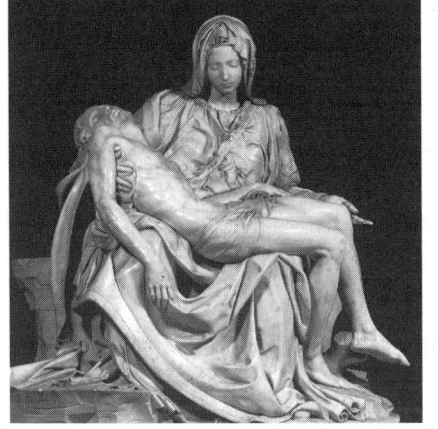

"The Pieta"

Questions:
1. What is the name of this piece of sculpture?
2. Who created the *"Pieta"* and what does it mean?
3. How do you spell *Michelangelo?*
4. When and where did Michelangelo live?

Lesson #149: *Jesus on the Cross*   Many great artists have done artwork of the crucifixion of Jesus. The *"Pieta"* shows Mary with Jesus after he was taken down from the cross. For this assignment, draw your own "Pieta" picture. Do this with your black pen.

#8 The Reformation Albrecht Durer "St. Michael Fights the Dragon"

During the same period as the Renaissance in Italy, northern Europe was experiencing the *Reformation*. This was a time when Martin Luther was alive and many of the Christian people rebelled against the powerful authority of the Roman Catholic Church, especially those in northern countries like Germany and the Netherlands. Albrecht Durer (all-breck door-er) was born in 1471 into a Christian family in Nuremberg, Germany. Many consider him the *"Luther of Art"* because of his Christian sentiments. This picture is a scene from the book of Revelation that shows Michael and his angels fighting the dragon and his angels (Revelation 12:7). The drawing is an *etching*. Etchings were a form of printmaking where the artist etched, or carved, the picture onto a surface with fine instruments and then made prints of it. This was very popular during the time of Albrecht Durer because the printing press had recently been invented, which made it possible to print and sell many of the pictures. Notice the fine detail and lines in the picture. German artists were noted for their patience and skill with detail.

Questions:
1. What is the name of the picture?
2. What is the name of the artist?
3. How do you spell *Albrecht Durer*?
4. What was the *Reformation*?
5. What is an *etching*?

"St. Michael Fights Against the Dragon"

Lesson #150: *Drawing a Dragon* Throughout the history of Christianity, dragons have often symbolized Satan and demons. For this assignment, find a picture of a dragon and draw it. See if you can make changes to it, making it more creative. You may want to draw from a picture of a crocodile or alligator. Do your drawing with your black pen.

#9 The Dutch Reformation   Rembrandt van Rijn   "The Prodigal Son"

Rembrandt van Rijn (reen) was a Christian man who was born in Leyden, Holland in 1606. He never traveled but remained in his own country his entire life. Like Durer, he was also very influenced by the Reformation and is noted for doing more paintings and drawings of scenes from the Bible than any other artist. During the Reformation, the northern countries in Europe did not believe in adorning their churches with religious pictures. Church authorities felt it was a form of idol worship. Therefore, many of Rembrandt's paintings from the Bible were done for his own enjoyment. Also, like Durer, he was a master at etching.

"The Prodigal Son"

Questions:
1. What is the title of this picture and who was the artist?
2. What period of time did Rembrandt live during and in what town was he born?
3. What is one thing he is noted for in art?

Lesson #151: *The Prodigal Son* Read the story of the *"prodigal son"* (Luke 15:11) and do a drawing of it with your colored pencils.

#10 19th Century   Jean-Francois Millet   "The Gleaners"

Jean-Francois Millet (mill-lay) was born in 1814 and raised on a farm in the small village of Gruchy, France. He grew up in a Christian household and was homeschooled by his grandmother and uncle, a pastor in a small church. As he grew older, he decided to become an artist and eventually left the farm to study art in Paris. However, Millet was never happy with the city life and after several years relocated in a country village named Barbaizon, where he spent the rest of his life. He liked to paint the common workers doing ordinary duties that filled their days. This type of art was called *"genre"* (shawn-rah) painting. Notice the painting of *"The Gleaners."* It is a picture of the meek working the land. Do you know who *gleaners* were? In the book of Ruth they were the poor who would pick up, or glean, what the harvesters left in their fields after the harvest.

"The Gleaners"

Questions:
1. What is the title of this picture?
2. Who painted it and how do you spell his name?
3. What does *genre* mean?

Lesson #152: *"The Gleaners"*   The book of Ruth is a wonderful story to read and many students love to do illustrations from this delightful story. For this assignment, read the story of Ruth and do a drawing of something from the story you especially like.

#11 Gustave Dore   "Daniel in the Lion's Den"

Gustave Dore (goo-stahv door-aye) was born in Strasbourg, Germany in 1832. He grew to become one of the most prominent artists in his country. Like Albrecht Durer and Rembrandt, he was also a master of etching. Many times he was commissioned to illustrate stories from the Bible like this picture, *"Daniel in the Lion's Den."* If you look carefully you can see all the details he placed in the picture. Also notice that all the shading was done with *lines.* This is what you have been learning in *I Can Do All Things* and is the method that most of the masters used in their drawings. Even though many of Gustave Dore's paintings and drawings were of the Bible, he never considered himself a Christian. He was raised a Catholic and spent most of his latter years spending his money lavishly. Remember, just because an artist does beautiful pictures from the Bible, does not necessarily mean that he is a Christian.

"Daniel in the Lion's Den"

Questions:
1. Who was the artist of the picture?
2. What is the title of the picture?
3. How was it done?
4. How do you spell and pronounce Gustave Dore?

Lesson #153: *"Daniel in the Lion's Den"*   Another favorite story from the Bible that students like to illustrate is *"Daniel in the Lion's Den."* Many great artists throughout history have also liked to depict this story. Read Daniel 6:10-32 and draw your interpretation of it. Do you know how to draw a lion? You may want to copy one from a picture. Use your black pen and shade with lines.

#12 Impressionism   Edgar Degas   "Study of Dancers"

Edgar Degas (day-gah) was born in Paris, France in 1834. He was the son of a wealthy banker which afforded him all the time and finances he needed to be an artist. He joined a group of artists who had a new style of painting called *"Impressionism."* They received the name "Impressionists" because they were not as concerned with realism in their artwork as they were in creating an *"impression"* of what they saw. Their paintings were full of color and brush strokes. Most of the French Impressionists worked out of doors, but Degas liked to work indoors, capturing people doing their daily chores. He also liked to paint ballerinas, and spent much of his time at the dance studios. Likewise, Degas was a master of *pastels,* or chalks; and *composition* (the way he placed objects in his pictures). Notice the picture of the dancers. Two are far to the right in the foreground while the others balance the picture out by being far to the left in the background. The middle is left open. None of them look at the viewer but are busy learning the dance. In a way, Degas was much like Millet in his desire to capture people in their daily activities.

"Study of Dancers"

Questions:
1. Who painted the picture?
2. How do you pronounce *Edgar Degas?*
3. What does *Impressionism* mean?

Lesson #154: *Ballerinas* There are many reasons why Degas liked to paint ballerinas. They have wonderful color, movement and lines. Find a picture of a ballerina and draw it with your colored pencils, putting a lot of light colors in it.

#13 Impressionism   Vincent van Gogh   "Portrait of Joseph Roulin"

Vincent van Gogh was born in Holland in 1853. He was the son of a minister and his first desire was to be a pastor like his father. In his early 20's he had much zeal for Christ and also much compassion for the poor. Vincent's first ministry was with the poor coal miners in Belgium. Young Vincent had so much love for them that he started dressing like the poor people around him. When the church authorities came to visit him he was dismissed for his shoddy appearance. Broken-hearted and rejected, Vincent van Gogh spent the rest of his life painting and living as an artist. Van Gogh's paintings are so different from any other artists before him because of his great sense for color. Color was so much more to him than just the blue of the sky or the red of a barn. To him it all had symbolic meaning. His choice of bright, vivid colors and his bold brush strokes have made him one of the world's most popular painters. Van Gogh loved to work in the open fields where he could feel the energy of the sun and the vibrant colors of nature. He also liked to do portraits of his friends, like this one of the postman, Joseph Roulin.

"Portrait of Joseph Roulin"

Questions:
1. How do you spell *Vincent van Gogh?*
2. What style of art did he do?
3. What else can you say about his life?

Lesson #155: *Colorful Flowers* Colored markers are great to use in coloring like an Impressionist because of the bright colors and bold strokes. Color a picture of flowers with your colorful markers.

#14 Carl Block   "Study of Christ"

Carl Bloch (block) was a Danish, Christian artist who was born in 1834 in Copenhagen, Denmark. His father wanted him to attend military school and serve as an officer for a career, but young Carl fell behind in his academics as he was always preoccupied with art. He eventually dropped out of military school and enlisted in an art school. Carl Bloch is noted for doing some of the most beautiful portrayals of Jesus in the history of art. Unfortunately, it is difficult to find books on him. The best way to see works by Carl Bloch is to look in a big, old Bible and, more times than not, you will find many of his wonderful paintings of Christ and stories from the Bible. Notice the etching that he did, *"Study of Christ."* Even in this drawing, you have an idea of how he saw and portrayed Jesus.

"Study of Christ"

Questions:
1. Where and when was Carl Bloch born?
2. How do you spell and pronounce his name?
3. What is he most noted for as an artist?

Lesson #156: *Portrait of Jesus* What do you think Jesus looked like? Was he handsome? Rugged? Happy? Sad? It is difficult to say because during the times of Jesus the Jewish people did not believe in making a portrait of another person. However, Isaiah 53 gives us a fairly good description of Him. Read the chapter and then do your own drawing of Jesus. Draw lightly with pencil and then go over it with your black pen.

#15 Pre-Raphaelites "The Hidden Treasure" by John Everett Millais

John Everett Millais (mill-lay) was born in England in 1824. As a young man he became one of a small group of artists known as the *"Pre-Raphaelites."* Their desire was to return to a style of art that was popular before the time of the great Italian artist, Raphael (before the 1500's). They believed that the art before that time was more simple and spiritual. Thus, *"Pre-Raphaelite"* has come to mean "before the time of Raphael." This small group of artists also called themselves *"The Brotherhood"* and one of their main goals was to glorify God in their artwork. Sadly, all of them departed from this wonderful goal with the exception of one, Holmon Hunt. Notice the picture by Millais, *"The Hidden Treasure."* It is an etching and part of a series of illustrations he did on *"The Parables of Our Lord."* The illustration has a beautiful message but, like Dore, Millais did not necessarily lead the Christian life.

Questions:
1. What is the name and meaning of the picture?
2. What is the artist's name and how do you pronounce it?
3. What was the name of the group of artists he belonged to?

Lesson #157: *The Parables of Our Lord* For this assignment, select one of your favorite *parables* from the Bible and do an illustration of it. First, draw it lightly in pencil and then go over it with your black pen, doing all the shading with lines just as the great masters did.

"The Hidden Treasure"

#16 Frederic Remington   American Western Artist   Cheyenne Scout

Frederic Remington was born in 1861 in the small town of Canton in upstate New York. Like Carl Bloch, he was sent to a military school as a young boy. Yet, young Frederic also had aspirations of being an artist. At the age of 17 he entered Yale University but was only interested in the art class. He was one of only two students in the class. Eventually his heart was won by the wild West and he began many journeys there to capture a life and times that has long since passed by. Like most of the great artists, Remington was prolific, creating hundreds of paintings and drawings of cowboys and Indians during his lifetime. Remington was so authentic in his pictures that many motion pictures have used his paintings as models for costumes in movies of the Old West. Notice the drawing of the *"Cheyenne Indian Scout."* Remington also drew excellent illustrations of horses and quick-action scenes. Frederic Remington and Charles Russell are noted as two of the greatest American artists of the Old West.

"Cheyenne Indian Scout"

Questions:
1. What is the title of the drawing?
2. Who was the artist and how do you spell his name?
3. What was he famous for?

Lesson #158: *Drawing Cowboys and Indians* For this assignment, draw a cowboy or Indian using only your brown and black colored pencils. This will give it an old western effect. If you can, also draw a horse. Frederic Remington drew hundreds and hundreds of horses during his lifetime. Drawing a horse is not easy and takes much practice.

#17 American Artist   Winslow Homer   "Waiting for a Bite"

Winslow Homer was born in 1836 in Boston. His family prospered from his father's mercantile and shipping business. However, when Winslow was a young man, most of the family's fortunes were lost investing in gold speculations in the California gold rush and he never received a college education. Nor did Winslow receive any art lessons, so he taught himself to draw and paint. Early in his career he became an illustrator for *Harper's Weekly* and was eventually commissioned to do illustrations of the Civil War. Winslow Homer spent nine months in Paris and several months in the Bahamas, but his heart was in New England, where he would spend most of his great career in the beautiful seclusion of Prout's Neck, Maine. Like Millet and Degas, he was a *genre* painter, capturing the real essence of what American life was like, especially in the outdoors. The picture of the *"Waiting for a Bite"* is a typical Homer scene of Americans doing things outdoors. Homer was greatly inspired by the rough New England sea and did many oils and water-colors of this beloved subject matter.

"Waiting for a Bite"

Questions:
1. Who did the picture of the *"Waiting for a Bite"*?
2. How do you spell *Winslow Homer*?
3. What did Homer like to draw and paint?
4. Where did he spend most of his life?

Lesson #159: *Outdoor Activities* For this assignment, draw an activity that is done outside, like fishing, hiking, or camping. Start lightly and then color it in with your colored pencils when finished.

#18 Modern Artist Georges Rouault "Portrait of Christ"

Georges Rouault (roo-alt) was born in a Paris basement in 1871. As a young artist he was influenced by the old, stained-glass windows that still adorn many of the great Gothic cathedrals on the avenues of Paris. He liked the simplicity of their bright and vibrant colors. Rouault was also influenced by the modern artists that were making themselves known at the beginning of the twentieth century. He joined a group of such artists who were known as *"abstract expressionists,"* better known as *"Fauvists."* This term means *"wild beasts"* and was given to them because of their abstract style of painting. However, Georges Rouault was most influenced by Jesus Christ. He was committed in portraying the sufferings of Christ on the cross and identifying with the sorrows of man, especially the poor and downcast. Look at *"Portrait of Christ."* Do you notice the influence of stained-glass in the basic shapes? Do you also notice the sad expression he has given the Messiah? Many Christians believe that all modern art is an abomination to God because it is not realistic. However, God can use an artist for His message no matter what the times or style may be.

"Portrait of Christ"

Questions:
1. How do you spell and pronounce *Georges Rouault?*
2. What style of art did he do?
3. What influenced his artwork?

Lesson #160: *Study of Jesus* You have already drawn one portrait of Christ in our lesson with Carl Bloch. However, Jesus, the Son of God, is many different persons all in one. He is the *"Lion of Judah,"* the *"Lamb of God,"* a *"man of sorrows"* and much more. For this assignment, draw Jesus in a simple way as Rouault has done and color your picture with colored markers. For the flesh of Christ, first color an orange circle and dip a wet brush into this to make a light flesh tone. Then, paint this light, skin color on your figure of Jesus.

Other Games to Play: "One... Two... Three..."

Another fun game is to line up all the picture cards in *chronological* order, meaning that you will start with the oldest, or most ancient artwork, and then go through history, placing them all in the order in which they were created.

Who Goes Where?

See if you can stack the artists in separate groups by the countries that they were born in. For example, you may want to have a pile for the Italian artists, one for the Dutch artists, another for the French artists and so on.

"Potato and Peas... van Gogh, please."

Discussing the great artists of the past is always delightful dinner conversation. See how many of the artists you can recollect (bring to memory) during dinner time. Have stimulating conversations about their artwork and other aspects of their lives. For example, Vincent van Gogh loved to paint sunflowers. When he was living in southern France, an artist friend came to visit and Vincent painted his entire room with bright sunflowers!

#1   Ancient Egypt:
    (2000 B.C.)

#2   Ancient Greece:
    "The Parthenon"
    (500 B.C.)

#3   Ancient Rome:
    "The Colosseum"
    (83 A.D.)

#4 Byzantine Art
(400 A.D. – 1200 A.D.)

#5 Early Renaissance (1400's):
"The Annunciation" by Fra Angelico

#6 The Renaissance: "The Last Supper" by Leonardo da Vinci

#7   The Renaissance:

   "The Pieta" by Michelangelo

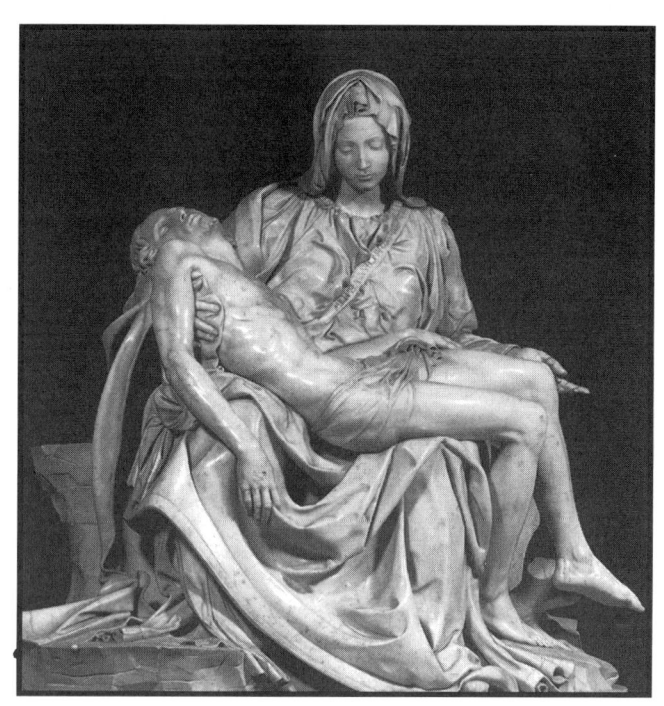

#8   The Reformation (1518 A.D.):

   "St. Michael's Fight Against the Dragon"
   by Albrecht Durer

#9   "The Prodigal Son" by Rembrandt van Rijn

#10 Nineteenth Century: "The Gleaners" by Jean-Francois Millet

#11 Nineteenth Century:
    "Daniel in the Lion's Den"
    by Gustave Dore

#12 Impressionism: "Study of Dancers" by Edgar Degas

#13 Impressionism:
"Portrait of Joseph Roulin"
by Vincent van Gogh

#15 Pre-Raphaelite:
"The Hidden Treasure"
by John Everette Millais

#14 "Study of Christ"
by Carl Bloch

#16   American Western Art:
      "Cheyenne Indian Scout"
      by Frederick Remington

#17   American Artists:
      "Waiting for a Bite"
      by Winslow Homer

#18   Twentieth Century Art:
      "Portrait of Christ"
      by Georges Rouault

Children's Art Journal

"Art comes to you proposing frankly to give nothing but the highest quality to your moments as they pass"   **Pater**

My ART Journal

by:

_____

If lost, please return.

My address is:

_____

_____

_____

_____

Place Photo or

Self-Portrait

My ART Journal

You have done several journal pages already. Now, let's learn more about keeping an art journal. Before beginning, personalize the first page of your art journal. Turn to the previous page. Print your name underneath "My ART Journal." Take your time lettering. We want your printing to be your very best. Below that, print your address and phone number on the lines provided. This is in case you lose your journal. When someone finds it, they will know where to return it. On the bottom of the page, place a photo of yourself in the figure box. It would really be special if your drew your portrait instead of using a photograph. Your drawing might be funny looking, but it will also be very special to you in time to come. Finally, do some drawings of things you like on the rest of the page. You can cut out some pictures of your artwork and paste them to the page but make sure to put some new drawings on the page. Use your colored pencils to color the page.

We will continue with some basic lessons in drawing and also some lessons in writing that will help in keeping your journal. There will be more "Doodle Pages" after some assignments. These are fun pages for you to draw and also write about whatever things you like.

"One of the greatest things in the world is to train ourselves to see beauty in the commonplace"
Charles Hawthorne

Lesson #161:

Let's draw another sun using your yellow and orange pencils. Remember, draw your circle lightly. Add the long sun-beams and all the shorter ones (A). Color with yellow and orange vertical lines. Can you give your sun a bright and cheerful face with your black pen? Draw your sun in (B).

B. Draw Sun Below _____

C. Large Circle   **D. Small Circle**   **E. Petals**   **F.**   **G.**

Can you draw another flower? First, light-ly draw a large circle using your yellow pen-cil (C). Draw a smaller circle in the middle of the larger circle (D). Then, draw the petals coming out from the smaller circle to the larger circle. This will keep your petals the same size (E). You can draw all different types of petals (F). Add a stem and leaves to your flower. The stem is two lines close together and not one skinny line. Draw your flower in G. Color with orange, red, and yel-low lines. Color the stem and leaves with blue, yellow, and green lines.

Let's overlap some flowers! It's just like overlapping balloons. Draw the circles lightly for each flower, and then darken the parts of the flower you can see (I). Draw and color your flowers below (J). Give them happy faces!

J.

I. Overlapping Flowers

224

Sunny Picture

Lesson #162:

Let's draw and color a sunny picture! Draw a picture of a happy sunshine, a house on a hill, two apple trees, a fence, and some flowers in front. Draw everything lightly with your yellow pencil, and then add lots of color using line to color and placing one color inside another. When you are finished, answer the questions below.

1. Did you enjoy drawing the picture? Why?

_____
_____
_____

2. Do you like the colors you used? Why?

_____
_____
_____

3. What did you have trouble with drawing, and what else would you like to draw?

_____
_____
_____

4. What is your favorite color? What is your least favorite color? Why?

_____
_____
_____

Penmanship: *"The art of writing with a pen; skill in writing."*

"I don't like to write."

Lesson #163: *Penmanship*

Learning to write is like learning to draw. You have a sheet of blank paper and either a pencil or pen. Everything you write is uniquely you, and everything you draw is uniquely you. You have your personal signature on everything you do. Writing can be very creative and lots of fun! We should all learn how to write in as nice a manner as possible. This is called *penmanship*. Many students do not like to write. However, the more you practice penmanship, the nicer your writing will be.

Practicing Lettering

Let's practice lettering. This will greatly help in the beauty of your writing. Print each letter of the alphabet two times. Use your colored pencils for this, and make the alphabet colorful with different colored letters!

a   b   c   d   e

f   g   h   i   j

k   l   m   n   o

p   q   r   s   t

u   v   w   x   y

z

Lesson #164: *Building a Vocabulary*

Building your vocabulary is very important. We should learn how to use a variety of words to express exactly what we want to say. For instance, how many times do you use the word *beautiful* to describe something. Are there other words that you could use besides *beautiful* ? Below is a list of some descriptive words that you might be able to substitute.

handsome	*attractive*	*lovely*
pretty	*divine*	*splendid*
wonderful	*excellent*	*superb*
exquisite		

Fill in the blanks. Select one of the words above to fill into each of the sentences below.

1. What a(n) _____ bouquet of flowers!

2. You certainly do have a(n) _____ house.

3. What a(n) _____ sunset!

Now write 5 sentences using one of the words above in each sentence to express what you want to say besides saying that it is *beautiful.* Make sure to use your best lettering.

_____

1. _____

_____

2. _____

_____

3. _____

_____

4. _____

_____

5. _____

_____

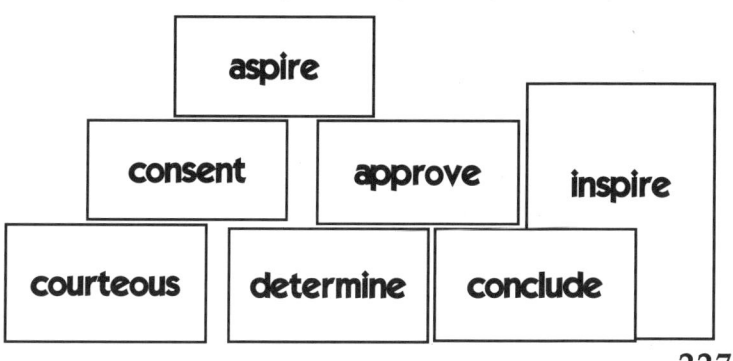

Continue to learn new words, and continue to build your vocabulary. The more words you learn, the better you will be able to express yourself.

Lesson #165: *Doodle Page*

It's fun time. For this assignment, fill the picture frames with more of your favorite doodles. Use your colored pencils to make your pictures bright and colorful!

Write About Your Doodles

Writing About Doodles: Can you write about your doodles? What do you like to doodle? What is difficult for you to doodle? Why did you color your doodles the way you did? What new words did you learn?

_____
_____
_____
_____
_____
_____
_____
_____
_____
_____
_____
_____

Lesson #166: *More Lon-n-n-n-n-n-g Lines*

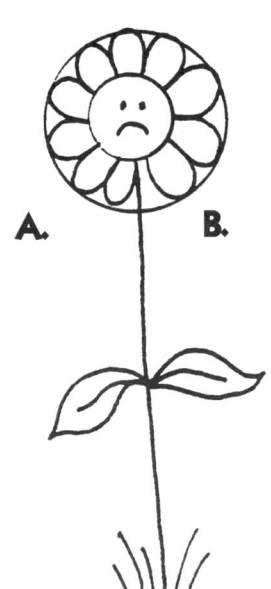

A.   B.

C.

Many students draw with skinny lines. They give flowers skinny stems (A), shoes skinny shoe strings (B), and even people skinny arms and legs (C). Complete the flowers by drawing the stems with a double line to make them thicker (D). Give each flower petals and a face. Next, complete the shoestrings from beginning to end with double lines (E).

Finally, complete the figure by adding meat to his bones, using a double line for his arms and legs (F). Do not use a ruler for drawing these lines. Draw lightly with your yellow or orange pencil, and then use darker colors.

E. Complete the Shoestrings

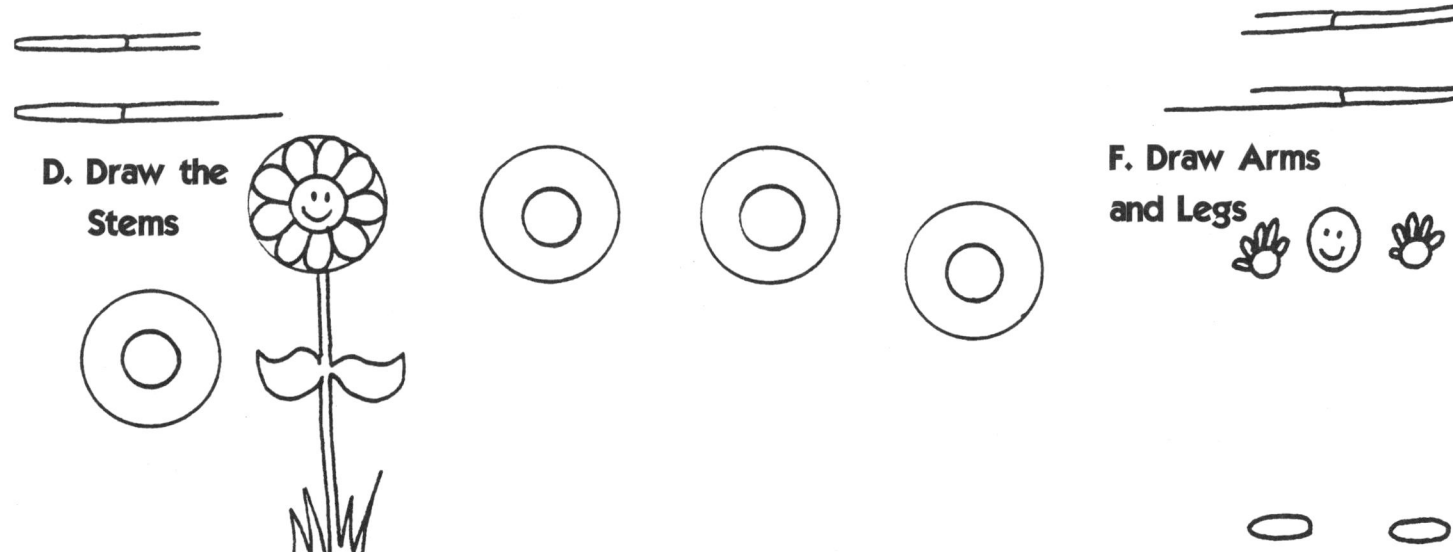

D. Draw the Stems

F. Draw Arms and Legs

Can you complete the drawings of the paint brush and pencil by connecting both ends with long lines (G & H)? On the bottom of the page, draw your own pencil or brush (I). Draw freehand, without a ruler.

G. Brush

H. Pencil

I.

Lesson #167: *Lettering & Writing/Using Guidelines*

Guidelines are light lines that we use to make sure all our letters are the same size. Using the guidelines below, print and write each word, and then draw the picture that goes with it. On the bottom of the page, make some guidelines for your name and write it or print it.

finger   draw here   apple   draw here   clown   draw here

Print: _____

Write: _____

mountains   Indian   draw here   raspberries   draw here

draw
here

Print: _____

Write: _____

Draw Guidelines
Here & Print or
Write Your Name

230

Lesson #168: *Picture Letters*

Let's draw a capital letter in each of the squares below. Give your letters a fancy design and place some nice patterns around them like: flowers, snowflakes, leaves, etc. Use different colored pencils to color each picture letter. Underneath each square, print and write two different words that begin with that letter. For instance, "K" is for kitten, which I printed, and for kite, which I wrote.

kite
kitten

Lesson #169: *Baby Lambs*

Let's draw some animals! We will start with a baby lamb. Use your light blue pencil for this. Do you know how to draw a cloud (A)? That's a good shape to start with for the body. Then, add an oval shape for the head. An *oval* is round, but not as round as a circle. Draw 4 short rectangular shapes for legs. Draw a little cloud puff for a tail, and a curly cloud puff around the baby lamb's head. Draw flappy ears and give him a pleasant face (D). Draw your baby lamb below (E). Color some grass and flowers behind him to make his wool look even whiter (the white of the paper). When you are finished, answer the questions and write a short story about your baby lamb.

A. Cloud   **B. Oval**   **C. Legs**   **D. Head and Tail**

E. My Baby Lamb

What is baby lamb's name?

What does he like to do?

Where does he live?

Does he have any friends?

What does he like to eat?

Can you write a story about your baby lamb?

_____

_____

_____

_____

_____

_____

_____

_____

_____

Lesson #170: *Kitty Cat*

Let's draw a cat. Use your light brown pencil, and draw your kitty cat in the figure box below. Start with circles, just like making a snowman, however, draw them next to each other, instead of one on top of another (A). Add a small circle to the front of the top circle, two smaller circles for eyes, and two curved stubby shapes for legs (B). For feet, add stubby hot dog shapes, draw a tail, and place two triangles on top of the head for ears (C).

Add toes by making smaller, stubby hot dog shapes, and add fluff to your kitty by drawing short strokes. Draw long whiskers with your black colored pencil, making sure they have a sharp point, quickly pulling long, thin lines out and away from the face. Practice drawing a fluffy texture with short strokes, and whiskers with long strokes on the kitty head below (D). Color the outside part of the eyes light yellow and light blue, blending them together. For the darker, middle part of kitty's eyes, use your dark blue pencil. Practice your colors on the kitty's head. You may also want to practice other colors on the kitty eyes below. Finally, is your kitty going to be a tabby with stripes? Or a Persian with a lot of fluff? Or a kitty with spots? Draw your kitty below (E) When finished, write about your kitty, using your best penmanship (F). What is her name? Where does she live? Who does she play with?

A.   B.   C.   D.

Kitty Eyes   ── E. My Kitty ──   **F. Write About Your Kitty Below**

_____

_____

_____

_____

_____

_____

_____

_____

233

Lesson #171: "Hoppy" the Happy Horse

Today we are going to draw *"Hoppy"* the Happy Horse. Do you know how to draw a horse? First, draw three circles, one for his hind quarters (A), one for the chest (B), and a smaller circle for the head (C). Connect the circles by drawing the neck, the back, and the belly (D). Let the back droop down between the two larger circles. Also, the neck is thinner near the head and thicker as it goes toward the chest, like the shape of a cone. Draw his nose by adding another similar shape to the circle. The ears are long thin, triangles that are curved. Also, another curved triangle goes inside each ear. Add the legs, hoofs, mane and tail. The eyes are shaped like almonds, and the nose has a tear drop shape for the nostril (E). Draw *"Hoppy"* below (F). Place him in a field with hills in the distance and flowers in the foreground. Can you write about *"Hoppy" the Happy Horse* (G)? What does he like to do? Who are his friends? Where does he live? What does he like to eat? What kind of horse is he?

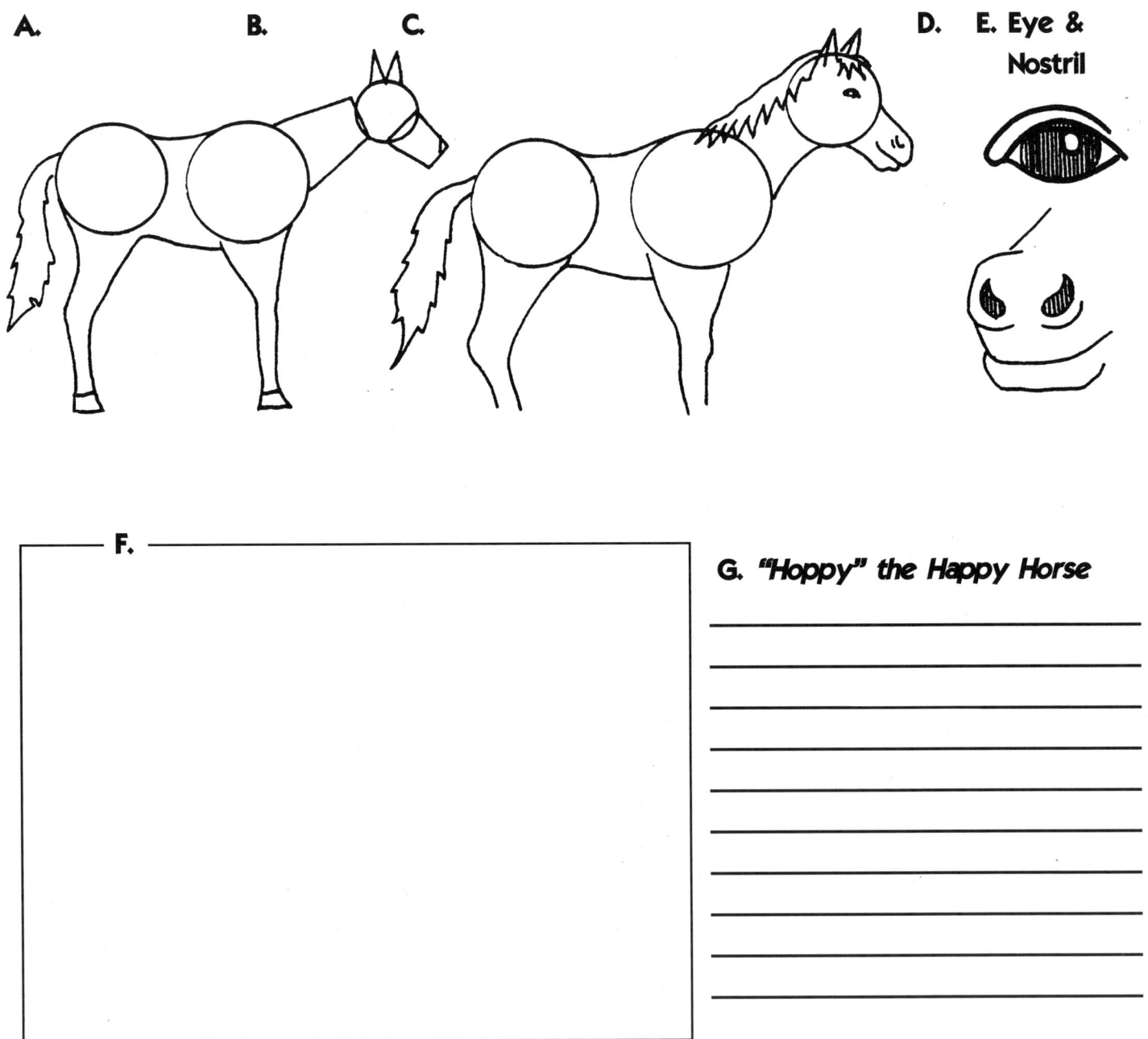

A.   B.   C.   D.   E. Eye & Nostril

F.

G. *"Hoppy"* the Happy Horse

Lesson #172: *Practicing Penmanship*

We have already practiced lettering. Now let's practice writing. Remember, in writing, all your letters should be on the same slant. Writing looks best when your letters are tilted a little to the right. Practicing these strokes is like practicing control with lines in drawing. Using the guidelines below, practice making each stroke five times. Make sure to have your strokes touch the top and bottom of the guidelines. Use a different colored pencil for each line of strokes. Take your time, making each stroke beautiful.

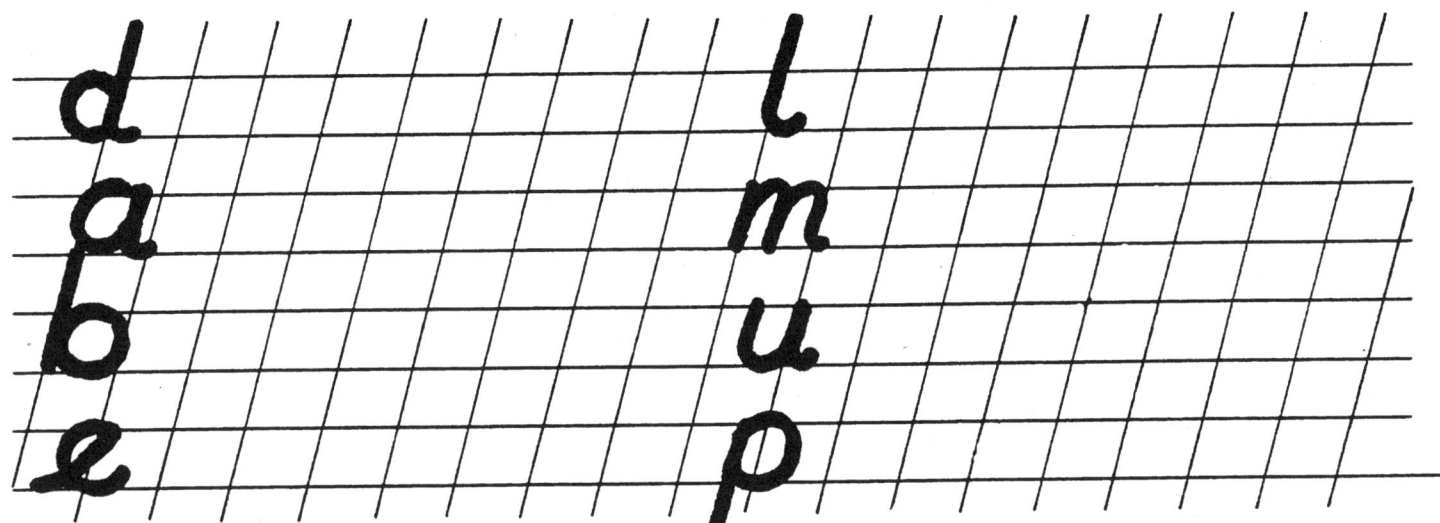

Finally, on the bottom of the page, write each word with your best handwriting. Use your guidelines and write with control. Color each word a different color from your set of colored pencils and then draw each object with your black pen.

car

house

dog

mouse

leaf

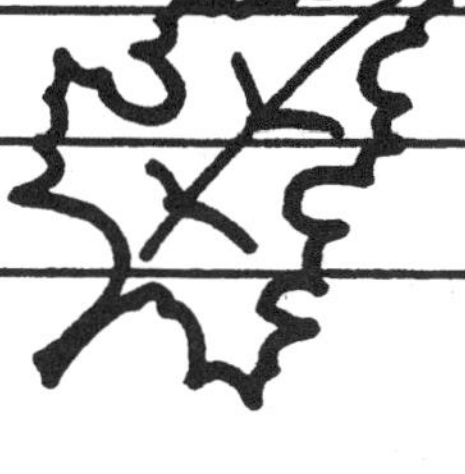

Lesson #173: *Funny People*

Let's draw some more funny faces! First, draw an oval. Remember, an oval is more egg-shaped than a circle (A), but is drawn in the same way, going around lightly four or five times. Draw five ovals below with your yellow pencil.

A.

Names: _____ _____ _____ _____ _____ _____

Funny Faces: Make funny faces out of each oval. Below is a gallery of eyes, ears, noses, mouths, and hair for you to use. See how funny your faces can be! Draw everything lightly with your yellow or orange pencil, and then go over the faces with darker colors. Write a name for each funny face underneath it.

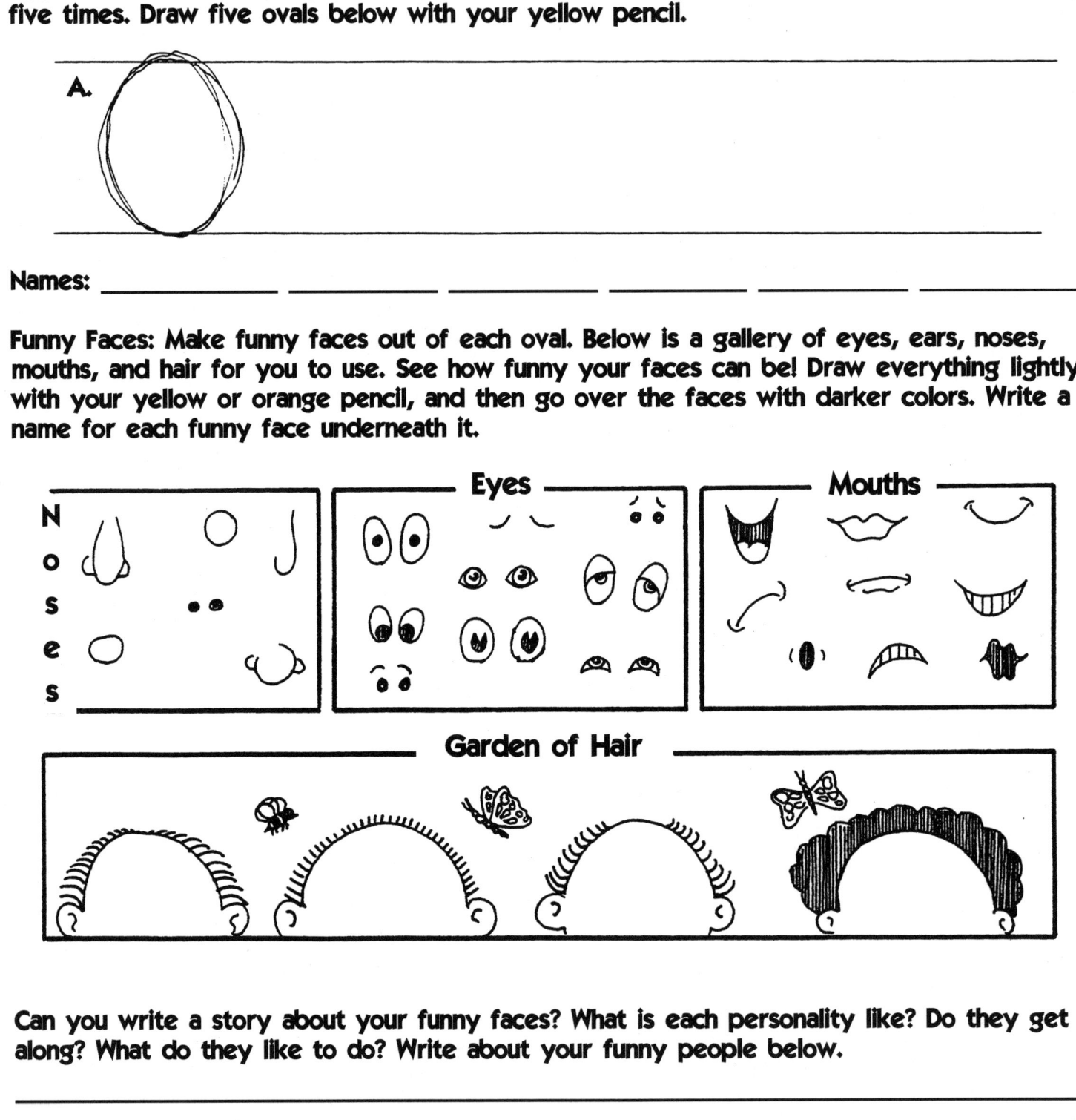

Can you write a story about your funny faces? What is each personality like? Do they get along? What do they like to do? Write about your funny people below.

_____

_____

_____

_____

_____

_____

Lesson #174: Complete the Story....

Let's write and draw a story. I will start the story, and you will complete it by filling in the blanks. After you have filled in the blanks, write an ending for the story. When you are finished, draw a picture to go with your story below.

"Once upon a time, there was a little girl named _____. She had a basketful of _____, and had just visited her _____. As she was walking home down a country road, she saw a bizarre, little _____ sitting in the shade of a _____. When she saw him, she said, 'Oh, my! I thought you were a _____.' He was very funny looking. His hair was _____, and he was wearing _____. Besides, he was very small, being only about the size of a_____. When the little girl looked at him closely, she noticed that there was a _____ on his nose! Well, he said to her, 'Don't be surprised. My name is _____. And I have been waiting here for _____ days. Will you please help me? I need to......'"

_____

_____

_____

_____

_____

_____

_____

_____

Lesson #175: My Favorite Pet

Do you have a favorite pet? Is it a dog? A cat? A bird? A fish? A horse? It could even be a cow or goat! Draw your favorite pet in the figure box below with colored pencils. Draw his surroundings, too. Does he live in the backyard, in the barn, in your home? When you are finished, write a description of your favorite pet beneath the picture. How old is your pet? What does it like to eat? What does it like to do? What do you like most about him or her? What do you like least?

My Pet's Name: _____

_____

_____

_____

_____

_____

_____

_____

_____

_____

_____

Lesson #176:

It's doodle time! Draw anything you like. Be creative and colorful. Don't forget to write about what you have drawn.

_____
_____
_____
_____
_____
_____
_____
_____
_____
_____
_____
_____
_____

Lesson #177: *Geometric Shapes*

Today we are going to practice drawing some more *geometric* shapes. Remember, geometric shapes are circles, squares, triangles, and rectangles.

Circle   Square   Triangle   Rectangle

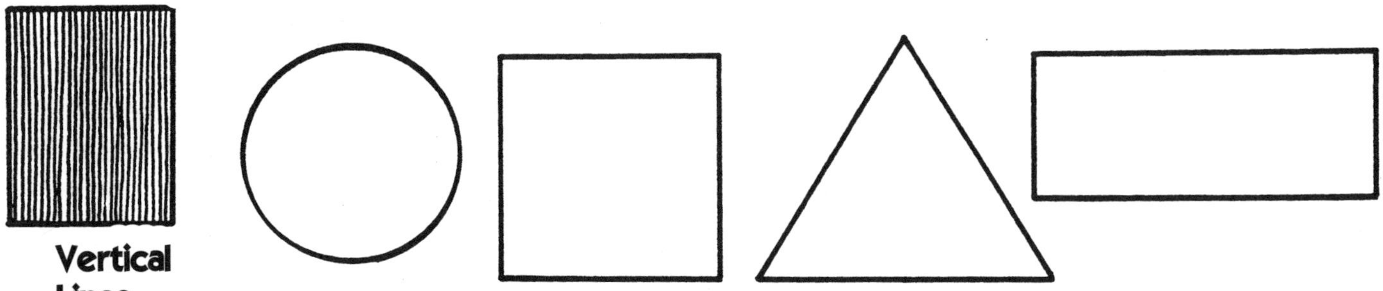

Vertical
Lines

A.

Can you draw a circle below like what you did previously? Remember, go around lightly four or five times, until you have the basic shape. Then, complete the drawings of the square, triangle, and rectangle below by adding lines to connect the sides. Do not use a ruler for this, but draw your lines *freehand* just like you did before. Practice drawing straight *vertical* lines in the long rectangle (A). Vertical lines are lines that go straight up and down, as shown above. Then, color the circle with red vertical lines, the square with blue vertical lines, the triangle with orange vertical lines, and the rectangle with green vertical lines.

Draw Circle Here

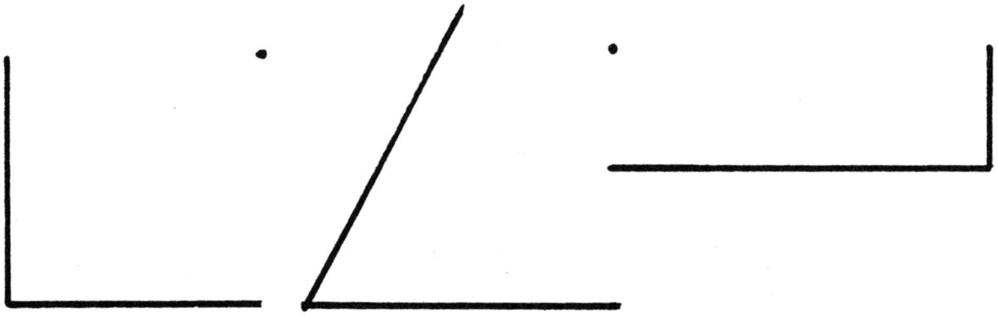

When you are finished drawing the geometric shapes, see if you can draw all the shapes by yourself below. Then, letter and write the name of each shape underneath them (B).

Circle   Square   Triangle   Rectangle

B. _____

_____

_____

Lesson #178: *Let's Draw a House!*

Drawing a house is only a matter of building block upon block. Start with a triangle (A), and add a square to it (B). Then, add a rectangle for the door, and squares for the windows (C). Finally, add the chimney to the roof with a cloud of smoke coming out of it. Let's make it a brick house. Do you remember how to make rows of bricks? Finish the rows of bricks below (D), and color with your orange and red pencils with horizontal lines. Can you add some curtains to the windows? A picket fence around the house? A tree and some hills in the background? Draw your house below (E). Then, color with your colored pencils.

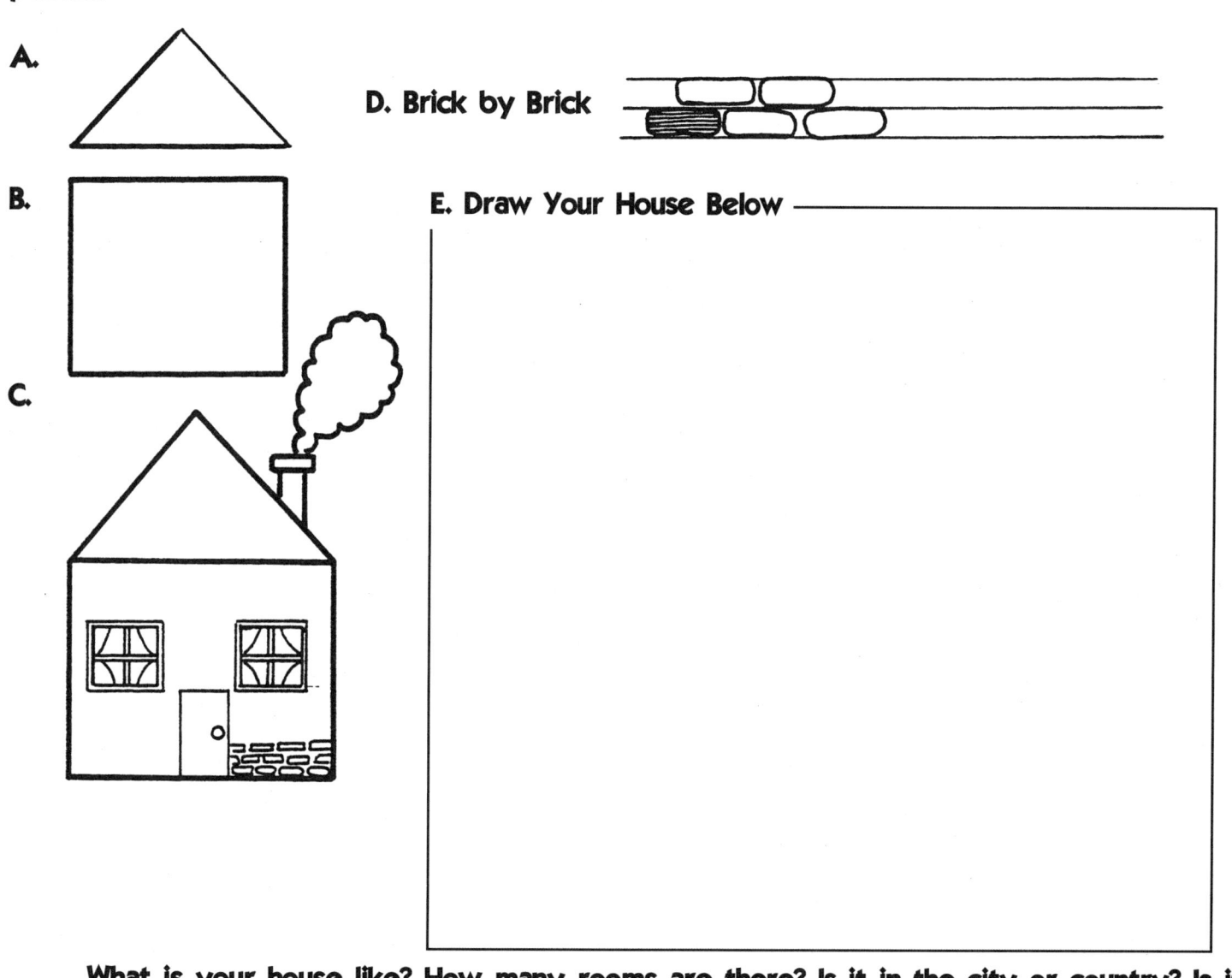

A.

D. Brick by Brick

B.

E. Draw Your House Below

C.

What is your house like? How many rooms are there? Is it in the city or country? Is it made of wood or stone? Do you have any trees around the house? Write about your house below.

_____

_____

_____

_____

_____

Lesson #179: City Along the Sky

Do you know what a city along the sky is called? It is called a *skyline*. Have you ever seen a skyline as you drive by a city? See if you can complete the skyline below by adding more windows to the buildings. Let's make this a night scene. Color the buildings with dark blue, red, and violet, using vertical lines. Color some of the windows yellow to show that the lights are still on. Color the sky a dark blue and purple, and the moon and stars yellow.

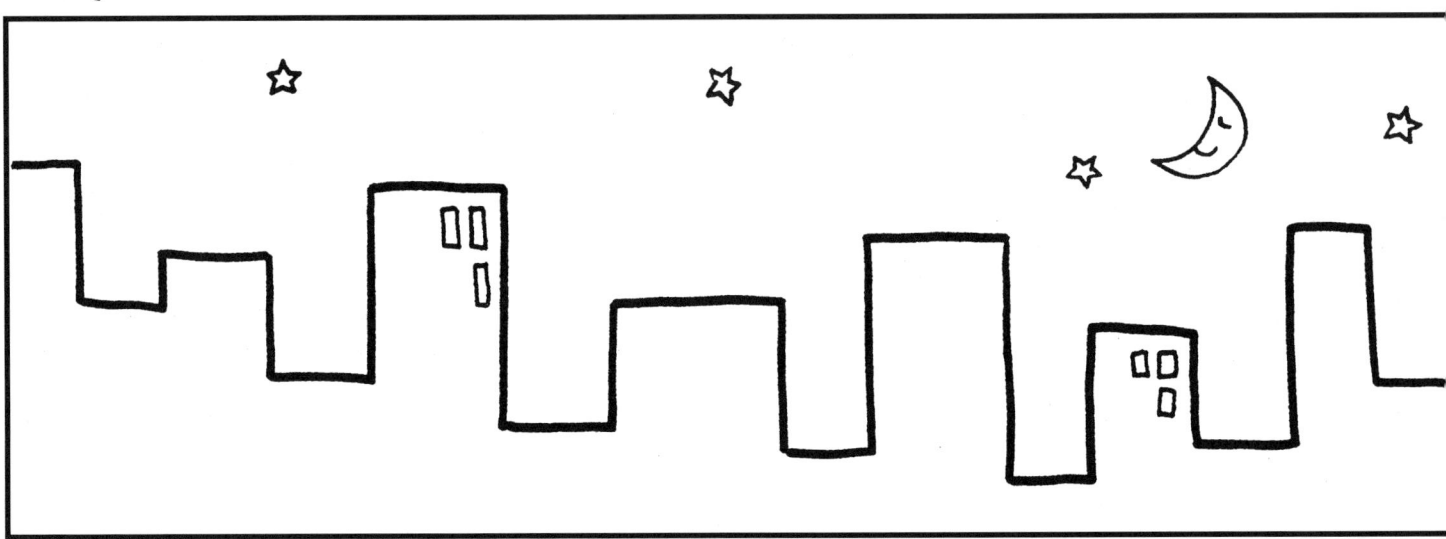

Can you draw your own skyline below. Draw different size buildings, like the ones above with your black pen. Add some domes and church steeples if you can. This time, let's color a sunset behind the city.

Do you like cities? Have you been to a lot of cities? What is your favorite city? Why? What cities would you like to go to? Write what you think about cities below.

_____

_____

_____

_____

Lesson #180: *Blue Skies & Sunshine*

Let's color a blue sky. First, lightly draw a bird and cloud, using your violet pencil in the figure box below (A). Color in a very light layer of light blue around them by extending your forefinger over the point of your pencil and coloring with a flat, light blue. Take your picture outside, and hold it up to the sky to see if your blue is too dark. Color your bird with red and dark blue horizontal lines.

Drawing a Bird   **Drawing a Cloud**   A. Draw Your Bird & Cloud Above

Lesson #181: *Coloring Sunlight*

Let's draw a tree and color it in sunlight. First, draw your tree in the figure box below with your yellow pencil. Then, draw your sun in the upper right corner. Draw a crescent moon shape across the center of your tree and an oval cast shadow under your tree. Color the half of the tree closest to the sun, along with the grass that is not in shade with a bright yellow. Then, go over the tree and the grass with your light green pencil. Keep it very light, so you can see the yellow in the sunny areas. Add blue to the shaded side of the tree and the shadow on the ground with your dark blue pencil.

**Draw Tree & Crescent Moon
& Shadow under Tree**

Color with Yellow & Green

Shade with Yellow, Green, & Blue   **Draw Your Sunny Tree Above**

Lesson #182: *Coloring with Browns & Black*

When you color with browns and black, it makes your pictures look darker. Many students tend to color too much with these two colors. Students should learn how to make more colorful pictures without using brown and black all the time. Let's see if you can make some nice colors below without using your browns and black. Color one tree trunk with orange and violet vertical lines. Then, try yellow, orange, and red on another. You may also want to try yellow, orange, and blue; or orange, red, and violet; or even orange, red, and dark blue. These colors will not look like the colors of your brown pencils, but will make some nice colors that can brighten up your pictures, and give you more variety. Finally, see if you can make a black by using your dark blue, red, and green pencils, and crosshatching to color inside the broken windows. Color the window pane with the nicest brown you made. Print the colors you used underneath each.

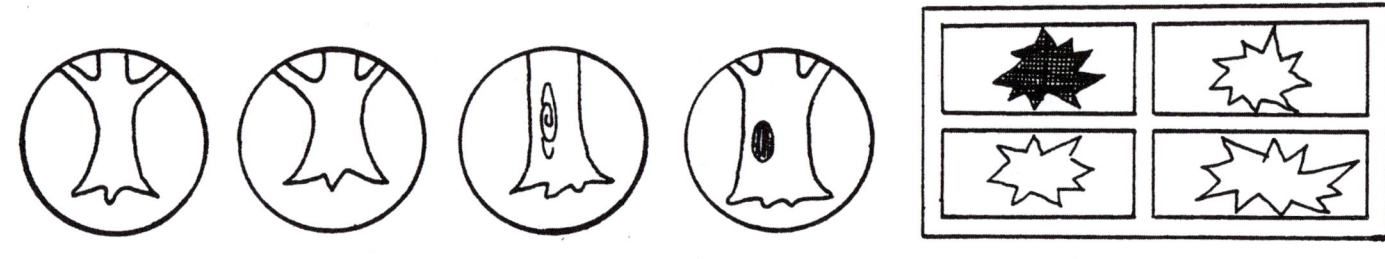

However, browns and blacks are great drawing pencil. Take your black drawing pencil, and draw the objects below.

Draw Here

Draw Here

Draw Here

A. Color in Before Drawing

B.

Using only light brown, brown, and black, draw the picture of the teddy bear (B) in A. Before beginning, lightly color in the entire figure box with your light brown colored pencil, coloring with the broad side of the point. Then, draw the bear with your dark brown and black pencils. What do you think of your drawing?

Lesson #183: *Let's Go Outside!*

For today's assignment, let's go outside and color a sunset! You have to wait for the time to be just right. Keep looking out the window until you see a lot of colors in the clouds. Color your picture below. When you are finished, write about the experience. Did you like coloring a sunset? What did you like best? What was the most difficult? Try to use other creative words to describe the sunset besides *beautiful*. Can you draw colorful designs in the picture frame? Make sure to place the date above your picture.

Lesson #184: *Boys & Bugs/Girls & Flowers*

It is really wonderful to go outside and draw! That is where there is a real treasure chest of delightful things. You may want to go outside and draw some bugs. Make sure to draw them LARGE! You may want to also draw some flowers. Make sure to put lots of color in them! If it is too cold to go outside, select some pictures to copy from. Use your colored pencils, and color with line.

Other Nature Studies: There are many other things that you may want to study and draw from nature: stones, a leaf, a branch, acorns, or even a tree in the distance. When it is time to work in your journal, you may want to go outside and draw the things around you!

Are You Ready to Start Your ART Journal?
* Monday & Thursday *** Monday & Thursday *

Are you ready to start with your art journal? It is probably best to work in your journals only two days a week. This will give you lots of time to think about what you want to write and draw when the time comes. Monday and Thursdays are good days for keeping journals.

"I don't know what to write."

Many students do not know what to write about in their journals. Again, writing takes *practice*, just like drawing. The more you practice, the better you will become at it, and the more you will like it. Below is a list of things you can write about in your art journal:

1. Date each page.
2. How do you feel today? Are you happy, sad, excited?
3. What have you learned today?
4. Did anything happen today that was interesting?
5. What type of artwork did you do?
6. What would you like to learn in am?
7. What do you have the most trouble with in drawing?
8. Are you going to do anything exciting in the future?
9. What books have you?
10. What's the weather like?

"Can-Do"

Build Your Vocabulary

Building Your Vocabulary

A. New Word:

excellent
excellent
excellent

On the bottom of each page will be a new word for you to learn. Write or print the word three times on the lines provided and see if you can use the word in a sentence when doing your journal writing. Let's say that your vocabulary word for the day is *excellent*. Write or print the word three times (A), and use the word in a sentence (B).

B.

My teacher said I did excellent today.

_____

_____

_____

_____

_____

_____

_____

_____

_____

_____

_____

_____

_____

Print
Discipline
3 Times Here

"Can-Do"

New Word:

discipline: having good habits for learning.
"Jacob has great discipline when learning how to draw and write."

Date: _____

_____

_____

_____

_____

_____

_____

Practice!
Practice!
Practice!

New Word:

_____

_____

_____

confidence: being certain about something.
"Rachel has much confidence in being able to draw horses."

New Word:

_____

_____

_____

Date: _____

_____

_____

_____

_____

_____

_____

_____

flourish: to grow strong and succeed.
"If a garden is well kept, it will flourish and provide a lot of vegetables."

Date:

New Word:

enrich: to make something more beautiful.
"Paul can enrich his art journal by drawing pictures in it."

Date: _____

_____

_____

_____

_____

_____

_____

_____

New Word:
_____
_____
_____
_____

attitude: the feeling that one has about something.
"Josiah has a great attitude when it comes to learning to write well."

Date:

_____
_____
_____
_____
_____
_____
_____
_____
_____
_____
_____
_____

aspiration: a strong desire to do something great.
"Mark has the aspiration to be a great artist."

New Word:

_____
_____
_____

_____

_____

_____

_____

_____

_____

_____

_____

_____

_____

_____

_____

_____

_____

_____

_____

_____

New Word:

_____

_____

_____

_____

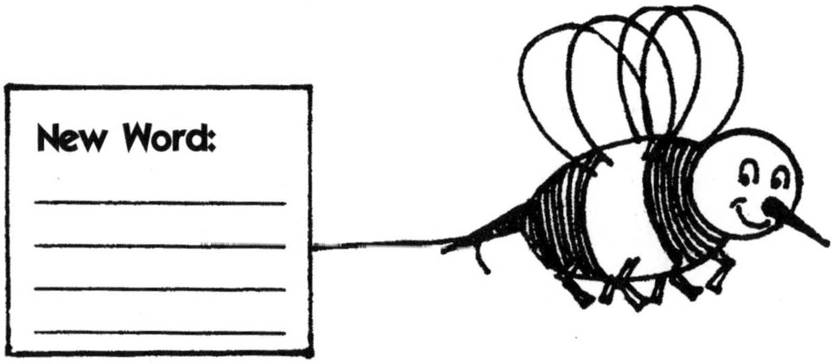

humble: a modest opinion of oneself.
"Timothy was humble when he found out his picture won first prize in the art show."

Examination
&
Glossary

Ellipse

Overlapping

Texture

"Study to show thyself approved." 2 Timothy 2:15

Color Examination

I. Color your answers to the questions below with colored pencils (5 points each).
Then see if you can check your answers using the book and glossary.

1. Do you know what the three primary colors are? Color each of the three balloons with a primary color.

2. Do you know what the three secondary colors are? Color in each of the three shapes below with the correct secondary color.

Yellow & Red Make

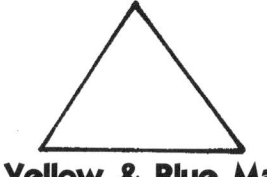

Yellow & Blue Make

Red & Blue Make

Vertical Lines   Horizontal Lines   Diagonal Lines

3. Can you color with line? Color the three clown heads with lines, using vertical lines in the first, horizontal lines in the second, and diagonal lines in the third. Use any colors you like and be colorful!

5. Color the picture above with warm colors.

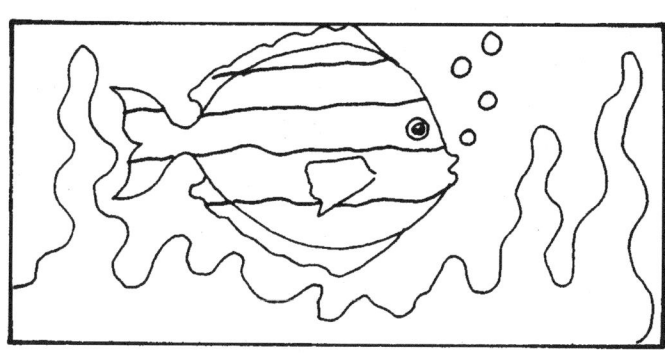

6. Color the picture above with cool colors.

4. Do you know your color wheel? See if you can color in the six pie sections on the color wheel below. Make sure to place the correct secondary color between the two primary colors that make it.

Color Wheel

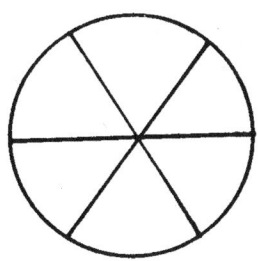

7. Color the tree with pointillism.

II. Choose the Correct Answer. Select One (5 points each):

1. A monochromatic painting uses how many colors? Select one:

> One   Two   Three

2. A Color Chart is:

> A. A map with lots of colors.
>
> B. A chart that you use to show how to mix colors.
>
> C. A wheel with colorful pie sections on it.

3. Three warm colors are:

> A. Red, Blue, and Yellow.
>
> B. Red, Green, and Violet.
>
> C. Yellow, Red, and Orange.

III. True or False. Place a "T" next to each true statement and an "F" next to each false statement (5 points each).

1. Ellipses are squares seen on an angle.

2. Red, yellow, and green are the three primary colors.

3. Red and yellow make orange.

4. When painting, always add a little of the light color into the dark color.

5. Vertical lines go straight up and down.

6. Cool colors are blue, violet, and green.

7. A still life is drawing animals when they aren't moving.

8. A monochromatic picture is a picture done only with red, yellow, and blue.

9. Texture means to draw something and make it look like it feels.

10. Highlights are the areas on things you draw and paint that shine the most from the light.

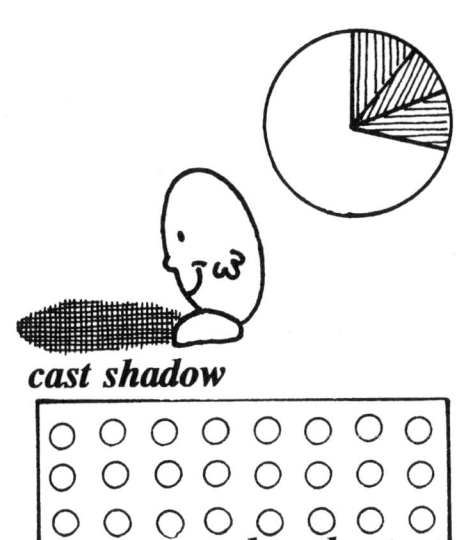

Glossary

1. **Analogous Colors:** *Any three colors that are next to each other on the color wheel.*

2. **Cast Shadows:** *The shadow that is cast by an object on the ground or other surface.*

3. **Color Chart:** *A chart used for understanding how to mix different colors.*

cast shadow

color chart

4. **Contour Line:** *A drawing that is done with one continuous line.*

5. **Color Wheel:** *A wheel with pie sections of different colors that is used to understand color better.*

6. **Cool Colors:** *Blue, violet, and green.*

7. **Ellipse:** *A circle seen on an angle.*

8. **Free-Hand:** *To draw something without the use of a ruler, compass, or any other object.*

9. **Geometric Shapes:** *Shapes such as a circle, square, triangle, and rectangle.*

10. **Guidelines:** *Lines used to make letters the same size.*

11. **Highlight:** *The bright area on an object caused by the reflection of light.*

| Vertical | Horizontal | Diagonal |

12. **Lines:** *Lines placed next to each other for drawing or shading. They can either be vertical, horizontal, or diagonal lines.*

mediums

13. Medium: *Different art materials you can use to draw and color with, such as watercolors, colored pencils, markers, etc.*

14. Monochromatic: *To color a picture with shades of just one color.*

15. Overlapping: *Placing one object slightly in front of another to show depth.*

overlapping

16. Pointillism: *To draw or color with dots.*

17. Secondary Colors: *Colors that are made with the primary colors. Red and yellow make orange; yellow and blue make green; and blue and red make violet.*

still life

18. Still Life: *To draw or paint objects that do not move, such as a vase of flowers, a book and some fruit.*

19. Technical Drawing: *To draw with the use of a ruler, compass or anything else that assists in drawing straight lines or curves.*

20. Texture: *To draw something and make it look like it feels. For instance, to draw the grain on a piece of wood, or the little holes in a sponge, or the fur on an animal.*

texture

21. Tones: *Different shades of the same color.*

light   dark

22. Warm Colors: *Warm colors are red, yellow, and orange.*

Doodle Page

Place your creative doodles
in the picture frames below

What Do We Recommend Next?

Now that you have finished *I Can Do All Things*, How Great Thou ART Publications would like to introduce you to many other delightful art books that you may want to study from next. For example, if you are still under the age of ten, we recommend *Lambs I & II Books of Art* or *The Wonderful Art of Drawing Horses*. If you are now over the age of ten and really like art, then we recommend a great art book, *Feed My Sheep*. Below is a brief description of each. For other curriculum, videos, and bundle packages see next page.

Lambs Book of Art I & II   Ages 8 thru 13

These award winning, one-year curriculum have been a favorite with homeschooling families for years and are a delightful introduction to art. Subjects include color theory, drawing, anatomy, perspective, nature studies, portraits, cartooning, lettering, creative writing, and much more. The Lambs Book of Art II complements Lamb's I with more lessons on the same level and you can start with each or use both to extend your program.
A one year curriculum
(Ask about our specials and bundle package!)

The Wonderful Art of Drawing Horses Ages 8 & Up

Homeschooling children love to draw horses! What better way to teach students the fundamentals of drawing and color theory than by having them draw and color one of God's most beautiful creations. Lessons may be done directly in the text or copied for in home use. Over 75 daily lessons.
A one year curriculum
Bundle Package
(text, sketchbook, colored pencils, black drawing pen, drawing pencil set, sharpener and kneaded eraser)

Feed My Sheep   Ages 10 & Up

This best selling curriculum is a comprehensive art text and workbook containing over 250, illustrated, step-by-step lessons. The recommended weaving in and out of the chapters will provide the student with a little drawing, painting, penmanship, art appreciation, etc...during any given month. Over 300 pages in a spiral-bound, softcover text includes 17 heavy cardstock paint cards.
A 4 Year Curriculum
Bundle Package
(includes text, paints & brushes, colored pencils, black drawing pen, drawing pencil set, sharpener and kneaded eraser)

Order Today! 1-800-982 DRAW (3729)

How Great Thou Art Publications Presents...
Barry Stebbing's Complete ART Curriculum

Ages 3 Thru 13

Baby Lambs Book of Art
(Ages 3 Thru 5)
Not a coloring book! Teaches beginning drawing, beginning color theory, beginning lettering, beginning addition and subtraction, and beginning writing - all in a fun way with art! Over 128 pages 8 1/2"x11"

Joseph the Canada Goose
Children ages 4 thru 8 will love this delightful story about a Canada goose with a broken wing named Joseph and his relationship with a lonely old farmer named Elmer Thatcher. What makes this book unique is that every page has an art lesson to go with it. Text includes 100 pages with over 45 art lessons. Recommended materials are a set of colored pencils & a black drawing pen.
•**Bundle Package!** Text, Prismacolor colored pencils, and a fine black drawing pen all for 1 low price!

Little Annie's Art Book of Etiquette & Good Manners
(Ages 4 Thru 9)
An adorable text that teaches the social graces with scripture along with simple art assignments. Lessons on dinner etiquette, being a good listener, saying "Please and Thank You," obeying your parents, writing thank you cards, refinement, spending quality time away from the television and much more! All with fun and easy art lessons.

The Children's Art Journal
This text is recommended for students ages 6 thru 10. This text offers 50 basic art lessons teaching fundamentals of drawing & color theory along with a 70 page beginning journal in the back of the text. Journaling encourages good penmanship and helps.

I Can Do All Things
(Ages 6 Thru 11)
A Basic Beginning Art Book! Learn to draw, color and paint with these easy step by step lessons. A complete curriculum with over 250 pages and 170 art lessons, includes 38 8 1/2" x 11" paint & Marker cards.
• **Supplies for ICD:** Paints & Brushes, 12 "Prismacolor" Colored Pencils, Watercolor Markers, # 7 Brush, Fine Pen, Kneaded Eraser & Sharpener.

I Can Do All Things Video
Over seven hours of instruction in a four tape series covering most of the lessons in the text. Includes an "I Can Do All Things" book.
• **Video Bundle Package!** Same as above Bundle plus 4 Video Set.

Now Available on DVD!
The same great teaching aid now on 4 menu driven DVD's.

Lamb's Book of Art I
(Ages 8 Thru 13)

Teaches a well rounded foundation in art. Subjects include color theory, drawing, perspective, nature studies, anatomy, portraits, cartooning, lettering, creative writing and more.

Lamb's Book of Art II

Instill creativity in your children. Lamb's Book of ART II. A continuation of Lamb's Book of Art I. Over 70 Lessons.

Lamb's Book I Video
Great teaching tool! Over 4 hours of instruction. Covers the 70 lessons in the Lamb's Book of Art I. Barry demonstrates how to use color, draw cartoons, learn perspective, study nature and much more. Three tape series includes a Lamb's Book I.

Inquire about DVD's

Ages 8 Thru Adult

The Wonderful Art of Drawing Horses
(Ages 8 Thru Adult)
Homeschooling children love to draw horses! What better way to teach students the fundamentals of drawing & color theory than by having them draw and color one of God's most beautiful creations. This text has been written for those students who have the desire & determination to draw horses correctly (and learn a little about them along the way)! Lessons may be done directly in the text or copied for in-home use. For Ages 8 & Up / Over 75 daily lessons.
•**Special Bundle Package!** Text, sketchbook, "Prismacolor" colored pencils, fine black pen, drawing pencil set, pencil sharpener & kneaded eraser.

God & The History of Art
A Godly Perspective to Art History
(Ages 10 Thru Adult)

Learn drawing, painting and art history at the same time! God & The History of Art focuses on those periods of art that strived to glorify God such as Early Christian, Byzantine, Romanesque, Gothic, and Early Renaissance. God & The History of Art is filled with art lessons that complement the period of time, or artist, that is being studied. Examinations cover each period of art. The art lessons teach basic fundamentals in drawing, painting, and color theory. A great program for a well rounded education in art.

Also Available for God & the History
•**Additional Paint & Marker Cards**
(Recommended one set per student)
•**Supplies for God & History:** Paints & Brushes, 12 "Prismacolor" Colored Pencils, Watercolor Markers, # 7 Brush, Ultra Fine Pen, Drawing Pencil Set, Kneaded Eraser & Sharpener.

Feed My Sheep
(Ages 10 Thru Adult)
An Art Curriculum that will last for years!
•Over 100 lessons just on Beginning Drawing

•A practical course in Art appreciation
•Beginning paint lessons •Nature Studies
•Perspective •Penmanship •Academia
•Anatomy • Portraits •
Over 300 pages 8 1/2" x 11"
Also Available for Feed My Sheep
Additional Paint Cards (Recommended one set per student)
Supplies for FMS: Paints & Brushes, 12 "Prismacolor" Colored Pencils, Ultra Fine Pen, Drawing Pencil Set, Kneaded Eraser & Sharpener.
Paint Cards Included Not just paint by numbers! Barry Stebbing has constructed a series of seventeen (17) educational and enjoyable painting exercises. Each is on a sturdy 8 1/2" x 11" white poster board ready for painting!

Feed My Sheep Videos
Over nine hours of instruction in a seven video series instructed by artist/teacher Barry Stebbing. Learn drawing and painting, nature studies, portraits, perspective and more! A must for every serious art student! Includes a Feed My Sheep text with Paint Cards
Video Bundle Package! Text w/paint cards, & video set plus all the art supplies needed to complete this 4 year course.

Feed My Sheep is now available on DVD!
The same great teaching aid now on 7 menu driven DVD's.

Ages 10 Thru Adult

The Student's Guide to Keeping an Art Journal
(Ages 10 Thru Adult)
Did you know that Leonardo da Vinci completed over 5,000 journal pages in his lifetime? Journaling is a wonderful & creative way to help your children improve their drawing and writing skills. Beginning a journal course will also help to instill creativity in your children by encouraging them to do independent studies and to draw from life! In the Students Guide to Keeping an Art Journal, Barry discusses what to write about, what to draw, having a theme, and much more as he invites students into the world of art Journaling. This newly revised text also includes over 40 art lessons.

How Great Thou ART I
(Ages 12 Thru Adult)

Teaches a strong foundation in Art: learning the basics of drawing, especially drawing from life. Subjects include: beginning drawing, anatomy, portraits, pen and ink, nature studies, perspective, graphics and more. Students can work directly in text.
Sketchbook included in back. Over 65 daily Lessons / Over 100 pages 8 1/2" x 11".

How Great Thou ART II
(Ages 12 Thru Adult)

A complementary ART text for How Great Thou ART I. Does not matter which text you start with, simply more daily lessons in beginning drawing, pen and ink, perspective, nature studies, graphics and more. Also includes an introduction to lettering and calligraphy.

How Great Thou ART I & II Video
Anyone Can Learn To Draw!
(Over 4 1/2 hours of instruction in 3 tapes)
Learn To Draw! Covers the lessons in How Great Thou ART I & II on beginning drawing, especially from life. Barry goes over many of the fundamentals of drawing such as: line, ellipse, axis line, values, shading, light source, proportions, anatomy, perspective, portraits and much more! A must for every student serious about drawing. Includes both books.
Inquire about DVD's
Teacher's Manual...
For How Great Thou ART I & II
The How Great Thou ART I & II manual has been created to give thorough guidance and instruction for each lesson in the two texts. The manual will give the teacher a thorough understanding of many of the finer nuances that go into instruction of the assignments.

Book of Many Colors
(Ages 12 Thru Adult)

Learn all about color through the use of colored pencils, markers, pastels, watercolors, oils and acrylics! This book has over 250 pages and includes 30 8 1/2" x 11" heavy index Paint & Marker cards. A great book for anyone serious about color theory & painting.

The Book of Many Colors Video Set
(Ages 12 Thru Adult)
Finally a video set designed for the Homeschooling family that focuses on color theory and painting! The videos compliment the Book of Many Colors text and cover many of its assignments. Over 4 hours of instruction in a three video set which includes the Book of Many Colors text.

Inquire about DVD's